Jean Manco took a broad interdisciplinary approach in her work, integrating the very latest research in DNA studies with archaeology, history and linguistics to delve into the deep history of Europe and its peoples, bringing new and often controversial conclusions to a wide audience. She had a particular interest in archaeogenetics and what they can tell us about migrations of people in the past, which came to fruition in *Ancestral Journeys: The Peopling of Europe from the First Venturers to the Vikings* and *The Origins of the Anglo-Saxons: Decoding the Ancestry of the English*, both published by Thames & Hudson.

JEAN MANCO

BLOOD
OF THE
CELTS

THE NEW
ANCESTRAL
STORY

with 102 illustrations

For my sons Tristan and Simon

Frontispiece *This statuette of a bearded and mustachioed Gallic warrior, wearing a torc around his neck (c. 0 BC/AD), was found at St Maur-en-Chaussée, Oise, France.*

First published in the United Kingdom in 2015 by
Thames & Hudson Ltd, 181A High Holborn, London WC1V 7QX

www.thamesandhudson.com

First published in 2015 in the United States of America
by Thames & Hudson Inc., 500 Fifth Avenue, New York,
New York 10110

www.thamesandhudsonusa.com

This compact paperback edition first published in 2020

British Library Cataloguing-in-Publication Data
A catalogue record for this book is available from the
British Library

Library of Congress Control Number 2015932471

ISBN 978-0-500-29587-8

Printed and bound in Ukraine by Unisoft

Contents

Prologue

Today Celtic languages cling to precarious life on the northwest fringes of Europe. [1] Delve into the pre-Roman past and we find Celtic spoken across the continent. The heritage of the Celts turns up beneath the trowels of archaeologists from Portugal to Romania, from Scotland to Spain.

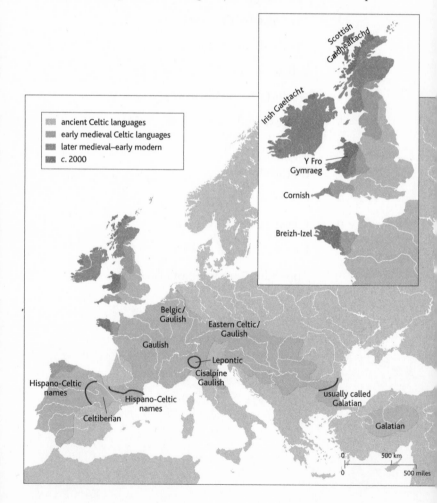

ancient Celtic languages
early medieval Celtic languages
later medieval–early modern
c. 2000

Scottish Gàidhealtachd
Irish Gaeltacht
Y Fro Gymraeg
Cornish
Breizh-Izel

Belgic/ Gaulish
Eastern Celtic/ Gaulish
Gaulish
Lepontic
Cisalpine Gaulish
Hispano-Celtic names
Hispano-Celtic names
Celtiberian
usually called Galatian
Galatian

0   500 km
0   500 miles

1 *(opposite) Celtic languages were widespread before most Celtic-speakers were enveloped by the Roman empire. Centuries of Roman rule ensured that the Continental Celts switched to speaking Latin. Celtic languages survived only in the British Isles. The Celtic language of Britain was taken to Brittany by British settlers. Another British settlement in northwest Spain did not long retain its Celtic tongue.*

2 *(right) The Celtic love of curvilinear design is displayed in this bronze mirror from Desborough, Northamptonshire (50 BC–AD 50). It is one of the finest examples of a type of Iron Age object that was exclusively made in Britain. The complex pattern may have been laid out using a compass.*

There are many books on the Celts. Their liquid, swirling art fills lavishly illustrated volumes. Works of deep scholarship explore their language and literature. For over a century archaeologists have been triumphantly publishing a wealth of discoveries that can be linked to the Celts. [2] Indeed the very enthusiasm in the last century for all things Celtic fed a backlash in the 1990s. A few exasperated archaeologists produced books assuring us that there was no such thing as a Celt – or certainly not in the British Isles. Scholars of Celtic studies were unshaken and even more productive. In the first decade of this century an ambitious project by the Centre for Advanced Welsh and Celtic Studies at the University of Wales culminated in the publication of a five-volume historical encyclopedia of Celtic culture and an atlas for Celtic studies.

Why then is there a need for another book? The fast-moving field of genetics has opened up new vistas on the past. Ancient DNA is replacing argument over who the Celts were and where they came from. At the same

Deduced timeline for the prehistory of the Celts

Approximate date	Archaeology	Language
3400 BC	Yamnaya culture on the European steppe	Proto-Indo-European
3100–2800 BC	Yamnaya movement up the Danube	Alteuropäisch/Old European
2200–1700 BC	Late Bell Beaker	Early Celtic, Italic and Ligurian
1200–750 BC	Bronze Age Hallstatt (Hallstatt A & B)	Celtic
750–600 BC	Early Iron Age Hallstatt C	Celtic

Timeline for the historical Celts

Approximate date	Archaeological period	Historical event	Date
600–460 BC	Final Hallstatt (Hallstatt D)	Inscriptions in Lepontic (Celtic) began	c. 600 BC
		Argantonios of Tartessos lived before	540 BC
		Hecataeus of Miletus referred to Massalia (Marseilles) as near Celtica	c. 500 BC
460–260 BC	Early La Tène	Herodotus mentioned *Keltoi* at the head of the Danube and in western Iberia	c. 450 BC
		Gauls ejected the Etruscans from the Po Valley	c. 400 BC
		Celtic mercenaries in Greece	369–368 BC
		Alexander the Great met a Celtic delegation	335 BC
		Celtic incursion into Thrace	298 BC
		Gauls entered Asia Minor, where the Greeks called them *Galatoi* (*Galatae* in Latin)	c. 280 BC
		Celtic attack on Delphi	279 BC
260–150 BC	Middle La Tène	Wars between Attalus I of Pergamum and the Galatians of Asia Minor	233–232 BC
		Roman victory over the Boii, Insubres and Gaesatae in Italy	225 BC
		Start of the Roman conquest of Iberia	218 BC
		Final defeat of the Cisalpine Boii	191 BC
150–50 BC	Final La Tène	Founding of the Roman *Provincia Gallia Narbonensis* in southern Gaul	125 BC
		Caesar conquered the remainder of Gaul	58–51 BC
		Caesar made two sorties into Britain	55–54 BC
AD 43–410	Romano-British	The Roman conquest of Britain	AD 43–84
		End of Roman Britain	AD 410
AD 410–800	Early medieval	Death of St Columba	AD 597

time some scholars are taking a fresh look at other kinds of evidence. The traditional conviction that the Celts arose in Iron Age Central Europe has been challenged. Historians meanwhile have been picking apart some of the best-known narratives of that elusive period from the time of St Patrick to that of Kenneth MacAlpin, and weaving their threads together again in new patterns. If revisionism has gone too far in places, it has still ignited fruitful debate. The aim here is to present a new multidisciplinary synthesis, tracking the Celts from their distant origins to their modern descendants through genetics, archaeology, history and linguistics.

As Irish historian Eoin MacNeill sagely said in 1920, there is no Celtic race, any more than there is a Germanic race or a Latin race, if by 'race' we mean some set of physical features that clearly distinguishes one from another. Roman observer Tacitus was convinced that the Germani all had 'wild blue eyes, reddish hair and huge frames'.[1] Finding that the Caledonians of northern Britain fitted the same description, he supposed that they were of Germanic stock. By contrast the swarthy faces and curly hair of the Silurians of south Wales he attributed to Iberian descent.[2] Another Roman author describes the Gauls as very tall, with white skin and blond hair, which is exactly the way other Classical authors portrayed the Germani. As MacNeill pointed out, what would most strike a Roman observer in northern Europe would be a higher percentage of paler colouring than he saw in Italy. Seizing on what is actually a matter of degree, stereotypes were created. We are still prone to this today. So it needs to be said that what MacNeill surmised in 1920 we can now prove. He felt that all the present nations of Europe are a mixture of the same ancestral components in varied proportions. He was right. As we shall see, there are three main components to the modern European gene pool. They came from ancient hunter-gatherers, early farmers and a Copper Age people. The modern Irish have a mixture of all three, as do the modern Germans and Italians. Any genetic differences are far too subtle to talk in terms of a Celtic race.

MacNeill's definition of a Celt was an ancient person known to have spoken a Celtic language.[3] That is the principle followed in this book, though I see no reason to exclude modern Celtic-speakers. The terms Insular Celts and Continental Celts are used to distinguish between those who inhabited the British Isles and those who lived on the continent of Europe.

What place does genetics have in this? We find correlations between languages and DNA signatures. The reason is that children usually learn their first language from their biological parents. Biology and language do not always go hand in hand. A child could be adopted, or could have parents of two different language origins and so could grow up speaking a completely different language from that of one or both biological parents. Then there are the seismic shudders through society that leave whole populations speaking a different language. Even so, the link between language and DNA occurs often enough for us to see patterns in the data.

This book does not attempt to describe or explain every aspect of the Celts. The primary focus is on the web of migration that over the ages criss-crossed a continent and took to the sea. The intertwined strands of that story show us how complex is the answer to what seem simple questions of origins and identity.

Since the Celts are here defined as those speaking a Celtic language, it is appropriate to open with their words, albeit in translation. So Chapter 1 displays the Celts of the British Isles in full voice in the early Middle Ages. Then in Chapters 2 to 4 we work backwards in time to find the deepest origins of the Celts and their ancestors, before turning forwards again to trace them down to their modern-day descendants in the British Isles and Brittany.

It is a story of sunlight and shadows, as indeed is all of human history. None of our ancestors lived in a fairy tale, though they might have the wit to invent one. Prising fact from fiction is one of the tasks of the historian.

CHAPTER ONE

The Voices of the Celts

Emer, daughter of Forgall the tricky, wife of Cú Chulainn, made
    speech:—
'I am the standard of women, in figure, in grace and in wisdom;
None mine equal in beauty, for I am a picture of graces.
Mien full noble and goodly, mine eye like a jewel that flasheth;
Figure, or grace, or beauty, or wisdom, or bounty, or chasteness,
Joy of sense, or of loving, unto mine has never been likened.
Sighing for me is Ulster,– a nut of the heart I am clearly –
My spouse is the hound of Culann, and not a hound that is feeble;
Blood from his spear is spurting, with life-blood his sword is
    dripping;
Finely his body is fashioned, but his skin is gaping with gashes,
Wounds on his thigh there are many, but nobly his eye looks
    westward;
Bright is the dome he supporteth and ever red are his eyes,
Red are the frames of his chariot, and red are also the cushions;
Fighting from ears of horses and over the breaths of men-folk,
Springing in air like a salmon when he springeth the spring of
    the heroes,
Rarest of feats he performeth, the leap that is birdlike he leapeth,
Bounding o'er pools of water, he performeth the feat of nine men;
Battles of bloody battalions, the world's proud armies he heweth,
Beating down kings in their fury, mowing the hosts of the
    foemen.'[1]

This proud lady is easily the winner in the 'Ulster women's war of words'
at *The Feast of Bricriu*, an Irish tale written down in the Middle Ages. Her
status was high, for her husband Cú Chulainn was the great hero of the
Ulster Cycle of tales. Her contest is linguistic. The wives of other warriors
had proclaimed their own rank and beauty and the deeds of their husbands.
Emer proves her worth with a flow of eloquence to outdo theirs.

In this one snippet of a tale, we see Celtic-speakers much as ancient Greek and Roman writers portrayed them – valiant, boastful, fond of feasting and lovers of language, beauty and wisdom. The Romans left their most detailed commentary on the Gauls, as we shall see, but here we have a matching picture of the Irish. No stereotype can truly mirror a multitude of individuals. Yet the voices of Celts long gone can reveal the values of the elite for whom songs were sung and pedigrees recited. The Roman legions brought literacy to many a Celt, but at a price. Celtic-speakers turned into Latin-speakers within the Roman empire. So the Celts of Continental Europe, where Roman influence was strongest, left us nothing that could be called literature in a Celtic tongue. There are inscriptions, curse tablets and suchlike fragments, but no connected narrative. We turn then to the poetry and prose of those Celts whose language was not lost to Latin.

Heroic ideals

Ireland remained outside the Roman empire; the Roman province of Britannia was on its northernmost fringes. Thus Celtic languages survived in the British Isles. There we find not only tales in Gaelic, but also heroic poetry written in Brittonic, once spoken over most of Britain and the ancestor of Welsh. The collection of death-songs called Y *Gododdin* sprang from northern Britain though it was preserved in Wales. Here is the elegy for a lord of Dumbarton:

> He rose early in the morning:—
> When the centurions hasten in the mustering of the army
> Following from one advanced position to another
> At the front of the hundred men he was the first to kill.
> As great was his craving for corpses
> As for drinking mead or wine.
> It was with utter hatred
> That the lord of Dumbarton, the laughing fighter,
> Used to kill the enemy.[2]

Once again we see admiration of courage. A lord was expected to lead his men into battle, not plan tactics from the rear. We can picture this 'laughing fighter' charging exhilarated at the enemy. He was the type of man who would become a leader, for he could inspire others to follow. This was not a society of nation states, with taxation supporting standing armies.

Through the lens of *Y Gododdin* we can glimpse a tribal structure similar to that which the Romans had encountered among the Celts. Indeed the tribal name Gododdin is the Middle Welsh version of Votadini, recorded in the Roman period. The tribe lived between the Firth of Forth and the River Wear. [see 87] Today their former territory is partitioned between northeast England and southeast Scotland.[3]

One of the strongholds of the Gododdin lies beneath the present castle on Edinburgh Rock.[4] Under the name Eidyn it features in *Y Gododdin*. Here a war-band feasted before the major battle celebrated in these verses. A chief who lavished meat and mead on his followers could expect feats of heroism in repayment. As one verse declares: 'The trees of battle were trampled – vengeance in payment for mead.'[5] Among the feasting warriors were men both of Gododdin and from further afield. War-bands were often of mixed origin. The lord of Dumbarton had come to Eidyn from the neighbouring Brittonic kingdom of *Alt Clud*, with its stronghold at Dumbarton overlooking the River Clyde.

The lord of Eidyn, leader of the war-band, was the son of a man with the English name Wolstan.[6] The Angles of Deira, in what is now east Yorkshire, were his enemies.[7] This enmity can be explained by the power struggles between the various bands of Angles and Saxons who had poured into Britain after it lost the protection of the Roman empire. Some Angles became neighbours of the Gododdin when they settled north of Hadrian's Wall, founding the kingdom of Bernicia. They then annexed the fellow-Anglian kingdom of Deira to the south, but in AD 616 the exiled heir of Deira successfully fought back, taking both kingdoms. The royal heirs of Bernicia sought refuge with the Picts or Irish.[8] So it would be no surprise to find one of their retinue among the Gododdin, thirsting for vengeance. The main battle commemorated in *Y Gododdin* is generally dated about AD 600, but a date during the period of Deiran control of Bernicia, AD 616–33, would explain why the enemy across the border from the Gododdin are the Deirans in the earliest form of the elegies.[9]

Another of the fallen commemorated in these verses was Heini son of Neithon, renowned for killing 100 gold-torced chieftains before he joined the band at Eidyn.[10] Here we have a man with a Celtic name slaughtering men wearing the Celtic symbol of the noble warrior. That tells us that warfare among Celts was not unusual either. War is a common theme in early Irish literature. Here are just the first few stanzas of a poem attributed to Laidcenn mac Bairceda:

> It ill beseems me to forget the affairs of every famous king, the careers of the kings of Tara, mustered tribes on the warpath.

> A noble battle-hero, fair and tall was Moen, Labraid Longsech; a cruel lion, a lover of praise, a mighty lover of battle.

> A fair warrior was Ailill in battles against the frontiers of Crothomun; Abratchaín shook the ranks of the field of Ethonmun.

> Dreaded master of Ireland was glorious Oengus Amlongaid. He dwelt upon the slopes of Tara: with his own will alone he conquered it.[11]

The style and archaic language of this poem places it among the earliest surviving Irish verses, from the late 6th century or early 7th century. The tradition of preserving knowledge orally in verse had come into contact with Christian literacy. Poetry began to be written down.[12]

Celtic poetry was not all blood-soaked. Bards retained by a lord to sing his praises might be limited in their official repertoire, but some poetry could be composed simply for pleasure. This pair of quatrains was written by a scribe in Old Irish in the margin of a Latin grammar that he was copying *c.* 845. It captures the delight in writing in the open air, amid foliage and birdsong.

> A hedge of trees surrounds me,
> A blackbird's lay sings to me;
> Above my lined booklet
> The trilling birds chant to me.
> In a grey mantle from the top of bushes
> The cuckoo sings:
> Verily—may the Lord shield me!—
> Well do I write under the greenwood.[13]

The Book of Taliesin preserves some of the oldest poems in Brittonic. Many of them are attributed to Taliesin, court poet to the 6th-century King Urien of Rheged in what is now the north of England. One poem from the collection, 'The Fold of the Bards', alludes in a round-about way to poetic contests, like the 'Ulster women's war of words' that opened this chapter. This extract boasts of the poet's skills:

> I am a harmonious one; I am a clear singer.
> I am steel; I am a druid.
> I am an artificer; I am a scientific one.
> I am a serpent; I am love; I will indulge in feasting.
> I am not a confused bard drivelling.[14]

Druids

Caesar linked the memorizing of verses particularly to a privileged class among the Celts, the druids, who acted as judges, priests and teachers.[15] How we would love to have an authentic account by a druid of his activities. Instead we have a view of druids from Classical sources, which may be biased. On the other hand we have modern fantasy woven around a long-bearded figure with an aura of power.

The wickedly entertaining Terry Pratchett had a druid flying a megalith through the clouds to patch up an astronomical stone circle which had developed a hardware glitch.[16] Pratchett managed thereby to satirize targets ancient and modern. One old story was that the great wizard Merlin had transported the stones of Stonehenge from Ireland, though on ships rather than by magical levitation.[17] Archaeologists may protest that the shadowy Merlin (if he lived at all) dates from a time long after the construction of Stonehenge, and so did druids. Yet nothing seems to shake the popular perception of a link between druids and megaliths. [3]

The druids in early Irish literature are rather different. One is persistently praised as good and marvellous in the Ulster Cycle of tales:

> At that time a certain *féinnid* [a warrior living apart from his tribe]
> came from the south of Ulster, performing *féinnidecht* [war-like
> deeds] across Ireland, with a band of three times nine men: his
> name was Cathbad, the wondrous druid. He had great knowledge,
> and magic [*druídecht*], and manly strength; he was of the Ulaid by
> birth, but had run off from them.[18]

3 *Antiquary John Aubrey surveyed Stonehenge in the late 17th century and considered it the work of natives of Britain, rather than the Romans. He knew from Classical texts of pre-Roman British priests called druids and so attributed Stonehenge to them. This 18th-century engraving of a druid in a grove by Stonehenge, holding a sickle and mistletoe, is in this antiquarian tradition.*

The tale goes on to relate how Cathbad took a princess of the Ulaid to wife by force and was granted territory by her father, the king of Ulster. A son was born to the princess, Conchobar mac Nessa, who became a king of Ulster in his turn, while Cathbad became the chief druid at his court – a position of the highest status. The warriors of Ulster fell silent when King Conchobar rose to speak; yet the king waited for Cathbad to open the proceedings.[19] So Cathbad was far from venerable when we first meet him as a fiery young warrior. His hands were stained with blood. The Ulster Cycle is full of marvels, but Cathbad usually has no part in them. He stands out in one way though. He is portrayed as having the gift of prophecy.[20]

Druids as prophets appear in a 7th-century *Life of Patrick*, where they foretell his coming as no glad tidings for them.[21] Indeed the gradual rise of Christianity in Ireland rendered druids redundant as priests and teachers.[22] We find Celtic Christian saints credited with the gift of prophecy. Since the Church had taken over the religious functions of the druids, prophecy would also logically fall within its sphere. The Christian tradition enveloped it easily, with its roots in Old Testament prophets. The far-famed St Columba or *Colum Cille* (died 597) was credited with many prophetic revelations.[23] 'He was a sage, a prophet and a poet' says an elegy written shortly after his death.[24]

Other powers associated with druids, such as control over nature, also appear in the early hagiographies of Irish saints. A fascinating passage in the Life of the 6th-century saint Mochuda presents a magical contest between a druid and the saint, in which the saint triumphed by causing an apple tree to blossom instantly and then fruit.[25] St Columba too contested with druids, we are told. In his mission to convert the pagan Picts of northern Britain, he faced particular opposition from Briochan, foster-father and tutor to King Brude. On one occasion Briochan aimed to prevent the saint from sailing away on Loch Ness by making the wind unfavourable. Columba foiled him by sailing anyway, and the wind swung round to support him.[26]

Though the powers of druids are presented as magical, prediction is what we expect from modern scientists. The understanding of natural forces enables a meteorologist to predict the weather, for example. The knowledge gleaned by living through many a season, stored up and passed down from druid to druid would have been invaluable.

Literature and archaeology

Of all the rich legacy of early Irish literature, the *Táin Bó Cúailnge* (Cattle Raid of Cooley) stands out for its length and fame. It forms the core of what is known either as the Ulster Cycle of tales, after the home of its hero, or the Red Branch Cycle, from the name of the banqueting hall at Emain Macha, the royal centre of Ulster. It tells of an heroic clash of arms. Medb, queen of Connacht, and her husband Ailill take an army to Ulster to steal a great brown bull, the Donn Cúailnge. The men of Ulster being struck by a debilitating curse, it is left to the young Cú Chulainn to defend the province. [4] He takes his stand at a ford, engaging one Connachtman after another in single combat until reinforcements arrive.[27]

Medieval Irish monks treated Cú Chulainn as an historical personage, attempting to work out dates for him long before their own time.[28] Modern scholars generally see the story as pure fiction. Indeed, statistical analysis of its network of social relationships reveals a pattern akin to that of the superheroes of the Marvel comics.[29] Could the *Táin* have any basis in fact?

Conflict between the peoples of Ulster and their southern neighbours is suggested by the remains of protective earthworks, of which the Black Pig's Dyke is the best known. [see 67] This is not one long frontier, but discontinuous stretches that probably protected points of easy access for cattle raiders. These fortifications included a massive timber palisade, probably made of oak tree trunks. Radiocarbon dating of remains of the palisade near Scotshouse in Co. Monaghan could be no more precise than somewhere between 500 BC and 25 BC.[30]

Fortunately, tree-ring dating can pinpoint felling years with some precision. Close study of the Dorsey earthwork in South Armagh reveals two successive lines of defence.[31] The southern one can be dated to 95 BC and the northern one to 140 BC.[32] So it is most likely to be part of the same works as Black Pig's Dyke. Navan Fort in Armagh can be identified as Emain Macha in the Ulster Cycle. Its occupants around 100 BC felt the need for a bank and ditch around the top of the hill. Within, a large circular building was erected. The massive central post has been dated by tree rings to 95 BC.[33] So there was a burst of defensive activity in the year 95 BC. This is not to say that the events of the *Táin Bó Cúailnge*, complete with their magic and marvellous cast of characters, are fully historical. The difference between the surviving versions of the tale show that it was elaborated over centuries.[34] While enthusiasts see the *Táin Bó Cúailnge* as a window on the Iron Age,[35] sceptics feel that the lifestyle it portrays would fit as comfortably just before the arrival of Christianity in Ireland in the 5th century AD.[36]

Tree-ring dating has sprung another surprise. Here is a snippet of a tale thought to be entirely mythological:

> These are the four things
> which Eochaid Airem chose
> from the many manly-seeming companies,
> with abundant shields and swords:
> A causeway across the bog of the Lámraige,
> a wood across Bréifne, without difficulty,
> the fair removal of the stones of great Mide,
> and rushes across Tethna.[37]

Eochaid Airem is described as king of Tara. The story itself is set in a supernatural world. It forms part of the Mythological Cycle of Irish tales

4 *Cú Chulainn, the hero of the Ulster Cycle of tales, is pictured riding into battle in his chariot, with his charioteer beside him.*

about pre-Christian kings. So the appearance of an Eochaidh Aireamh in the *Annals of the Four Masters* as a king of Ireland reigning between Anno Mundi 5070 (*c.* 142 BC) and Anno Mundi 5084 (*c.* 116 BC) was dismissed as non-historical.

True annals are contemporary with the events they record. Monastic annals might begin as jotted notes in the table used to calculate the date of Easter, as reminders of memorable years, such as that in which a king died. Transferred later to separate manuscripts, they could be continued by one scribe after another. The Irish annals provide a contemporary record of Irish history for over a millennium, from the middle of the 6th to the early 17th centuries AD. Annalists could make mistakes, but the fact that they were recording events as they happened makes annals one of the most reliable sources for historians. However, the *Annals of the Four Masters* is a compilation made in the 17th century. It aimed to gather together all the Irish annals surviving at that time. Since it includes annals now otherwise lost, it is an immensely valuable source.[38] Yet its prehistoric section is not based on any annal. In common with many another chronicle composed retrospectively, it attempted to date events from miscellaneous sources.

No wonder that Eochaid Airem's causeway was seen as imaginary – until, that is, an impressive timber causeway was uncovered at Corlea. [5] It was built in 148 BC across the boglands of Longford, close to the River Shannon.[39] Richard Warner, then archaeologist at the Ulster Museum in Belfast, argued that the name Lámraige in the tale is preserved in the townland name Laragh, close to Corlea. So the Corlea trackway could be identified as the work of Eochaid Airem. In fact Warner defended the whole prehistoric section of the *Annals of the Four Masters* by attempting to fit reported events to tree-ring dating.[40] This met with a shower of cold water from J. P. Mallory, who was teaching archaeology at Queen's University Belfast. How plausible is the concept of oral memories passed down over thousands of years? The Corlea trackway, being much closer in time to literacy, could be the one diamond in a heap of broken glass.[41]

5 *The massive Iron Age causeway at Corlea, Kenagh, Co. Longford, Ireland, crosses boglands close to the River Shannon. It was built from split planks laid on top of raised rails and was solid enough to carry wheeled traffic.*

Pseudo-history

The tradition of a learned class who memorized verse has encouraged the optimistic idea that authentic history could have been passed down orally for thousands of years, finally to emerge in the work of medieval historians. Yet it is rare for such histories to make any reference to drawing on oral sources. A common theme instead is a frustrated search for native written records. It begins in the Dark Ages with Gildas complaining that if there ever were any British records of Britannia as a Roman province, they must have perished in the towns burnt by the Saxon enemy or accompanied those Britons who fled to distant lands.[42] Gildas was primarily a religious writer, whose sermonizing *Ruin of Britain* was preserved among Christian literature. So it survived as a precious resource for historians from a period of British history otherwise almost mute.

In the 8th or early 9th century the first attempt at a history of Britain, the *Historia Brittonum*, was composed. In a prologue in one manuscript copy of it, the author, named as Nennius, disciple of St Elbotus (presumed to be Elfod, bishop of Bangor), blamed the dull British for casting away knowledge of their past. He tells us that he had heaped together all he could find, 'partly from traditions of our ancestors, partly from writings and monuments of the ancient inhabitants of Britain, partly from the annals of the Romans, and the chronicles of the sacred fathers'.[43] The result was mainly pseudo-history. One modern authority deems the prologue a forgery and the authorship of the work therefore unknown. Yet the prologue's strictures on the failure to record the past find echoes elsewhere.

Here is an exasperated Irish would-be historian, writing in the late 9th or early 10th century:

> The foolish Irish race, forgetful of its history, boasts of incredible
> or completely fabulous deeds, since it has been careless about
> committing to writing any of its achievements.[44]

Geoffrey of Monmouth (died 1154/5) was similarly frustrated. He was probably of Breton stock. William the Conqueror had granted Monmouth Castle to a Breton and it descended in his family until after Geoffrey's time. So Geoffrey's parents may have been part of the entourage of the Breton lords of Monmouth.[45] The Bretons and Welsh spoke similar Celtic languages. No wonder Geoffrey of Monmouth wallowed in nostalgia for a golden Celtic past. As a cleric in Oxford, he searched keenly for any clue to that past. According to him, he could find little until his friend Walter, archdeacon of Oxford, gave him a 'very ancient book written in the British language'. Geoffrey tells us that he set himself to translate it into Latin,[46] claiming that the result was his *History of the Kings of Britain*, completed about 1138.[47] Geoffrey traced the royal line from one Brutus of Troy, whom he imagined to be the founder of Britain, through a host of supposed pre-Roman sovereigns to three genuine 7th-century kings of Gwynedd starting with Cadfan, whose gravestone is in Llangadwaladr church on Anglesey (see also p. 178). [6] Geoffrey devoted most space to a detailed and loving treatment of Arthur, that shadowy symbol of resistance by the Britons to the Anglo-Saxons, which has ensured the eternal popularity of his book. The phenomenal success of the Arthur legend is fascinating. It has been endlessly adapted over the centuries to appeal to different audiences. Geoffrey converted a Dark Age battle-leader into an imperial Arthur who could rival the creators of Continental empires, thus giving the British as proud a history as that of the Greeks and Romans. Some scholars of Geoffrey's time entertained their readers at his expense,[48] but such critical voices were drowned in the wave of delight.

Alas, the *History of the Kings of Britain* was one long exercise in fantasy writing for the greater glory of the nation. Far from being the translation of

6 *The gravestone of King Cadfan (d. c. 625) built into the north wall of the nave in Llangadwaladr church, Anglesey. The inscription reads* Catamanus rex sapientisimus opinatisimus omnium regum *('King Cadfan, most wise and renowned of all kings').*

7 The Historia Brittonum *was the first attempt at a history of Britain, written in Latin. In this copy dated 1105 in the British Library, the large capital 'B' halfway down the page begins a section on the origins of the British and Irish. In translation, it begins: 'The island of Britain is so called from one Brutus, a Roman consul.'*

a single book, it draws on many sources, both Classical and Welsh, changing and elaborating to suit Geoffrey's purpose.[49] His key British source may have been a manuscript similar to one now in the British Library. [7] This contains the *Historia Brittonum*, from which he took the pseudo-history of Brutus and a list of Arthur's battles, the *Annales Cambriae* (*Welsh Chronicles*), which mention Arthur, and Welsh royal genealogies.[50]

Much of Geoffrey's work was simple supposition from place-names. For example, he imagined that London must have been founded by a King Lud and Leicester by a King Leir. Both cities were actually of Roman foundation.[51] Geoffrey was following in a long tradition of creating origin stories from names. Places were indeed sometimes named after the person who first settled there. So it was tempting to imagine that from every place-name, country name or tribal name an ancestor could be conjured up. Then storytellers wove legends about him.

Isidore of Seville (d. 636), who wrote an 'encyclopedia' of information gathered from Classical sources, wryly reported that 'Some suspect that the Britons were so named because they are brutes [brutus in Latin]'.[52] The Historia Brittonum deftly turned insult into boast, asserting that Britain derived its name from one Brutus, a Roman consul. Brutus is represented as the grandson of the Trojan prince Aeneas. There could be no clearer proof that this tale drew on Classical sources rather than local folk memory. The Aeneid was the Roman answer to the Greek Iliad, that stirring epic poem peopled with gods and heroes, and telling of the 10-year siege of Troy. Virgil created his own epic around Aeneas, a character in the Iliad who survives the fall of the city and was therefore available for further poetic adventures. Virgil has his hero buffeted around the Mediterranean until he found shelter at last in Latium, home of the Latins. There Aeneas became king by a combination of conquest and marriage politics. Thus Virgil provided a glorious origin for the Roman people. Tagging a Brutus on to the genealogy of Aeneas created an equal status for the British with much less effort.[53]

Since Christianity and literacy were so closely linked, it was generally the scholarly religious who began to shape origin stories for the Celts of Britain and Ireland in the Middle Ages. It was natural for them to turn to the Bible for ancient history. Genesis narrates the story of a deluge which only one family survived – that of Noah, with his three sons Shem, Ham and Japheth and their wives. Their descendants supposedly populated the earth.[54] The biblical offspring of Ham covered an impressive swathe of lands from Mesopotamia through Palestine to northeast Africa. The biblical Shem is presented as the forefather of the Assyrians, Elamites and Hebrews. Japheth's brood seem to be those Indo-Europeans who were known to the Hebrews. They lived in a semicircle around the Fertile Crescent: to the east were the Medes, to the north on the steppe ranged the Scythians and Cimmerians, while the Hellenes lay to the northwest in Greece, Cyprus and western Asia Minor.[55]

The Romano-Jewish historian Josephus (AD 37–c. 100) provided some more geography:

> Japhet [sic], the son of Noah, had seven sons: they inhabited
> so, that, beginning at the mountains Taurus and Amanus, they
> proceeded along Asia, as far as the River Tanais [Don], and along
> Europe to Cadiz; and settling themselves on the lands which

they light upon, which none had inhabited before, they called the nations by their own names.[56]

As newly Christian nations began to search for their origins, increasingly complex genealogies from Noah were created.[57] The *Historia Brittonum* provides a descent of Brutus from Japheth via his son Javan, which is the word used throughout the Old Testament for the Ionian Greeks of western Asia Minor.[58] This no doubt seemed logical to those trying to forge a link to the people of Troy.

Another pseudo-history painted on a biblical backdrop has fascinated generations. *Lebor Gabála Érenn* (*The Book of the Taking of Ireland*), compiled in the late 11th century, tells a stirring story of invaders battling for Ireland. It opens with a synopsis of Genesis, starting with the creation of heaven and earth and proceeding inevitably to the offspring of Japheth. This time two sons of Japheth are mentioned: Magog, whose 'progeny are the peoples who came to Ireland before the Gaedil', and Gomer, 'of him are the Gaedil and the people of Scythia'.[59] Gomer is the name used in the Bible for the Cimmerians, occupants of the steppe north of the Black Sea, later known as Scythia.[60] Isidore thought Gomer was the ancestor of the Gauls, possibly because no other son had a name beginning with G.[61] Similar thinking may account for the choice of Gomer as ancestor of the *Goidel*, a name that the Irish used for themselves no earlier than the 7th century AD, which helps to date the *Lebor Gabála Érenn*. The name was adapted from the Brittonic name for the Irish.[62]

Magog is mentioned in Ezekiel (38–39) as the land of a powerful potential enemy:

> Gog of the land of Magog.... You will come from your place in the far north, you and many nations with you, all of them riding on horses, a great horde, a mighty army.

The description fits the Scythian horsemen who took over the European steppe from the Cimmerians. Their incursions south of the Caucasus were the bane of established states of the Near East. Josephus made the logical identification: 'Magog founded those ... who are by the Greeks called Scythians.'[63] So Scythia was seen as the starting point for both the Gaedil and their predecessors in Ireland.

Genetics: the first clues

Genetically the Irish do not cluster close to Iberians, despite the claims in some origin myths (p. 28). Instead they overlap with their nearest neighbours, the British.[64] How do we know? The studies that came to this conclusion compared samples of DNA from living people. But what exactly did they look at? In the nucleus of every human cell are the 23 pairs of chromosomes that hold the code for the creation of a human being. One of each pair is inherited from each parent; 22 pairs of your chromosomes are gender neutral. The other pair dictates whether you are born male or female: two X chromosomes and you are a girl, but an X and a Y for a boy. Together these 23 pairs of chromosomes are known as the genome. Each chromosome is made up of two strands of DNA that coil around each other in the famous spiral staircase or double helix.

The code itself is composed of just four nucleobases, written as A, T, C and G. Most of our DNA is shared with all other human beings, but there are locations where the genetic code varies between individuals, for example I might have a T where you have a C. Such a location is known as a Single Nucleotide Polymorphism (SNP, pronounced 'snip'). The studies which found that the Irish cluster with the British compared many SNPs across the genome. It may make matters clearer to focus on one particular chromosome.

Only males carry a Y-chromosome. So mutations on this chromosome enable us to track descent from father to son. Picture an unbroken chain of life from your earliest male ancestor through countless generations to your paternal grandfather and your father down to you, if you happen to be male. Your Y-DNA should be exactly the same as your father's. But sometimes there are faults in replication. You could see it as a typing error in the chains of letters along the DNA. Such errors, often called mutations, can tell us a lot. The pattern of mutations in your Y-DNA places you in a haplogroup.

Western Europe is saturated with a particular Y-DNA signature, which has been labelled R1b1a2a1a2. [see 23] This name fits the haplogroup on to a Y-DNA 'family tree' or phylogeny. [8] From R descends R1, from R1b descends R1b1 and so on. Since these 'relative' names change as new mutations are discovered and the tree changes, it is common to identify a haplogroup also by the mutation which defines it, which is unchanging. So you may see R1b1a2a1a2 written as R1b1a2a1a2 (P312) or R1b-P312 for short.

The subclade (subgroup) R1b1a2a1a2c (L21) is overwhelmingly common in Ireland and north and west Britain. [9] It is found at its densest concentration in those parts of the British Isles where the Celtic languages lasted longest. In France it is strongest in Brittany, named after the Britons who settled there. Y-DNA from a burial at Hinxton, Cambridgeshire, dating to the last decades before the Roman conquest belongs to R1b-L21.[65] A link is clear between R1b-L21 and the Insular Celts.

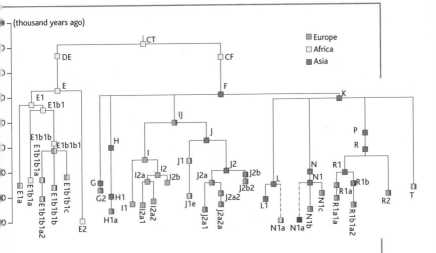

(thousand years ago)

8 (above) A section of the phylogeny of Y-DNA showing the haplogroups common in Europe from 80,000 years ago to the present day. These descend from the ancient CT, mainly via F. The root of the tree (not shown here) is even more ancient, going back to ancestral haplogroup A in Africa. R1b, common in western Europe, is a relatively young haplogroup.

9 (below) The distribution of Y-DNA R1b-L21 suggests that it travelled down the Rhine and into the British Isles, where it is now densest in the regions least affected by later arrivals. The high level in Brittany may reflect the Dark Age migration of Britons, after whom Brittany was named.

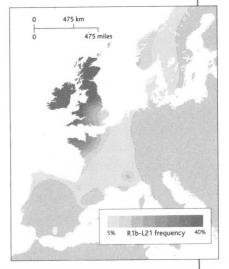

Outside the British Isles, R1b-L21 of British and Irish types can be explained by migration from the Isles, but this does not account for all the R1b-L21 in France and the Low Countries. It is a working theory that R1b-L21 entered the British Isles from this direction. Ancient DNA is needed to confirm it. The light dusting of L21 in Galicia may be a relict of those Britons who settled there in the Post-Roman period, or those who may have moved there in the late Bronze Age. Some subclades of R1b-L21 can be associated with specific surnames or families (see Appendix).

As it chances, the European steppe is now regarded as the homeland of the Indo-Europeans, as we shall see in Chapter 4. But in the *Lebor Gabála Érenn* the idea perhaps built on the geography of Josephus for the sons of Japheth moving westwards into Europe from the River Don to Spain.

A related idea appears as early as AD 731, when Bede began his *Ecclesiastical History of the English People*. He records a tale that the Picts came from Scythia.[66] The *Historia Brittonum* culled from Irish scholars an Irish origin story that starts with a Scythian nobleman and his kin exiled in Egypt at the time that the Israelites escaped Egyptian captivity. After many years wandering in Africa these supposed exiles landed in Spain. There they stayed and multiplied for a thousand years before moving to Ireland. Thus a parallel was created with the wandering Israelites seeking the Promised Land. Waves of arrivals from Spain culminated in three sons of a Spanish soldier (*miles hispaniae*) reaching Ireland with thirty ships.[67]

The *Lebor Gabála Érenn* elaborates on this story. The Scythian nobleman becomes Fénius Farsaid, who brought the Irish language from the Tower of Babel. His character is based on one Fenech, who appears as the leader of the descendants of Japheth at Babel in an obscure Hebrew text. Fenech was evidently seized upon because of the fortuitous similarity between his name and the word *Féni*, an Old Irish term for the Irish people. The Latin *miles hispaniae* (soldier of Spain) was converted into a name, Míl Espáine, and a mass of fake genealogy was grafted on to the scheme. His sons Éber and Erimón divide the kingship of Ireland between them. Both these names are also artificial, being derived from the name of Ireland in Latin (*Hibernia*) and Gaelic (*Ériu*). Éber, presented as the founding father of the Eóganacht, takes the southern half, while Erimón takes the north. This division supplants a more ancient concept of Ireland being divided into five parts. So it was probably cooked up in the 8th century AD to give a respectably ancient ancestry to the newly dominant dynasties of the Uí Néill and Eóganacht. Essentially it is a learned fiction, but it incorporates some genuine Celtic names, such as *Fir Domnann*.[68] For them we have some independent evidence (see p. 156).

Like Geoffrey of Monmouth's fanciful work, the *Lebor Gabála Érenn* was accepted for centuries as an accurate history. Modern scholars are less credulous. R. A. Stewart Macalister, who translated the *Lebor Gabála Érenn* into English in the mid-20th century, declared that: 'There is not a single element of genuine historical detail, in the strict sense of the word, any-where in the whole compilation.'[69]

Linguistic and genetic evidence conclusively rule out a Scythian ances-try for the Celts, as we shall see (p. 78). Though some probable input from Iberia into the Celts of Ireland or Britain will emerge in Chapter 5, modern DNA suggests that this was overlain by a stronger migration pulse down the Rhine (see Genetics box, pp. 26–27). So in the next chapter we cross the choppy English Channel to what was once Gaul.

Overview

- Ireland and Wales preserve the earliest literature in Celtic languages.

- Key features of the Insular Celts that emerge from this literature are:

  - Heroic values and leadership by warrior chiefs.

  - Love of nature, feasting, language, beauty and wisdom.

  - High status accorded to druids as prophets, sages, teachers and priests.

- The *Táin Bó Cúailnge* is fiction, but its core conflict between the peoples of Ulster and their southern neighbours fits archaeological evidence.

- The medieval Irish, Welsh and Picts had no true knowledge of their origins, which were too far in the past for recollection. So origin stories were developed by early Christian scholars, using Genesis and Classical sources.

- The genetic evidence links Ireland to Britain more than Iberia, but complications will emerge in Chapter 5. In Chapter 2 we follow the more obvious trail to Gaul.

CHAPTER TWO

The Gauls and Celtic

The Gauls are very tall with white skin and blond hair, not only blond by nature but more so by the artificial means they use to lighten their hair. For they continually wash their hair in a lime solution, combing it back from the forehead to the back of the neck … this treatment makes the hair thick like a horse's mane. Some shave their beards, while others allow a short growth, but nobles shave their cheeks and allow the moustache grow until it covers the mouth…. In both journeys and battles the Gauls use two-horse chariots which carry both the warrior and the charioteer. When they encounter cavalry in battle, they first hurl their spears then step down from the chariot to fight with swords. Some of them think so little of death that they fight wearing only a loincloth, without armour of any kind…. Their trumpets … are of a peculiar and barbarian kind which produce a harsh reverberating sound suitable to the confusion of battle.[1]

Thus wrote Diodorus Siculus between about 60 and 30 BC, but he was relying on older sources. When Caesar conquered Gaul in 58–57 BC, he did not encounter chariots in warfare. They had dropped out of use in favour of cavalry. But when Gauls battled the Romans in northern Italy in 225 BC, they did indeed use chariots in battle and some fought naked.[2] [10]

We tend to visualize Gaul as equivalent to modern-day France. We talk of Gallic cuisine or expressive Gallic gestures, when we mean French. The Gaul of Caesar's day did include all of mainland France, but it also stretched eastwards to the Rhine, encompassing what is now Belgium and Luxembourg, the Netherlands south of the Rhine, and those parts of Germany and Switzerland west of the Rhine. From the Roman perspective, this region was Transalpine Gaul (Gaul on the other side of the Alps). Since Gauls had spread over the Alps into northern Italy by then, there was also a region known to the Romans as Cisalpine Gaul. [see 1]

10 A denarius minted by the Roman moneyer Lucius Hostilius Saserna in 48 BC. The bust of a Gallic warrior appears on the obverse, his hair thickened with lime and combed back. The reverse depicts a naked Gallic warrior standing in his chariot, holding a spear and small shield, while a crouched charioteer, perched on the pole, drives the horses with a whip.

Caesar famously declared that Gaul was divided into three parts, inhabited by the Belgae, the Aquitani and 'a people who call themselves Celts, though we call them Gauls'. Each, he said, had a different language.[3] In fact the name Belgae has a Celtic etymology and there were Celtic place-names in their territory in Roman times,[4] so their linguistic differences from the Gauls cannot have been dramatic. By contrast the Aquitani of southwestern Gaul appear to have spoken a language ancestral to modern-day Basque. Yet another language, not noted by Caesar, was spoken by the Ligurians along the southern coast of Gaul. Enough evidence survives of the language of the Gauls themselves for linguists to recognize it as belonging in the same family as Breton, Welsh and Gaelic. Centuries earlier, seagoing Greeks had encountered *Keltoi* on the Mediterranean coast at Narbo (Narbonne) and near Massalia (Marseilles). The earliest surviving record of these *Keltoi* comes from Hecataeus of Miletus (c. 500 BC).[5]

Ancient Greek knowledge of Central Europe was much vaguer. Herodotus (c. 484–425 BC) had heard of Celts beyond the Pillars of Hercules (Strait of Gibraltar) and he knew, probably from Hecataeus, that the River Ister (Danube) rose in the land of the Celts, but his geography seems absurd to modern readers. He thought that the river rose at the city of Pyrene, which he envisaged somewhere in Iberia.[6] Aristotle (384–322 BC) made it clear that Pyrene in this passage was intended to be the Pyrenees.[7] Before we mock such ignorance, we should recall that ancient Greek geographers were pioneers, trying to make sense of information coming from sailors and traders. There were huge gaps in their knowledge. That could lead to a mental map of one region being stitched directly to that of another, without realizing that there was a lot of territory in between. The Danube actually

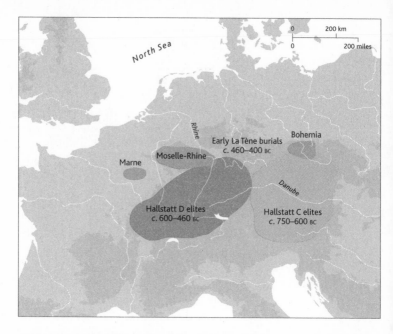

11 *The Iron Age phases of the Hallstatt culture (Hallstatt C and D) encompassed the upper reaches of the rivers Danube and Rhine. Early La Tène culture centres sprang up on the northern fringes of the Hallstatt elites.*

rises from two sources in the Black Forest mountains of southwestern Germany, and is swelled by tributaries from the Alps. The Alps are not mentioned by Greek authors until the 3rd century BC.[8] Herodotus, however, does list the tributaries of the Danube from east to west, the last one of which he names as the Alpis, rising north of the land of the Ombricians (Umbrians of Italy) and flowing north to join the Danube.[9] Here it seems we have one of the Alpine tributaries. So we can ignore the red herring of Pyrene and accept that Celts were living north of the Alps around the head of the Danube.

In the 19th century scholars identified two successive cultures at the right place and time to correspond to these historical Celts. Johann Georg Ramsauer was in charge of the salt mines at Hallstatt in the Austrian Alps in 1846 when he discovered a cemetery nearby. [see 46] Instead of simply plundering it, as antiquity-hunters of his day were wont to do, he carefully excavated and recorded his findings. The people buried there had been salt miners too. Odd items that they left in the mines – clothing and wooden tools – were wonderfully preserved by the salt. So this early foray into archaeological methodology remains one of the most remarkable sites ever linked to the Celts. We now know that it belongs mainly to the 7th and 6th centuries BC.[10] When similar artifacts were found elsewhere, they were naturally identified as in the style of Hallstatt, so the site gave its name to a culture eventually found to be widespread over Central Europe. [11] It began in the Bronze Age, centuries before the salt mine at Hallstatt, but its later phases (c. 750 to c. 475/450 BC) fall into the Iron Age.[11]

The same process decreed that a site at La Tène, on Lake Neuchâtel in Switzerland, should be forever associated with the next phase of the Central European Iron Age (c. 460 BC to mid-1st century BC). In 1857 local collector Hansli Kopp noticed some timber piles driven into the mud of the lakeside. Groping between them, he found about 40 weapons. It was a sign of the riches to come. Over the following decades, this extraordinary site yielded over 3,000 artifacts. The flowing forms of the decorative metalwork attracted most attention, but the oxygen-free lake mud also preserved wooden objects, including a complete chariot wheel.[12] [12, 13] The chariot was to prove a key distinction between the earlier Hallstatt culture and La Tène.

12 (opposite) *Stylized animals enliven an iron scabbard (3rd century BC) from La Tène in Switzerland. The style is confidently fluid and playful.*

13 (right) *This spoked wheel with iron tyre was discovered at La Tène. It was preserved by the oxygen-free mud of this lake site.*

By the time of the 1871 International Congress of Prehistoric Anthropology and Archaeology in Bologna, objects in the same style as found at La Tène had been dug up in France and northern Italy. The Italian finds were crucial. The Roman historian Livy described the Gauls crossing the Alps in waves to settle in the Po Valley, driving out those Etruscans who lived there.[13] So the cemetery of an intrusive people in the ruins of the Etruscan town of Marzabotto could be firmly identified as Celtic.[14] The La Tène culture could thus be seen as the material manifestation of the Celts. It could be tied not only to historical events, but also to descriptions of the Celts, such as that which opens this chapter, mentioning the Celtic chariot.

Chariots

The essential feature of the chariot was its speed. The first wheeled vehicles were heavy wagons with solid wheels. They were tough structures, ideal for transporting farm produce or use as a mobile home. The invention of the spoked wheel reduced the weight. Given a stripped down superstructure without a driver's seat, a single axle and the power of fast horses, these wheels could flash along.

The chariot was the sports car of its era for its speed and manoeuvrability. In the Bronze Age of the Near East, Egypt and Greece it was the vehicle favoured by royalty and a warrior elite. Since these civilizations left records behind, we know that maintaining a chariot force was hugely expensive, requiring specialist chariot warriors, charioteers, horse-trainers, grooms and chariot-makers. Chariots were used in war and peace. A mobile archery platform could be used for hunting. More ornate versions featured in ceremonies. It was a versatile vehicle.

Among the Celts the chariot appears in high-status burials, mainly of warriors with their weapons.[15] Since wood usually decays in the soil, the remains of chariots are more often recognized by their metal fittings. Celtic chariot burials were discovered in the Marne department of France in the 1870s, such as that of La Gorge Meillet.[16] [14] Marne has subsequently proved to be rich in chariot burials of the early La Tène period.[17] [see 55]

The Continental Celts left us no descriptions of chariots. So we are faced with a paradox. Some of the best Celtic-language sources for chariots were written in Ireland, where no complete chariot has been found, though wooden wheels have survived at the remarkable wetland site at Edercloon,

14 *Chariot burial of La Gorge Meillet, in the French department of Marne, excavated in 1876. The body of a warrior had been laid on the floor of his chariot, and slots cut in the ground for the wheels to fit into. The wooden wheels had decayed, but the iron tyres and bronze axle bands and hub caps remained. The rectangular cut of the burial is typical of those found in Marne. The grave was richly equipped with iron sword, javelin and knife, and a bronze helmet.*

Co. Longford, starting with a Late Bronze Age solid wheel and continuing to Iron Age and medieval spoke wheels.[18] Furthermore the earliest surviving version of the *Táin Bó Cúailnge* may have been first committed to writing in the 8th century AD.[19] So there is a gap of over a millennium between the earliest Celtic chariot burials and this literary epic. That gap in time narrows if we consider the last evidence for chariots, rather than the first. Though Caesar mentions no chariots in Gaul, his forces came up against massed ranks of them in Britain in 54 BC.[20] Chariots were still in use by Britons resisting the Romans in AD 60–61. Who can forget the image of an enraged Boudica rousing up rebellion 'in a chariot with her daughters in front of her'.[21] Even in post-Roman Britain, one of the warriors celebrated in Y Gododdin had a war-chariot.[22] In Ireland a king escaped in a chariot from a battle in AD 563.[23]

Sadly, the texts of the Táin Bó Cúailnge that survive are not the original manuscript, but versions written down in the 12th century, garnished in glorious detail, wherein scholars detect the hand of medieval scholarship. A wonderful description of the war-chariot of Cú Chulainn, laden with precious metals, comes into the category of such later embroidery.[24] By this time Irish scholars were well versed in Latin literature, which included versions of Greek epics. Cú Chulainn was dubbed 'the Irish Achilles' by Celticist Alfred Nutt at the beginning of the 20th century, for his correspondences to Homer's hero.[25] The chariot of Cú Chulainn was drawn by two swift horses, one grey and one black, who are given a supernatural origin.[26] In the Iliad, Achilles has yoked to his chariot the 'fleet horses, Xanthus and Balius, that flew swift as the winds, horses that the Harpy Podarge conceived to the West Wind, as she grazed on the meadow beside the stream of Oceanus'.[27]

Xanthus means 'yellow' and Balius 'piebald', but they can be depicted as white and black, for example on a Greek hydra of the 6th century BC.[28] Isidore of Seville refers to one black horse and one white being yoked together in the two-horse chariot.[29] So is the Irish chariot merely a literary device?

Chariots are carved on six high crosses in Ireland. That might seem evidence enough that they existed. However, these scenes seem to depict a story from the Ulster Cycle, 'The Phantom Chariot of Cú Chulainn'. In this tale the hero reappears 450 years after his death to convince Loegaire, king of Tara, to convert to Christianity.[30] Proof that the Irish chariot was no phantom comes from the Irish law codes. They refer to a vehicle called a carpat. This is the same word translated as 'chariot' in early Irish literature. We can imagine a more workaday vehicle than that driven by the hero of the Táin.[31]

Another lively debate has surrounded chariot burials found in Britain. Doubts have been expressed about any connection with the Continental Celts, yet a tribal link leaps to the eye. Since the Celts were largely illiterate in pre-Roman days, it was ancient Greek and Roman authors who first recorded tribal names. The Geography of Claudius Ptolemy, written in Greek

c. AD 150, provides the framework of our knowledge. It is a shaky scaffolding by comparison with a modern atlas, but it was revolutionary in its day. Crucially, Ptolemy supplied geographical co-ordinates to locate towns. This was the start of scientific mapping.[32]

Ptolemy located the Parisi in two areas, both of which have chariot burials. The Continental tribe, called the Parisii by Caesar, is easily identified by the town that Ptolemy assigned to them, Lutetia Parisiorum – present-day Paris. The British tribe had a settlement called Petuaria, usually identified as Brough-on-Humber in Yorkshire.[33]

At the end of the last century, two Celtic chariot tombs dating to 300 BC were uncovered during runway construction at Charles de Gaulle Airport at Roissy, on the northern outskirts of Paris. In layout both were similar to the chariot burials which begin earlier in the Marne region. [see 14] They were rectangular in plan, with the deceased laid flat on the platform of their chariots. Slots were cut in the ground to accommodate the wheels. One burial was that of a warrior with weapons.

The other was exceptional. [15] Here had been laid to rest a man without weapons. His chariot was sturdier than that of the warrior and ornamented with decorative bronzes of rare quality. So it was built for status rather than speed. A strange collection of objects lay scattered between the wheels. They were probably amulets, which had been kept in a pouch around the man's neck. Could this be the tomb of a druid?[34] The high status of druids in the Irish tradition (see p. 16) is confirmed by Classical writers. Thus Diodorus Siculus:

15 *The most remarkable object from an unusual chariot burial at Roissy, on the outskirts of Paris, which may be the last resting place of a druid. This perforated bronze, a swirl suggesting fantastic animals with outstretched wings, was created by the lost wax method. Surviving fibres show that it formed the cover of a wooden vessel.*

> The Gauls have highly honoured philosophers and theologians
> called druids.... They do not sacrifice or ask favours from
> the gods without a druid present, as they believe sacrifice
> should be made only by those supposedly skilled in divine
> communication.... The Gauls obey with great care these druids.[35]

On the other side of the English Channel we find the Arras culture of the Yorkshire Wolds, in the region where Ptolemy located the Parisi. [see 55] This culture combines La Tène material with chariot burials. Where we find not only artifacts but also burial rites transplanted from one place to another, it is reasonable to suspect migration. People tend to prefer the burial practice familiar to them. Yet these burials are distinctly different from those at Roissy. Typically, the Arras vehicles were dismantled and the deceased buried in a crouched position. So it has been argued that there is no connection with the Parisii of Gaul.[36] Six of these typical burials were certainly of people who lived locally all their lives. The clues lie in the isotopes in their bones and teeth, which are characteristic of those living on a chalk soil like that of the Wolds.[37] So they were not a group of migrants from Gaul. Who their ancestors were is another matter.

The burials most typical of the Arras culture can be dated to around 200 BC.[38] Earlier chariot burials have now been discovered in Britain, causing considerable excitement. One dating to c. 355 BC was found at Ferry Fryston in Yorkshire.[39] This chariot was buried intact with slots dug to accommodate the wheels, like those of the Marne region and Roissy. Ferry Fryston seems connected to the Arras culture – perhaps the earliest manifestation of it. The occupant of the chariot came from a region of ancient granites.[40] That might fit Scotland, in view of the discovery of an even earlier chariot burial at Newbridge, near Edinburgh. [see 55] This is dated to the 5th century BC – placing it within the earliest La Tène period. Here, if anywhere, we might hope for a migrant from Gaul. Unfortunately all traces of a human body had completely disappeared. So there was no opportunity for either isotope or DNA analysis.[41]

Trump of war

> The Romans ... were dismayed by the discipline of the Celtic
> army, and intimidated by the blare of countless enemy horns
> and trumpets. With the Celts all chanting battle-hymns at the
> same time as well, there was so much noise that the sound
> seemed not just to ring out from the trumpets and the men,
> but to echo from the very hills around them.[42]

Thus wrote the Greek historian Polybius about the Gauls advancing into
northern Italy in 225 BC. The eerie sound of the war horn has now been re-
created, thanks to an astonishing discovery. It has long been known that
the Celts used a long, slender trumpet called a carnyx, with a bell shaped
like an animal head. They were played upright, as we see on the Gundestrup
Cauldron. [16] Carnyces were not exclusive to the Celts. They are depicted
with captured Dacians on Trajan's Column in Rome. The Dacians may have
adopted them from Celts who had expanded into their region in the 4th
century BC (see Chapter 7).

16 *An interior panel of the huge Gundestrup Cauldron shows a procession of warriors (below)
towards a god-like figure (on the left), with (on the right) trumpeters playing the carnyx.
Though found in Denmark, the cauldron looks like Thracian silverwork, but the carnyces and
the helmets topped by animals are typically Gaulish. Probably the cauldron was made where
Celtic and Thracian peoples lived close together at the time of its production between about
150 BC and 0 BC.*

As we know from warfare in times closer to our own, the trumpet can be used to relay the orders of commanding officers over the din of battle. So it was with the carnyx. The great hero of the Gauls, Vercingetorix (see pp. 151–52), who rallied Gallic tribes in one last attempt to repulse Caesar in 52 BC, sounded the trumpet (presumably the carnyx) to lead his men into battle.[43]

The problem for eager re-enactors was that only a few segments of carnyces had been found prior to 2004. The finest fragment was a boar's head from Deskford, northeast Scotland, found in 1816. Since it was made from recycled Roman metal, it can be dated to the Roman period in Britain. In 1992 a replica of the complete instrument was created, reconstructing the missing parts mainly from depictions. This was the brainchild of musicologist Dr John Purser, keen to bring the music of the past alive.[44] But without a complete ancient instrument, could we be certain of the replica's accuracy?

Then suddenly a wealth of evidence was unearthed from just one find-spot. In September 2004 a mass of metalwork was discovered in a pit at a Gallic shrine at Tintignac in the Limousin region of central France. Objects had been broken to put them out of use by mere mortals. They included swords and scabbards, iron spearheads, the metal parts of a shield and armour, and bronze helmets, one in the form of a swan. Finally, in the bottom of the pit, were fragments of no fewer than seven carnyces, as tall as a man. Six have boars' heads and one a snake's head.[45]

The Limousin region takes its name from the Limovici tribe, whom Ptolemy identified, together with their town of Augustorium, now Limoges.[46] Southeast of Limoges lies the present-day town of Naves. The remains of the sanctuary are nearby. The Romans were generally tolerant of the religions they encountered within their expanding empire. So their conquest of Gaul did not see the shrine at Tintignac deserted. On the contrary, a monumental Romano-Gallic complex was erected, which included a theatre.

The earlier Gallic shrine of the 1st century BC at Tintignac was simpler. Like most Gallic structures, it was timber-built. It seems to have played an important part in the life of the tribe. Traces were uncovered of gatherings for animal sacrifices and banquets, including libations to the gods – usually of imported Roman wine. A small circular building was probably a temple. Beside it was the pit with its extraordinary contents, which propelled the site on to the international stage.[47] The contents of the pit look like the spoils of war. That fits Caesar's description of the habits of the Gauls:

When they have decided to fight a battle they generally vow to Mars the booty that they hope to take, and after a victory they sacrifice the captured animals and collect the rest of the spoil in one spot. Among many of the tribes, high piles of it can be seen on consecrated ground; and it is almost an unknown thing for anyone to dare, in defiance of religious law, to conceal his booty at home or to remove anything placed on the piles. Such a crime is punishable by a terrible death under torture.[48]

The Romans generally equated Celtic gods with whichever member of their own pantheon seemed closest in character. A bewildering variety of Celtic deities is known from inscriptions to them. Many seem local or tribal. Several were conflated by the Romans with Mars. In the absence of an inscription, we cannot be certain which war-like god was honoured at Tintignac. We can only be thankful that religious feeling preserved so many carnyces for modern scholars.

Though none of the Tintignac carnyces was buried complete, it proved possible to piece together one boar's head carnyx from the hoard. [17] The result may seem surprising. The Gundestrup Cauldron creates the

17 The bell of a carnyx found at a Gallic shrine at Tintignac, France, is in the shape of a boar's head. Fragments of seven carnyces were found in a pit at this site.

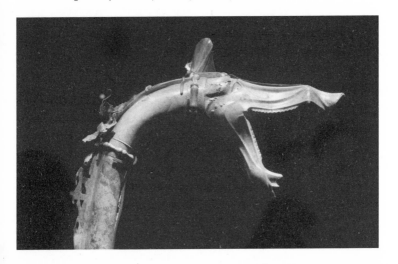

18 A coin of Tasciovanus, king of the Catuvellauni c. 20 BC to c. AD 9. A riding warrior holds aloft a carnyx.

impression that the carnyx-players were facing forward, which would suggest that the instrument was curved at the base where it was blown. The Deskford reconstruction and a number of others were therefore given a curved mouthpiece, though depictions on coins show a straight tube. [18] The Tintignac mouthpiece was not curved. Christophe Maniquet, the archaeologist in charge of the excavation, was curious to find out exactly what sound a carnyx produced. In 2011 a brass copy was made of the restored Tintignac carnyx so that it could be tested. It proved difficult to play, and not as powerful as a modern brass instrument. The closest modern instrument is an alto saxhorn.[49]

Migration mystery

Just the few examples above show that in the last centuries BC there was a similarity of culture between the Gauls and the island Celts. Indeed, that similarity was remarked upon by Julius Caesar.[50] There might seem to be a simple explanation. It has been supposed by many authors that the Celts spread out from Central Europe with the La Tène culture. In this model the first Celtic-speakers to set foot in Britain would have arrived c. 450 BC and in Ireland not much before 300 BC.[51] This theory had a strong appeal. It was underwritten by Classical sources and La Tène is solidly identified as Celtic (p. 34). As we shall see in Chapter 7, Greek and Roman historians vouch for movements of the Gauls in various directions during this period. The arrival of chariot burials in Britain we can certainly date to the La Tène period. It seemed a neat fit. Yet La Tène had an insignificant impact on southern Ireland and most of Iberia, where Celtic languages were spoken from as far back as we can delve with historical sources.

Here we turn to the ancient Greeks, literate and adventurous before the Romans took to the seas. Herodotus tells us that the Phokaeans were the earliest Greeks to make long voyages by sea. Phokaea (now Foça, in modern Turkey) was one of a number of Greek colonies in Asia Minor. The Phokaeans opened up Iberia to trade with the Greek world. Perhaps they were enticed by a traveller's tale. In around 630 BC Kolaios, a merchant captain on the Samos to Egypt route, was blown so badly off course that he ended up beyond the Strait of Gibraltar at Tartessos. This wealthy city was virgin territory for Greek traders at the time, and Kolaios returned home with a huge profit from his cargo.[52] The fame of Tartessos had already spread across the Mediterranean. This mineral-rich region in what is now south-western Spain had attracted the Phoenicians before the Greeks. By the 8th century BC the Phoenicians had founded the city now known as Cadiz in order to trade with Tartessos around the Lower Guadalquivir. Phoenician traders were visiting the Huelva area in the previous century.[53] Phokaea created its own colony c. 600 BC on the Mediterranean coast of what is now France at Massalia, modern Marseilles, facilitating their trade outside the Mediterranean. In the 4th century BC the Greek historian Ephorus describes 'a very prosperous market called Tartessos, a famous city, with much tin carried by river, as well as gold and copper from Celtic lands'.[54]

The Phokaeans reported that the king of Tartessos was called Argantonios.[55] This name is Celtic, derived from the word *arganto* (silver).[56] Names from this root are attested in Roman times all over Hispania and further afield, such as the Caledonian chieftain Argentocoxos, meaning 'silver-limbed'. On the other hand Argantodannos is found on Gaulish coinage, referring to the official in charge of minting coins.[57] So Argantonios could also be a title. That might make sense of the strange claim by Herodotus that he ruled for 80 years and lived for 120. New traders arriving might not realize that they were dealing with a series of men with the same title. However, Herodotus also reports that Argantonios was dead before the Phokaeans abandoned their home city in Asia Minor, when it was under siege by the Persians. That was in about 540 BC.[58]

This does not necessarily mean that the language of Tartessos was Celtic. Celtic-speakers could simply have taken control of trade in those precious metals that came from their own territory further inland. Celticist John Koch has argued that inscriptions in the Paleohispanic southwestern script, adapted from the Phoenician alphabet and dating from between the 8th and

Genetics: ancient DNA

Today scientists can extract genetic code from the remains of people who walked the earth thousands of years ago. Early studies of ancient DNA focused on mitochondrial DNA (mtDNA), since it was easiest to extract. This is found not in the cell nucleus, but in energy-generating mitochondria throughout the rest of the cell. Since there are up to a thousand mitochondria per cell, it is the most abundant human form of DNA in terms of copies. That made it the natural first choice for pioneers trying to extract DNA from ancient bones and teeth. MtDNA is passed down from mother to child. Men do have mitochondrial DNA – it comes from their mothers. But they cannot pass it on.

Table 1 *The first appearance of each Y-DNA haplogroup so far found in European ancient DNA up to the Copper Age.*

Period	Date	Place	Haplogroup	Source
Palaeolithic	37,500 cal. BP	Kostënki 14, Russia	C* (M130)	Seguin-Orlando 2014
Mesolithic	6100 BC	Loschbour, Luxembourg	I2a1 (P37.2)	Lazaridis 2014
	5800 BC	La Braña-Arintero, Spain	C1a2 (V20)	Olalde 2014
	5700 BC	Motala, Sweden	I2a1a1a* (L672)	Haak 2015
	5700 BC	Motala, Sweden	I2c2 (PF3827)	Haak 2015
	5600 BC	Sok River, Samara, Russia	R1b1* (L278)	Haak 2015
	5250 BC	Yuzhnyy Oleni Ostrov, Karelia, Russia	R1a1* (M459)	Haak 2015
Neolithic	5740 BC	Alsónyék-Bátaszék, Hungary	H2 (L281)	Haak 2015
	5600 BC	Alsónyék-Bátaszék, Hungary	G2a2b (S126)	Szécsényi-Nagy 2015
	5250 BC	Els Trocs, Spain	I2a1b1 (L161)	Haak 2015
	5250 BC	Derenburg Meerenstieg, Germany	F* (M89)	Brandt 2013
	5100 BC	Karsdorf, Germany	T1a (M70)	Haak 2015
	5100 BC	Halberstadt, Germany	G2a2a (PF3185)	Haak 2015

6th centuries BC, are in the Tartessian language and that this is Celtic.[61] Both suppositions are contested. Only four of the around 90 inscriptions in this text come from the Tartessian region. Most are from southern Portugal. Their content is so meagre as to severely hamper identification of their language,

The results overturned cherished beliefs. The standard view at the end of the 20th century was that Europeans are mainly descended from European hunter-gatherers. Ancient mtDNA revealed an influx of farmers from the Near East in the Neolithic, whose haplogroups predominate in modern Europeans.[59] A new generation of technology has made it possible to extract ancient Y-DNA, which confirms the influx of farmers. Haplogroup I, found in hunter-gathers, represents less than one-fifth of the present European population, while C1a2, found in a Spanish hunter-gatherer, is vanishingly rare in modern Europeans.[60] The first farmers brought new Y-DNA haplogroups such as G2 from the Near East, while the R1a and R1b that dominate Europe today are first found in Russian hunter-gatherers and did not arrive in Central Europe until the Copper Age.

Period	Date	Place	Haplogroup	Source
Neolithic	5100 BC	Halberstadt, Germany	G2a2a1 (PF3170)	Haak 2015
	5000 BC	Avellaner Cave, Spain	E1b1b1a1b1a (V13)	Lacan 2011
	5000 BC	Balatonszemes-Bagódomb, Hungary	I1 (M253)	Szécsényi-Nagy 2015
	3750 BC	La Mina, Spain	I2a2a1 (CTS9183)	Haak 2015
	3200 BC	Esperstedt, Germany	I2a1b1a (L1498)	Haak 2015
Copper Age	3200 BC	Ötztal Alps, Italy	G2a2a1a2 (L91)	Keller 2012
	3100 BC	Lopatino I, Sok River, Samara, Russia	R1b1a2a2* (CTS1078)	Haak 2015
	3100 BC	Lopatino I, Sok River, Samara, Russia	R1b1a (P297)	Haak 2015
	3000 BC	Lopatino I, Sok River, Samara, Russia	R1b1a2a* (L23)	Haak 2015
	2550 BC	Kromsdorf, Germany	R1b1a2 (M269)	Lee 2012
	2400 BC	Esperstedt, Germany	R1a1a1* (M417)	Haak 2015
	2250 BC	Quedlinburg, Germany	R1b1a2a1a2 (P312)	Haak 2015

and Koch's solution is controversial.[62] The fact remains that we have a man with a clearly Celtic name in Iberia long before the La Tène period.

The earliest known names for Britain and Ireland are also Celtic. These names were familiar to seafarers before La Tène material arrived in either island. Or so it appears. As we head backwards from the La Tène period, historical sources disintegrate into tantalizing snippets, acquired second-hand. In the 4th century AD a Roman named Rufus Festus Avienus laboured over a poem designed to display his erudition rather than personal knowledge: *Ora Maritima*. It describes the coast from Brittany to Marseilles, not in his own day, but drawing on authors from the 6th and 5th centuries BC. He credits Himilco with knowledge of what lay north of Brittany. This Carthaginian explorer was sent to investigate the remote northwestern shores of Europe around 500 BC.[63]

The *Ora Maritima* begins the poetic voyage by describing a high ridge known in an earlier age as Oestrymnis, facing south and sloping down to the sea. Beneath it lay the Oestrymnic Bay, in which islands called the Oestrymnides were widely spread. A tribe in what is now western Brittany was known as the *Ostimioi* to the Greek traveller Pytheas in the 4th century BC. So a modern translator is no doubt correct to identify Oestrymnis as the island of Ushant (*Uxisame* to Pytheas) off the extreme western point of Brittany. To the east of it is the Bay of Douarnenez. A chain of islands spreads from Ushant to the bay.[64] The *Ora Maritima* goes on to say:

> From here it is a two-day voyage to the Sacred Isle, for by this name the ancients called the island. It lies rich in turf among the waves, thickly populated by the Hierni. Nearby lies the island of the Albiones. The Tartessians were accustomed to trade even to the edge of the Oestrymnides. The Carthaginian colonists and people around the Pillars of Hercules frequented these waters. Four months scarcely is enough for the voyage, as Himilco the Carthaginian proved by sailing there and back himself.[65]

'Sacred Isle' is a misconstruction of the name of Ireland. In ancient Greek *hieros* meant 'sacred'. The Hierni are easily identified as the Irish and the Albiones as the people of Britain. The Irish name for themselves can be reconstructed as *Iwerni*, from the Irish name for Ireland, *Iverio* ('the fertile land'). That evolved into Old Irish *Ériu* and modern Irish *Éire*.[66] Albion corresponds to the Old Welsh *elbid* and Middle Welsh *elfydd*, with meanings 'world, earth, land, country, district'.[67] Here are Celtic names dating from two or three centuries before La Tène material appeared in Ireland.

Awareness of these flaws in the concept of Celtic spreading only with La Tène has generated new interest in an alternative model, proposed intermittently since the 1930s, in which the Bell Beaker culture was the vector for the earliest forms of Celtic.[68] Support for this model is starting to arrive from ancient DNA. Yet we shall see in the next chapter that a straightforward equation of Bell Beaker with Celtic may over-simplify a messier reality.

Overview

- Two successive Iron Age archaeological cultures, Late Hallstatt and La Tène, are found in the right place and time to correspond to Classical references to the Celts.

- The Gauls called themselves Celts. They spoke a language of the same family as Breton, Welsh and Gaelic.

- The La Tène culture spread to Britain. There are striking similarities in culture between Gaul and Britain, such as:

  - The use of chariots.

  - The use of a type of trumpet called a carnyx.

- This similarity encouraged the idea that Celtic languages spread from Central Europe with the La Tène culture. There are two problems with this theory:

  - La Tène material is barely found in Iberia or southern Ireland.

  - Celtic place- and personal names appear in the British Isles and Iberia before the La Tène period.

- So was the Bell Beaker culture the vector for the Celtic languages? Or is that an over-simplification? These questions are tackled in Chapter 3.

CHAPTER THREE

Bell Beakers and Language

> The change in the properties of copper by heat is really very
> startling; it is distinctly more dramatic than the effect of baking
> upon potter's clay.... Even more startling and mysterious were the
> transmutations involved in the extraction of the metal.... It was
> a stupendous feat ... to connect the green crystalline stones with
> the tough red metal. The recognition of the underlying continuity
> marked the beginning of chemistry.[1]

The seeming magic of metallurgy has seldom been more vividly conjured up than by the passage above from Vere Gordon Childe, published
in 1930. This influential archaeologist understood that the earliest smiths
were privy to powers that would have been awe-inspiring in their era. Metal
management lay at the centre of the Bell Beaker culture.

Bell Beaker (c. 2800–1700 BC) leapt across Europe, not settling everywhere,
but picking certain patches, often ones with ores to exploit. [19] It is recognized by its characteristic pottery, shaped like an inverted bell. Some later
cultures of the Bronze and Iron Ages were quite widespread within western
Europe, but none extended over the whole area anciently Celtic. This is
why a series of archaeologists have looked towards Bell Beaker for the
origins of the Celts.[2]

Is it really that simple? Bell Beaker in Italy covers an area where Celts
did not appear until they drove out the Etruscans from the Po Valley in
historical times (see Chapter 7). It also appears as far south as Sicily and
Calabria. Could it be that in its earliest stages Bell Beaker was associated
with both Celtic and Italic languages, or with an ancestor to both? If so
which ancestor? Could it be a type of Italo-Celtic,[3] or something even
earlier? We shall consider this question below, but first, what exactly was
Bell Beaker?

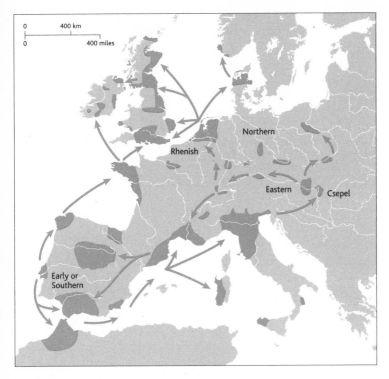

19 *Bell Beaker pottery spread by sea and river routes. It was probably made by women. So its dispersal may be partly linked to a search for marital partners among the scattered kin of a mobile Copper Age people.*

The bell-shaped pot

Bell Beaker pottery is distinctive. The inverted bell shape is decorated with horizontal zones of patterns, which can be incised or impressed into the wet clay. Where such pots are particularly well preserved, the white paste that was rubbed into incisions to pick out the pattern may still be visible. [20]

The concave sides of the typical Bell Beaker would make it easy to grasp, so archaeologists have usually seen it as a drinking vessel, hence the name 'beaker'. That image led to a vision of male drinking rituals cementing the culture.[4] Beer was thought to have arrived in Europe with Copper Age cultures such as Bell Beaker. Indeed the powerful appeal of alcohol was seen as one source of the influence of the Beaker folk. Vere Gordon Childe thought the heady fumes of beer could have drawn the earlier farmers of Europe into the Bell Beaker net.[5]

The popularity of alcohol can scarcely be denied. It features in countless cultures. Therein lies one problem with seeing it as the Bell Beaker liquid weapon. As scientific techniques in archaeology have advanced, the evidence for fermenting and brewing has been pushed so far into the past that beer is challenging bread as the presumed staple of early farmers. Perhaps as early as 9000 BC people gathered to feast and drink beer at the world's first megalithic monument, Göbekli Tepe in Anatolia.[6] In that case brewing techniques could have travelled into Europe with early farmers. Residues of alcoholic beverages have indeed been found in Neolithic Scotland.[7]

So Beaker folk could not have introduced beer to western Europe. They certainly drank it though. Chemical analysis of Bell Beaker vessels from tombs in the Ambrona Valley in Spain found residues of a primitive wheat beer.[8] Beer and mead (made from fermented honey) have been identified from other examples too, but not all Beakers were drinking cups. Some were used to smelt copper ores, others contain food residues, and yet others were funerary urns. Bell Beaker pots vary considerably in size. The largest, with a capacity up to 20 litres (over 4 gallons), were scarcely ideal for drinking.[9] So perhaps we should see the waist of the bell shape as a more general lifting aid. There would be less likelihood of such a pot slipping out of the hands of its bearer.

20 *Replica of a Bell Beaker found at Ciempozuelos, Spain. The incised patterns are picked out in white paste made of crushed bone.*

Bell Beaker ware is found as far east as Poland,[10] as far south as northern Morocco and as far north as Scotland,[11] northern Denmark[12] and even the southern tip of Norway.[13] Either its makers were mobile or this was a popular trade item. These days scientists can probe a pot's origins. In 2012 an almost complete bell-shaped beaker was uncovered at Cranbrook near Exeter in England. Under the microscope a geologist could identify the minerals in the clay as so local that the pot was probably made on the site where it was found.[14] This is typical for Bell Beaker in southwest England,[15] and fits a wider pattern. Local origin was the most common conclusion from testing a selection of Bell Beaker pottery in France.[16] This discovery triggered a systematic programme of testing Bell Beaker pottery from over a hundred sites in France, Portugal, Spain and Switzerland. It found that most pots were locally made, varying from just over 50 per cent to 100 per cent.[17] So while there was some movement of actual pots, in the main what moved was knowledge of how to make them.

This pottery was not wheel-thrown in a workshop. It was made in the home. So it is most likely that it was made by women. In a society in which women generally moved on marriage to the home of their spouse, the knowledge of particular pottery techniques and styles would travel too.[18] The genesis of Bell Beaker pottery has been much debated. That fraught question is discussed in Chapter 5, along with the origin of the whole culture.

Way of life and death

Bell Beaker folk ushered the Bronze Age into western Europe. They were the first metalworkers to enter the British Isles, homing in on the copper belts of Ireland and Wales. Around 2400 BC they left their characteristic beakers at a copper mine on Ross Island, in Lough Leane, Co. Kerry. This is the earliest known copper mine in northwestern Europe. There can be no doubt that it was created by incomers, for they brought with them an already advanced knowledge of metallurgy. These experts were probably looking especially for arsenic-rich copper ore, and they certainly found it at Ross Island. An arsenic-copper alloy made a tougher metal than pure copper. The prized ore was smelted on site into copper ingots, which could be moved elsewhere to be cast into finished objects.[19] Analysis of chemical composition shows that copper from Ireland was traded into Britain.[20]

From around 2200 BC Bell Beaker interest in Britain intensified as Cornwall was discovered to be a prime source for tin, the rare and precious component of true bronze. It has recently been realized that Ireland too had tin in the Mourne Mountains.[21] These resources gave the British Isles a head start in western Europe in making bronze.[22]

Tin was also available in western Iberia and the Erzgebirge Mountains in Central Europe. The abundant tin and copper of Tartessos (p. 43) might lead you to expect the earliest Iberian bronze in southwestern Spain. Instead it appears in the northwest of the peninsula, which was linked into a trade network that included the British Isles. At one site the whole process of metalworking is laid bare. High in the mountains of the District of Bragança in Portugal, the detritus of bronze-working has been found on the hilltop of Fraga dos Corvos. Here a small rural community tended their flocks, hunted deer, and made their own pottery and bronze axes around 1750–1500 BC. The pottery includes Epi-Bell-Beaker, a final, crude representative of the type. So in Iberia too we see Bell Beaker at the beginning of bronze-making.[23] This interesting site has inspired a novel in Portuguese titled *The First Alchemist*.[24]

Bell Beaker burials vary by region and status. It has long been noticed that in Iberia and Ireland, Bell Beaker people were willing to re-use Neolithic megalithic tombs. In addition, wedge-shaped tombs were dotted along the west of Ireland in the Bell Beaker period. These are undeniably megalithic in construction, but of Bell Beaker date and peculiar to Ireland. They usually contain more than one interment or cremation.[25] It has been supposed that this pattern of collective burials was exclusive to the southern and Atlantic zones of the Bell Beaker culture, while individual graves were the rule in the eastern Bell Beaker region. A recent review overturns this idea. It seems that the re-use of earlier monumental tombs was common throughout the Beaker territory. It is simply more visible in the zone with most monumental graves. Likewise, individual graves are also found throughout.[26]

Most people were buried quite simply, but burials of high-status individuals were more elaborate. A burial chamber could be timber-lined. Finely decorated Bell Beakers were placed in it by mourners. The deceased was clothed, but since fabric rots away, only imperishable objects such as the characteristic v-shaped buttons and archers' wrist-guards survive. Tanged arrowheads are usually found with wrist-guards. Archery equipment is typical of male burials, but one woman buried at Tišice in central Bohemia had arrows and a wrist-guard.[27]

A few burials are extraordinary. In the Bell Beaker necropolis at Hulín-Pravčice, Czech Republic, a group of large graves have inner structures and rich equipment. Besides the usual high-status set of objects, they all have copper daggers. (Copper knives are found in less than 6 per cent of Bell Beaker graves.) A profusion of jewelry made from gold, silver, electrum, amber and copper included a pair of gold spirals, probably used to bind the ends of hair plaits. Sets of stones among the grave goods are interpreted as symbolic of tools used by smiths. Mastery of metal could reap rewards.[28]

On the other side of Europe we find another honoured metalworker. The Amesbury Archer was buried near Stonehenge around 2350 BC. [21] His skeleton reveals that he was a man aged between 35 and 45, who must have been in constant pain in the last few years of his life. An abscess on his jaw had eaten into the bone. His left kneecap had been ripped off, perhaps in a riding accident, resulting in a bone infection. Had he come to Stonehenge in hope of a cure? Tim Darvill's vision of Stonehenge as a healing shrine has won little support among his fellow British prehistorians, yet the idea of places with special powers runs deep and it seems this massive monument drew people from far and wide. Isotope tests on the Archer's teeth and bones show that he spent his younger years in the Alpine region. Altogether around 100 objects were buried with the Archer, making his the richest Bell Beaker grave found in Britain. His mourners placed beside him five Beaker pots and two wrist-guards. Significantly, he was also buried with a cushion stone, thought to be used by metalworkers. He had no fewer than three copper knives. Two could be from northern Spain and the third from western France; it seems the Archer had travelled widely. His gold hair binders are the earliest gold artifacts found in Britain.[29]

A similar gold hair binder and cushion stone were found in a burial mound at Kirkhaugh in Northumberland in 1935, together with a bell beaker. The matching hair binder was found there in 2014. The grave lies on the edge of an orefield. So the man buried at Kirkhaugh could have been part of a team prospecting for copper in the north Pennines.[30]

Gold was prized by the Bell Beaker elite. It is too soft for practical uses, but its eternal glitter is ideal for ornament. Southwestern Iberia abounded in gold in the 3rd millennium BC. It was worked using the same technology as for copper.[31] Ireland had gold in the Mourne Mountains.[32] Britain too had several sources of the precious metal. No wonder then that we find a wealth of gold objects in the British Isles from between 2400 and 1400 BC. A type

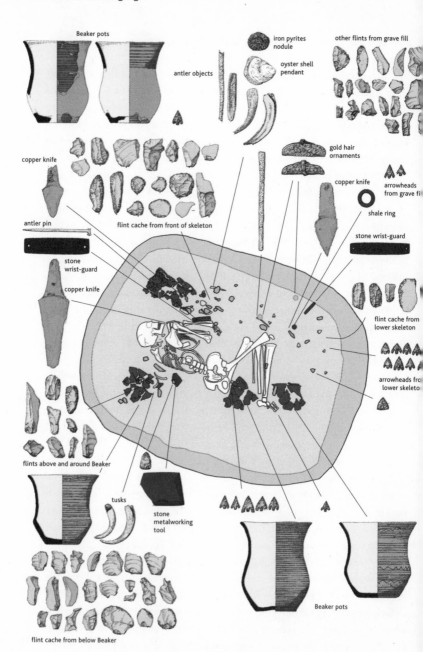

Beaker pots

antler objects

iron pyrites nodule

oyster shell pendant

other flints from grave fill

copper knife

gold hair ornaments

copper knife

arrowheads from grave fill

shale ring

antler pin

flint cache from front of skeleton

stone wrist-guard

stone wrist-guard

copper knife

flint cache from lower skeleton

arrowheads from lower skeleton

flints above and around Beaker

tusks

stone metalworking tool

flint cache from below Beaker

Beaker pots

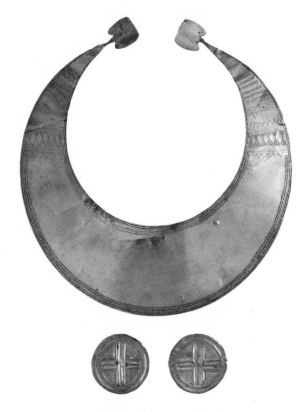

21 (opposite) *The burial of the Amesbury Archer. This man was buried near Stonehenge around 2350 BC with a rich array of symbols of his prestige. His grave goods included the arrowheads and wrist-guards that led his discoverers to name him the Amesbury Archer.*

22 (above) *A finely incised gold lunula and two gold discs found at Coggalbeg, Co. Roscommon in Ireland in March 1945, but unknown to scholars until they were revealed by a safe robbery in 2009. This hoard represents the first recorded association of a lunula and gold discs, long thought to represent the moon and sun.*

of golden collar or pectoral known from its crescent shape as a lunula is not found in burials and so was probably not a personal item, but something akin to a priestly pectoral which would be passed on to a successor. The finest are incised with complex geometric patterns related to Beaker pottery.[33] [22] Lunulae and golden discs are found along the entire Atlantic region from Portugal to the British Isles, though are particularly common in Ireland. We may see them as symbols of the moon and sun. Indeed discs and diadems appear right across Bronze Age Europe, suggesting a common perception of their significance.[34]

Mobility

When the Bell Beaker culture was first recognized, it was taken for granted that it arrived with immigrants. The anti-migrationism that arose in British archaeology in the 1970s changed the perspective. For decades afterwards Bell Beaker was viewed as a purely cultural phenomenon. The present century has seen the pendulum of opinion swing back, as evidence of mobility mounts.[35] We have already noted above (pp. 51, 53) that Bell Beaker arrivals at Ross Island must have been incomers, and that the Amesbury Archer certainly was.

Unfortunately isotope testing can only detect first generation migrants. A few metres away from the Amesbury Archer was the burial of a younger man, who was born in Britain and died a generation or two after him. The presence of a rare trait in the bones of their feet showed that the two were related.[36] Given that the Bell Beaker culture lasted many centuries, we would expect to find that the overwhelming majority of Bell Beaker burials were not of first-generation migrants. Indeed an isotope study of 250 individuals from all over Britain has shown exactly that, though local and regional mobility seems common.[37] A similar pattern of mobility appears in a study of Bell Beaker burials in Austria, Bavaria, Czech Republic and Hungary. Out of 81 individuals, 51 had moved during their lifetime.[38]

It has long been recognized that Bell Beaker skeletons in northern, central and eastern Europe had a different skull shape from previous people in these regions.[39] Initially this was taken as straightforward evidence of new arrivals. However, the position in which an infant is placed to sleep can affect skull shape, so DNA is a better guide to the degree of relationship between populations.

Celtic and Italic languages

The Celtic and Italic language families both belong within the huge family that linguists label Indo-European (Chapter 4). So they have similarities that go back to the common parent of all Indo-European languages. That

Genetics: Y-DNA R1b-P312

R1b1a2 (M269) was found in human remains from a Bell Beaker site in Kromsdorf, Germany.[40] This Y-DNA haplogroup has many subclades, generated by an explosive population growth. The growth spurt was assumed to date from the Neolithic,[41] before ancient DNA results made the Copper Age more likely. One subclade predominates in western Europe today: R1b1a2a1a2 (P312) or R1b-P312 for short. [23]

Any mutation happens first in just one person. So all men today carrying R1b-P312 or one of its descendants have a common ancestor. Where and when he lived we shall never know exactly. However, R1b-P312 has been found in a man of the Bell Beaker culture at Quedlinburg, Germany (see box pp. 44–45). Today the concentration of Y-DNA R1b-P312 falls most heavily where Celtic languages were once spoken and in Italy, the home of the Italic language family. We often find a correlation between Y-DNA haplogroups, which are passed down from father to son, and languages.

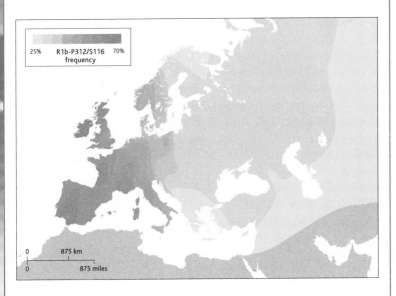

25%   R1b-P312/S116   70%
      frequency

0   875 km
0   875 miles

23 Y-DNA R1b1a2a1a2 (P312) is a large and widespread haplogroup, which predominates in regions of Europe where Celtic and Italic languages were once spoken. Some of the highest levels are in Wales and Ireland.

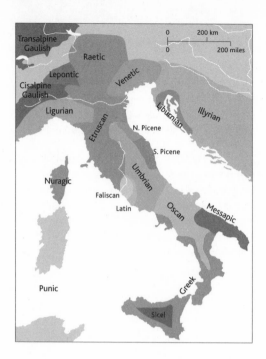

24 *The languages of the Italian peninsula and neighbouring territory c. 550 BC. Italic languages are picked out in colour.*

25 (opposite) *The density of Celtic place-names recorded in Classical sources. Such sources are more plentiful within the former Roman empire.*

is without question. As we shall see, there are some similarities shared just between Celtic and Italic which suggest a closer relationship.

Today Romance languages such as French, Italian, Spanish and Portuguese are spoken by many millions of people. They all spring from Latin, which was spread by the Roman empire. Before the rise of Rome, Latin was just one of a group of Italic languages confined to central Italy, sandwiched between Etruscans in the north and Greeks who had colonized southern Italy. [24] That picture was to change dramatically as the Romans gradually dominated the other Italic-speakers, then the Etruscans, and finally burst out of Italy to create an empire that engulfed much of Celtic-speaking Europe (Chapter 8).

We need mentally to turn back that Roman tide if we are to reconstruct the linguistic pattern of western Europe as far back as we can. Roman geographers recorded a wide scatter of Celtic place-names inside the empire and even beyond it. [25] The wealth of Celtic place-names in Gaul supports Caesar's observation that most of Gaul was Celtic-speaking before the

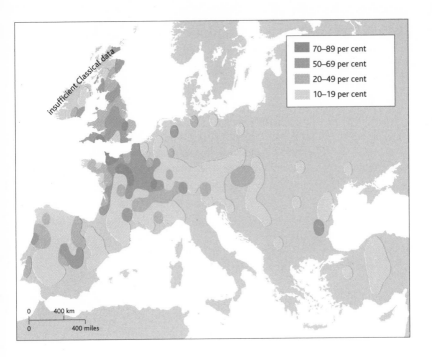

Roman conquest. Iberia too was well supplied with Celtic place-names in Roman times, though there are interesting gaps, which will be discussed later. The Romans also recorded many place-names of Celtic origin within their province of Britannia. The absence of Celtic place-names in western Ireland and northern Scotland on the map should not disturb us. It simply reflects the way that it was created. Patrick Sims-Williams analysed, by one-degree squares, what percentage of place-names noted in the *Barrington Atlas of the Greek and Roman World* (2000) could be derived from Celtic.[42] Those labouring on the *Barrington Atlas* had to contend with the limited data-gathering by Romans outside their own borders. Virtually all the information for Ireland comes from Ptolemy. Few of the Irish place-names he recorded can be located today with certainty, so the *Barrington Atlas* does not attempt to plot them all.[43] The Scottish Highlands were thinly populated, with few settlements known to Roman geographers, but Ptolemy tells us that 'From the Bay of Lemmanonia [Firth of Clyde] until the Varar estuary [Moray Firth] dwell the Caledonians, above whom is the Caledonian forest'.[44]

The tribal name *Calidonii* seems derived from Celtic *calet*, which has meanings including 'tough' and 'hardy', entirely suitable for the highlanders.[45] It is preserved in Dunkeld (9th-century Dun Chaillden) and Schiechallon.[46]

Next we need to peel away the layers of known migration before the Roman conquests. Celtic place-names in the Po Valley, the Balkans and around the Black Sea can be attributed to movements of the Gauls south and east into formerly non-Celtic territory after 500 BC (Chapter 7). By contrast, the scattered Celtic place-names east of the Rhine tell us that a Celtic language was in use there before the expansion of Germanic speakers from 500 BC. The name of the River Rhine itself is Celtic in origin.[47] It lay well within the zone of influence of both the Hallstatt and La Tène cultures. [see 11] According to an anonymous Greek poet of about 200 BC, the Rhine was a sacred river to the Celts:

> The bold Celts test their children in the jealous Rhine
> And no man regards himself as a true father
> Until he sees the child washed in the holy river.[48]

Untangling the story for Britain and Iberia is more complex. Roman writers tell us that Gauls moved into Iberia, and Belgae moved into Britain before the Roman conquest of those regions. The very fact that these migrations were known suggests that they were not in the far distant past for Romans. That is supported by archaeological evidence of culture changes in the early centuries BC (Chapter 7). Yet we saw in Chapter 2 that sea-going Greeks were recording Celtic names in Iberia and the British Isles long before that. So the pattern seems to be one of waves of Celtic migration, the earliest of which were before recorded history.

Italo-Celtic

The Celtic and Italic language families have similarities that suggest a common ancestor more recent than the parent of all Indo-European languages. They share the o-stem genitive singular ending in 'i', for example the Latin *viri* (of a man), and Primitive Irish *maq(q)i* (of the son). A joint innovation is the superlative suffix *-ismmo*, in such formations as Latin *maximus* (greatest), and the Gaulish place-name *Ouxisame* (highest). There is also a subjunctive morpheme *-ā-*, as in Latin *fer-ā-t* (he may carry) and Old

Irish *beraid* (he may carry). So some linguists argue for a common ancestor for the two families which they call Proto-Italo-Celtic. Non-linguists have sometimes misunderstood this to mean a type of Celtic. So it needs to be clearly stated that it is not. It is the proposed ancestor of both language families. The alternative explanation for their shared features is that Proto-Celtic and Proto-Italic developed in such close proximity that they influenced each other.[49]

The case for a common ancestor was first made in 1861, was then countered in 1929 and has oscillated in and out of favour since. Calvert Watkins of Harvard University forcefully made the case against in 1966. He pointed out the many dissimilarities between Proto-Celtic and Proto-Italic.[50] Indeed these suggest a comparatively short period of common evolution, followed by a long period of separate development, as argued by Dutch linguist Frederik Kortlandt.[51] This does not dispose of the common ancestor, whose existence has continued to garner support among linguists.[52] One good reason is that there are several lost languages, such as Ligurian and Lusitanian, that do not fit into either the Italic or Celtic branches, but are related. We could see them as descending from Proto-Italo-Celtic. They were also spoken within the regions colonized by Bell Beaker.

So could Proto-Italo-Celtic be the first language carried by the people of the Bell Beaker culture? This was the solution I previously favoured, since ancient Greek observers reported a coastal band of Ligurians all the way from northwestern Italy to western Iberia, where the Romans encountered Lusitanians.[53] But recent work suggests that the Lusitanians and their kin did not arrive in Iberia until the Late Bronze Age.[54] So we must look to a yet earlier language.

Old European IE (*Alteuropäisch*)

Hans Krahe noticed river-names across Europe which appear to be Indo-European, but do not fit any known Indo-European language. He called this the *Alteuropäisch* (Old European) hydronymy.[55] Krahe saw such names as evidence of a lost language ancestral to the western branches of Indo-European. Critical dissection left this idea bleeding to death. Specific archaic Indo-European river-names range from reflecting the original Indo-European parent to dialects of it that had not quite become fully fledged daughter languages.[56] Nevertheless Krahe's work is important. It helps us to realize how complex the process of language spread can be. Many parts of Europe seem to be like a linguistic layer cake. One wave of Indo-European was succeeded by another.

Place-names that can be identified as Indo-European, but neither Celtic nor Italic, are found in Iberia, particularly in the south. Most obviously there are many place-names starting with the letter 'p', which was lost in early Celtic. Modern place-name scholars generally class these as Old European.[57] This means that the first language of Bell Beaker communities in the west may have been a form of Indo-European too early even to have features specific to both Celtic and Italic.[58] So we need to press on further back, to the origins of the Indo-Europeans.

Overview

- The Bell Beaker archaeological culture (c. 2800–1700 BC) is characterized by:
  - Pottery shaped like an inverted bell.
  - Metalworking in copper (later bronze) and gold.
  - Mobility. It spread widely in Europe, and even into Morocco.
  - A focus on archery.
- The Bell Beaker culture is found in all regions of Europe where Celtic languages were subsequently spoken.
- Bell Beaker is also found where Italic languages were subsequently spoken, as well as languages such as Ligurian, which appear to be related to Italic and may derive from a common ancestor of Italic and Celtic.
- Place-names over the Bell Beaker region include some which are classified as Old European (*Alteuropäisch*), a dialect of Indo-European too early to fall into any particular branch of the family.
- So the earliest Bell Beaker makers may have spoken Old European. To better understand its origins, we turn in Chapter 4 to the Indo-European language family.

CHAPTER FOUR

The Indo-European Family

The Sanskrit language, whatever be its antiquity, is of a wonderful structure; more perfect than the Greek, more copious than the Latin, and more exquisitely refined than either, yet bearing to both of them a stronger affinity, both in the roots of verbs and in the forms of grammar, than could possibly have been produced by accident; so strong indeed that no philologer could examine them all three, without believing them to have sprung from some common source, which perhaps no longer exists: there is a similar reason, though not quite so forcible, for supposing that both the Gothic and the Celtic, though blended with a very different idiom, had the same origin with the Sanskrit; and the old Persian might be added to the same family.[1]

Thus spoke Sir William Jones (1746–1794) as he celebrated the third anniversary of the learned society that he had founded in Calcutta. The date was 2 February 1786, only about six months after he had begun to study Sanskrit, the ancient literary language of India. He had been a linguistic prodigy even as a child. The son of a celebrated Welsh mathematician nicknamed 'Longitude Jones' and a gifted English mother, the young William Jones not only learnt the customary Latin and Greek at Harrow School, but taught himself Hebrew and the Arabic script. At Oxford University he improved his Arabic and became fascinated by Persian. In his vacations he read European classics in Italian, Spanish and Portuguese. In 1770 William Jones entered the Middle Temple, London, to study law. As a barrister in Wales from 1775, he became a keen Celticist. So when he arrived in India in 1783 to take up a position on the Bengal supreme court, he was an outstanding linguist.[2]

The correspondences between Sanskrit and the Classical languages of Europe are striking. For example, the word for 'father' in Latin and Greek is *pater* and in Sanskrit is *pitar*. Likewise the word for 'mother' in Latin is

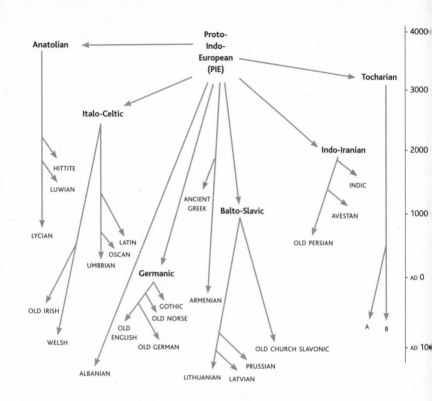

26 *A tree of Indo-European languages, adapted from Nakhleh, Ringe and Warnow 2005. The date scale indicates the estimated time that a group broke away from the Proto-Indo-European parent, so that its speech developed independently and became a daughter language, and then the estimated time of any splits in that daughter language. The first appearance of a language in writing is indicated by the names in small capitals. The names in bold, such as 'Balto-Slavic' and 'Proto-Indo-European' are the creation of linguists; these languages were not recorded in writing.*

mater, in ancient Greek is *meter* and in Sanskrit is *matar*. Such resemblances had been privately noted by others. Indeed a proposal that Latin, Greek and Sanskrit had a common origin had been sent to the French Academy by Jesuit missionary Gaston Coeurdoux (1691–1777) some years before the famous statement by William Jones, though it was not published until 1808. Coeurdoux and Jones took the same approach, looking for similarities not simply between words (for words can be borrowed between languages), but also in grammar. A methodology was born. Linguistics had entered the realm of science. By 1813 linguists had formulated a model of a language family labelled Indo-European.[3] It has been intensively studied since. [26]

So now we know that Celtic belongs to the Indo-European family of languages. [27] How do such families arise? In the days before modern communications, any language had to be spoken face to face, with the people you met day to day. The language of a community would gradually change. For example new words would be created, perhaps for new inventions, and everyone in the community would soon know them. If a group split from the community and moved so far away that it could not talk constantly to the parent group, then it would no longer be part of the parent language evolution. Instead it would develop its own dialect. Eventually the parent and child communities would speak different, though related, languages. As

27 Indo-European languages in AD 1500. From a Copper Age homeland on the European steppe, Indo-European languages spread far and wide. It is now the dominant language family in Europe. Names of non-Indo-European languages are in italics.

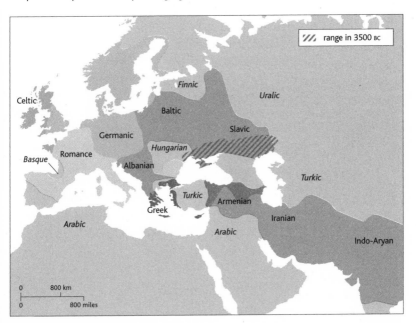

Sir William Jones surmised, the parent of all the Indo-European languages was long gone by his day. Linguists have painstakingly reconstructed it; it is known as Proto-Indo-European (PIE).

Indo-European homeland

Where was the birthplace of PIE? The lack of inscriptions or other ancient writing in PIE set free the wildest imaginations. As J. P. Mallory put it:

> This quest for the origins of the Indo-Europeans has all the fascination of an electric light in the open air on a summer night: it tends to attract every species of scholar or would-be savant who can take pen to hand.[4]

He took on the unenviable task of sifting the evidence. A scholar of both linguistics and archaeology, he gave equal weight to both. Other theorists have tended to make a linguistic case for which there is little or no archaeological support, or vice-versa.

Cambridge archaeologist Colin Renfrew argued that the Indo-European languages were brought to Europe by farmers from Anatolia in the Neolithic.[5] This was a bold and attractive hypothesis. There is little doubt that many of the language families spoken today spread with agriculture.[6] PIE certainly includes farming terms, but it reflects later innovations as well. The first farmers used digging sticks rather than ploughs. They had no wheels or wagons, no gold or silver. They kept cattle for beef, not milk and cheese. They did not make wine. They did not spin wool. Yet PIE had words for all these things.[7] So dating the spread of Indo-European as early as the first farmers did not appeal to linguists.

Regardless, the Anatolian model continued to have its supporters. Some biologists have claimed to prove it by applying a methodology from epidemiology.[8] Would that it were so simple. Any assumption that humans will behave exactly like viruses is doomed to crash against reality. Humans do not move randomly. They are capable of weighing up geography, climate, hazards and convenient routes. Worse still, the conclusion relied on computer models with a built-in bias. Advocates of the Anatolian homeland had always placed great weight on the primacy of the Anatolian branch of the Indo-European family in two respects: it was the first to split away from the parent and the first to be committed to writing. By devising a computer model that placed the Anatolian branch at the root on these grounds, the devisers simply gave the Anatolian homeland theory pseudo-scientific cladding.[9] An independent analysis failed to replicate their results.[10]

It is always exciting to find tangible evidence of a language – an inscription, a papyrus, a clay tablet with signs that we can decipher. It is a message from the past. It is easy to forget that for millennia our ancestors spoke to each other without putting anything in writing. Literacy goes hand-in-hand with civilization: a complex, centrally organized society run by a bureaucracy. The vocabulary of PIE does not fit an urban society with all the trappings of a legal system, officials and taxes. So we should not be surprised that it was never written down. The earliest languages attested in writing were those of the first civilizations. These included languages in Anatolia, such as Hattic, that were unrelated to Indo-European. As speakers of other languages came into contact with civilization, they too could adopt literacy. This was the pattern in Anatolia.

The Indo-European-speakers we call Hittites called their own language *Nešili*, meaning 'the language of Neša'. Kaneša (shortened to Neša) was the Hittite name for a town in central Anatolia known as Kanesh to the Assyrians. The site of Kanesh at Kültepe has been excavated, so we know the Assyrians had a merchant colony there. Assyrian merchants mention Hittite names in their texts, but the Hittites themselves left us no word until their king Pithana of Kussara conquered Kanesh 'in the night, by force', but without doing any damage. His son Anitta had an inscription made to record that moonlit drama and his own conquest of the Land of Hatti in central Anatolia.[11] In short, the Hittites turned to writing as they rose to power and acquired literate bureaucrats.

The crucial point linguistically is that Hittite took features from Hattic, but PIE did not.[12] There is no indication of PIE being in contact with any of the languages of Anatolia. The PIE homeland lay elsewhere.

The chief attraction of the Anatolian theory was its simplicity. If we look for a massive cultural upheaval across the whole of Europe, the coming of farming leaps immediately to mind. The pattern emerging from ancient DNA does indeed support mass migration in the Neolithic. Yet Copper to Bronze Age movements also stirred the European gene pool with startling results in Y-DNA (see box pp. 44–45), now supported by full genome comparisons (see box p. 73).

J. P. Mallory, and more recently David Anthony, championed the alternative hypothesis that PIE spread later, along with metallurgy, from the Pontic-Caspian steppes.[13] Put simply, PIE can be located in time by its vocabulary and in place by its neighbours. PIE-speakers created their own words for wagons and wheels, from Indo-European roots. These words were retained in a number of daughter languages, with changes characteristic of those languages, which is how linguists trace them to the mother language. So PIE cannot date before the invention of the wheel around 3500 BC.[14]

Crucially, PIE evolved in contact with Proto-Uralic, parent of the language family which includes Finnish and Saami. Farming vocabulary was absorbed from PIE and its offspring by Uralic. The Uralic family takes its name from the consensus view that the parent language developed near the Ural Mountains. So we can deduce that PIE was spoken somewhat to the south of Proto-Uralic, closer to the sources of farming.[15] PIE in turn borrowed words from more southerly languages. The words for 'bull' in PIE (*tawro-s) and Proto-Semitic (*tawr) are clearly related. This formed the crux of linguistic arguments in favour of a homeland for PIE in Neolithic Anatolia. Yet Proto-Semitic does not belong in that niche. Its lexicon places it in the Copper Age Levant.[16] So contact between PIE and Proto-Semitic fits neatly into the Copper Age, but what about the geography? There are linguistic clues that such words trickled through the Caucasus.[17] Culturally that is feasible. The Maikop culture of the North Caucasus (see below) was in contact with both Mesopotamia and the North Pontic steppe.[18] The conclusions from linguistics can be anchored in archaeology. The Yamnaya culture on the European steppe fits the type of society PIE leads us to expect (see pp. 72, 74). Then we see the influence of Yamnaya moving east and west to places where Indo-European languages later emerge (see pp. 75–78).

For the moment, though, let us continue our detective journey back in time. Indeed we take a massive leap to the age of mammoths. Today Y-DNA R1 dominates Europe, but it first appeared on its eastern fringes. Its ancestor R has been found in an ancient burial in Siberia. With this discovery another piece of the puzzle may have fallen into place. The relationship of Uralic to PIE runs deeper than the adoption of farming terms. The two languages share such fundamental vocabulary as the words for 'water' and 'name'. The explanation could be contact at an early stage, before Uralic and PIE were fully formed. A language ancestral to Proto-Uralic was probably spoken somewhere in the Sayan region of south-central Siberia.[19]

From Siberia to Europe

In the valley of the Angara River, which drains the massive Lake Baikal in central Siberia, a four-year-old boy was buried 24,000 years ago. His remains were discovered in the late 1920s near the village of Mal'ta and taken to the Hermitage Museum in St Petersburg (then Leningrad), Russia. It looks as though he was much loved. He was buried with a beaded necklace, several pendants and an ivory diadem. His people were reindeer and mammoth hunters. They carved Venus figurines from mammoth tusk, some of which are marked to suggest fur clothing. They lived at a time when the north was in the grip of vast glaciers and Siberian mountains were ice-covered. Hardy hunters clustered in the shelter of the pine-forested valleys of southern Siberia. At Mal'ta they lived in round huts with a central fire that would have given both heat and light. Perhaps the long winters encouraged art and craft, though no other Siberian site of the period can compare to Mal'ta in richness and diversity of art objects. Apart from the female figurines, there are bird carvings and the engraving of a mammoth.[20] [28] Mal'ta boy's people were creative. Mal'ta boy himself has given us something of great significance – his DNA. This has been analysed, with some surprising results.

Some 4,000 years after Mal'ta boy a new stone tool-making technique arose in his region, called pressure blade-making. It spread both east into North America and west to the borders of Europe.[21] [29] So could it have been invented by Mal'ta boy's relatives? The team who tested his remains also managed to extract DNA from a man who lived about 17,000 years ago at Afontova Gora, a site with pressure blade-making. Afontova Gora man was indeed similar genetically to Mal'ta boy (see box p. 70).

28 *Around 24,000 years ago a hunter scratched this image of a mammoth on a slab of mammoth tusk. It was found at Mal'ta in Siberia, along with other evidence of the creativity of the small band of people who sheltered there, such as female figurines and bird carvings.*

Pressure blade-making was a remarkable innovation. For millennia humankind created tools by directly striking a piece of flint. Breaking stones without striking them is more complicated. Obsidian was the preferred material. This volcanic glass fractures into pieces with curved surfaces and very sharp edges. Freshly cut obsidian is sharper than a surgical steel scalpel. By firmly clamping a piece of obsidian and then using a tool to apply pressure to the right spot a regular blade with parallel edges and constant thickness could be produced. The technique was still in use by Aztecs in Mesoamerica in historic times, as described by Spanish friars.[22]

The complexity of the technique makes it likely that it was passed on in families. So we may suspect migration along the trail of technology. [29] The pressure technique emerged around 20,000 BC in Mongolia, northern China and the Lake Baikal area of Siberia.[23] Moving westwards it arrived in the upper Volga region around 9600 BC.[24] Pressure blade-making spread north of the Black Sea from about 9000 BC.[25] The technique also travelled south of the Caspian into the Near East, where it was embraced by farmers. Long obsidian blades have been found at Çayönü Tepesi in layers dating to around 7000 BC.[26] Within 500 years the technology had arrived with farmers

---

Genetics: Mal'ta boy

We now know that the ancestor of the Y-DNA R1 so common in modern European men lived far from Europe. The Palaeolithic boy from Mal'ta in central Siberia was found to have carried Y-DNA R*, the ancestor of the whole R lineage. That alone would have made headline news. The multinational team who tackled Mal'ta boy's DNA went further, however, obtaining a full genome. The result was sensational. The boy was related not only to modern Europeans but also to Native Americans. Perhaps we should not be too surprised. The Y-DNA haplogroups R and Q are brothers, both descended from P. Some Q was to enter America across the Beringian land bridge, but it seems that R1 went westwards instead, to appear in western Russia from around 5600 BC (see box pp. 44–45). Mal'ta boy was unrelated to modern East Asians, whereas modern Native Americans have a clear relationship to the latter. So those relatives of Mal'ta boy who moved into Beringia must have mixed with an East Asian group somewhere along the way. A second genome was extracted from an adult male at Afontova Gora, a site to the west of Mal'ta and later in date. It proved similar to that of Mal'ta boy.[27] Together these two genomes were used to represent ancestral north Eurasians (ANE) in an analysis of the source populations of Europe (see box on p. 73).

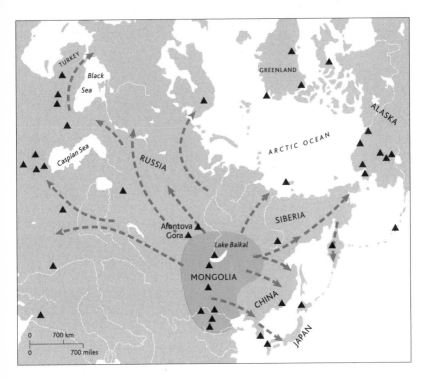

29 *Pressure blade-making spread east and west from an early centre in Mongolia, northern China and the region around Lake Baikal in Siberia. Its westward movement took it into the region around the Caspian and Black seas. Triangles mark findspots of pressure blades.*

on the coast of the Sea of Marmara in western Anatolia.[28] Dairy farming was developing in that region and crossed into Europe shortly afterwards. Around 4800 BC the innovatory Cucuteni-Tripolye culture formed north of the Black Sea, with pressure blades and great herds of cattle.[29]

A second craft innovation also spread west from Lake Baikal to the European steppe. The earliest pottery was made in the Far East, thousands of years before farming. The idea was carried westwards across Siberia by hunter-gatherers. This type of pottery reached the Samara region in the middle Volga River valley by 7000 BC. It diffused south and west into the valleys crossing the European steppe.[30] Genetic characteristics associated with Mal'ta boy and Afontova Gora man were present at Samara along with pottery (see box on p. 73).

The survival of male forager lineages as the Neolithic engulfed a territory would depend on the willingness of foragers to adopt farming. So let us home in on a visible transition from foraging to farming. In the forest-steppe zone the pottery-making foragers of Dnieper-Donets I transformed themselves into Dnieper-Donets II cattle farmers around 5000 BC.[31] Their ancient mitochondrial DNA is revealing. They carried not only a typical haplogroup for European foragers, but also some haplogroups found in European farmers, and, intriguingly, others normally found in Central Asia.[32] A pottery-making wife might have been sought after when the first pottery arrived in the region from Asia. A farming wife could have been equally welcome as Dnieper-Donets foragers encountered cattle-keeping neighbours. Indeed a wife could have arrived with a cow as dowry. This already mixed culture seems to be just one of the ingredients of the cultural *bombe surprise* that is Yamnaya, which raced across the steppe absorbing previous cultures. It eventually melded with the remnants of the Cucuteni-Tripolye culture.

The Indo-European lifestyle

There are about 1,500 reconstructed PIE roots and words. This must fall far short of the full language. Yet the PIE lexicon reveals a great deal about the lifestyle of its speakers. They were familiar with agriculture and metallurgy. As we have seen, they coined words for wheels and wagons. They talked of dairy products, sheep and wool. They had a concept of social ranking, but few words for specific occupations, or other clues to urban life. The lexicon reveals a Copper Age society, but not an urbanized state.[33] That is a match for the mobile, pastoralist Yamnaya (Pit-Grave) culture of the European steppe.[34]

Yamnaya (3400–2800 BC) is a rich blend of influences. At the time when Dnieper-Donets foragers were turning into farmers, the most advanced cultures in Europe were in the Balkans. Farmers had prospered on the rich, silt soils of the Lower Danube Basin. Hamlets in what is now Bulgaria, Romania and Serbia grew into solidly built villages of multi-roomed houses. This was the first region in Europe to take up copper-working. It was also the first in the world to work gold.[35] Before these Balkan cultures could evolve into civilizations, the sun set on them. A cold period afflicted Europe from 4200 to 3800 BC.[36] Balkan settlements were abandoned and Balkan metallurgy collapsed. Mines in Bulgaria ceased production. Some Balkan copper-workers may have fled westwards into Italy and Sardinia.[37]

Genetics: three main sources for Europeans

The last few years have seen a great leap forward in studies of ancient DNA. It is now possible to obtain entire genomes from ancient individuals. From comparison of these to modern Europeans, a pattern has emerged. The modern European gene pool was formed from three main source populations: western hunter-gatherers (WHG); early European farmers (EEF); and ancestral north Eurasians (ANE), who arrived in Europe later than the farmers.[38] Modern European populations are mixtures of the three components, in varying amounts. [30]

ANE represents a Siberian hunter-gatherer lineage, as represented by Mal'ta boy and the man from Afontova Gora. ANE admixture has been found in remains from the Samara district of Russia, between the Volga and the Urals. The earliest examples, from about 9,000 to 6,000 years ago, belong primarily to mitochondrial DNA haplogroups typical of European hunter-gatherers, but later ones of the Yamnaya culture include those associated with farmers.[39] Likewise, mitochondrial DNA from the Dnieper-Donets II culture and its Yamnaya successor both show mixed forager and farmer origins.[40] Yamnaya people did not carry 100 per cent ANE, but had enough of it to enable geneticists to trace their descendants in the Corded Ware and Bell Beaker cultures of the Copper Age.[41]

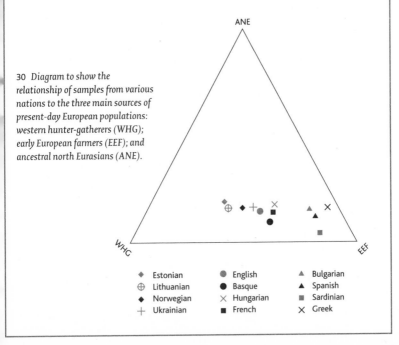

30 *Diagram to show the relationship of samples from various nations to the three main sources of present-day European populations: western hunter-gatherers (WHG); early European farmers (EEF); and ancestral north Eurasians (ANE).*

◆	Estonian	●	English	▲	Bulgarian
⊕	Lithuanian	●	Basque	▲	Spanish
◆	Norwegian	✕	Hungarian	■	Sardinian
+	Ukrainian	■	French	✕	Greek

The Cucuteni-Tripolye culture had emerged between the Carpathian Mountains and the Middle Dniester around 5200–5000 BC and spread gradually northeast until it bordered the Dnieper-Donets II culture.[42] It survived the climatic crisis by adapting its economy. The Cucuteni farmers were already keeping cattle for milk. So they had taken one step towards what archaeologist Andrew Sherratt called the 'Secondary Products Revolution'. Instead of just killing animals for meat, farmers began to keep them for renewable secondary products, such as milk, cheese and wool, and for transport and traction. Horses and donkeys could be ridden or carry a pack; oxen could pull a plough or a wagon. Thus more could be gained from stock and soil with no increase in human effort. Any society adopting this new way of life had a marked advantage in wealth and mobility.[43]

The earliest evidence of the wheel comes from the Late Cucuteni-Tripolye culture in the form of wheeled toys. The Cucuteni-Tripolye villagers by this time had begun to merge with the indigenous people to their east. Around 3600 BC this culture produced models of sledges harnessed with oxen.[44] By the inventive stroke of adding wheels, it seems that the sledge became the cart.[45] Meanwhile a simple type of plough called the ard, made of elk antlers, was devised by the Cucuteni-Tripolye farmers. Traces of yoking and harnessing on steer bones provide convincing evidence of animal traction.[46] Just as oxen had pulled sledges and the first ploughs, they were the early choice for wheeled vehicles.[47] Horses ran wild on the wide grasslands of the Eurasian steppes. They were tamed at around the same time that the wagon was invented, but not to run in harness. The first carts were heavy and slow-moving. Horses were fleet of foot and ideal for riding. Riders could control much larger herds of animals, and venture further with them.[48]

The Maikop culture (4000–3100 BC) of the North Caucasus introduced to the steppe the tough arsenic-copper alloy that did duty as bronze before the invention of true bronze (copper alloyed with tin). Maikop marked the burials of their chiefs with a mound of earth.[49] At the same time, the habit appeared nearby on the steppe. The Repin culture developed from around 4000 BC between the Volga and Ural rivers. Here began the characteristic burial type of Yamnaya, with the body laid in a crouched position under a round tumulus or barrow (*kurgan* in Russian).[50]

Around 3400 BC Yamnaya archaeology begins to be seen. This was a mobile, wagon- and tent-based herding economy adapted to the grasslands. Evolving between the Volga and Don rivers, Yamnaya spread rapidly over the whole European steppe.[51] The Yamnaya cultural package is distinctive. The most visible element today is the kurgan. It placed a new emphasis on the individual by being a single grave, rather than a collective grave often re-used. The difference is perhaps more one of initial intent, since many house secondary burials. We can guess that those few with rich grave goods, especially wheeled vehicles, were for honoured leaders of the community. The Kargaly copper ore deposits in the foothills of the southern Urals were exploited by Yamnaya people. Burial with tool-kits marked the special status of metalworkers.[52]

New weapon designs included the tanged dagger and the shaft-hole axe, which had been introduced by the Maikop metallurgists. The Yamnaya people wore woven clothes, gold or silver spiral hair rings (*lockenringe*), distinctive bone toggles and decorated bone discs.[53] The hair binders are found in pairs with both men and women, and would have been worn on the end of braids to keep them from unwinding. In the *Iliad* we find the Trojan hero Euphorbos with his tresses bound with gold and silver.[54] Cord decoration was common on pottery. The technical innovations of horse-riding, wheeled transport and metalworking were gradually adopted across Europe and Asia. Often they are accompanied by other Yamnaya character-istics, which consolidate the link to the cultural progenitor.[55]

Indo-European dispersal

Swings of climate played a large part in triggering movement from the steppe. The collapse of Balkan farming in the cold period from 4200 BC to 3800 BC left land vacated in the Balkans. Some steppe herders pushed into the marshes and plains around the mouth of the Danube for winter fodder and cover. The Cernavoda culture (4200–3500 BC) of the Lower Danube and eastern Bulgaria may represent the development of Proto-Anatolian.[56] This ancestor of ancient Hittite and Luwian had a PIE-derived word for thill or harness-pole, but seems not to have had a PIE-derived word for wagon or wheel, so it is logical to suppose that it left the parent lan-guage community after animal traction was in use for drawing sledges or ploughs, but before wheeled vehicles appeared. There are strong similari-ties in pottery and metal finds between the later stages of Cernavoda and some sites of northern Anatolia. Coastal seafaring around the Black Sea would be the obvious explanation. The Balkan-Anatolian network appears to be continuous and long-lasting.[57] So we may picture a gradual drift across into Anatolia.

A shift in the climate after 3200 BC may have encouraged another exodus from the European steppe. Conditions became colder and drier. In the forest-steppe belt the forest was reduced and the steppe expanded. The region was at its most arid between 2700 and 2000 BC.[58] The Yamnaya culture and its descendants spread far and wide along multiple routes.

The first Indo-European move east had all the boldness that would come to characterize the steppe nomads. A group set out from the Volga-Ural region to trek some 2,000 km (1,240 miles) to the high steppe of the Altai Mountains c. 3300–3000 BC. There they created the first mobile pastoralist culture east of the Ural Mountains.[59] An Indo-European language with archaic features crops up millennia later along the Silk Road, named Tocharian after the people known to the Greeks as *Tokharoi*.[60]

The next movement visible in the archaeology flowed to the western end of the steppes, integrating Yamnaya herders and Late Cucuteni-Tripolye farming communities into the Usatovo culture around the mouth of the River Dniester. This culture could be the first step along the road leading to the Pre-Germanic dialect splitting away. The next step was migration up the Dniester, which blended with the descendants of Balkan farmers to create the widespread Corded Ware or Single Grave culture (2750–2400 BC).[61] Ancient DNA samples suggest that people of the Corded Ware culture had on average three grandparents descended from Yamnaya ancestors.[62]

Proto-Germanic (the *immediate* ancestor to the Germanic language family) did not develop until about 500 BC. It has an interesting feature. Up to one-third of its lexicon is non-Indo-European. As Sir William Jones said in the quotation that heads this chapter, Germanic seems 'blended with a very different idiom'. Many of these non-Indo-European words are agricultural, and so must have been borrowed from a farming culture. Furthermore, traces of this same language can be found in the Greek, Latin and Celtic languages.[63] The common feature seems to be contact with Balkan farmers or their descendants.

We can certainly imagine some such contact within the massive migration up the Danube between about 3100 and 2800 BC. Yamnaya herders passed through the Usatovo culture into the Danube Valley, ending up in what is now eastern Hungary. The evidence lies in their kurgans. This was a true folk movement that left ten thousand burials.[64] In fact it is best considered

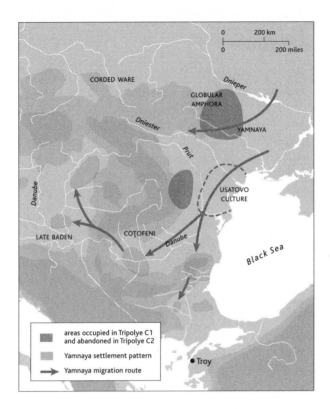

31 *Yamnaya movement up the Danube into the Carpathian Basin is generally taken to represent the spread of Proto-Italo-Celtic. Yamnaya movement towards Thrace could represent the ancestor of the 'Balkan group' of languages: Thracian, Greek, Armenian and Phrygian.*

as an extension of Yamnaya. In that Danubian arm of the expanding culture we can visualize the gradual development from Old European (*Alteuropäisch*) to Proto-Italo-Celtic.

Yamnaya settlements west of the Black Sea [31] suggest movement towards Thrace, where the ancestor of the Balkan group of languages (including Greek and Armenian) could have developed. Long before appearing in the south Caucasus around 600 BC, Armenian seems to have had a developmental period close to the ancestor of Greek.[65] At Plachidol in Bulgaria a particularly interesting Yamnaya-type cemetery of six tumuli was excavated in 1979. Two anthropomorphic stelae were found there. One female grave contained two solid wooden wheels.[66] From Plachidol and Ezerovo, near Varna, there is a trail of anthropomorphic stelae to Greek Macedonia and on to the Aegean island of Thassos and Soufli Magoula in Thessaly.[67] [see 33]

Steppe groups penetrated Late Cucuteni-Tripolye towns on the Middle Dnieper, together with elements of Corded Ware, creating a hybrid that gradually became its own distinct culture. This seems to represent the dialect which became Proto-Balto-Slavic.[68]

Towards the end of the most arid period on the steppe, a final expansion east of the Ural mountains apparently set the Indo-Iranian languages on their way. Here the first fortified settlements appeared on the Asian steppe, such as Sintashta and Arkaim (2100–1800 BC). The earliest evidence of chariots has been unearthed at Sintashta. These light vehicles with spoked wheels were in demand by the princes of the Near East by 2000–1900 BC.[69] The culture of Sintashta merged into the widespread Andronovo culture.

Andronovo gave birth to languages spoken today in India and Iran, but let us focus on the fate of those who remained on the steppe to emerge in history as Scythians, since several medieval pseudo-histories that we encountered in Chapter 1 claim them as the ancestors of the Insular Celts. By the 8th century BC the whole Eurasian steppe was inhabited by horse-riding nomads known to the Greeks as *Scythioi*. They were not a nation, but rather numerous tribes, all speaking dialects of an East Iranian language.[70] So the Scythians were not the ancestors of the Celts. They spoke languages from an entirely different branch of the Indo-European family. Furthermore, the predominant Y-DNA signature found in ancient Scythians was R1a,[71] while that of Celtic-speakers is R1b (see box pp. 26–27). In the next chapter we follow a trail of clues from the steppe to the homelands of the Celts.

Overview

- Proto-Indo-European (PIE) was the parent language of a large family of languages spoken today in both Europe and parts of Asia, including the Celtic branch.

- In prehistory any language had to be spoken by a group of people face to face. As groups of PIE-speakers moved away from the parent group, they developed daughter languages.

- A theoretical PIE homeland in Anatolia has been preferred by those who see the Neolithic as the most likely time for a new language family to spread. Yet PIE appears to be a later, Copper Age language, which did not develop in contact with any language of Anatolia.

- The theory of a PIE homeland in the Pontic-Caspian steppe is supported by archaeological evidence of Copper Age movements from this region to areas where speakers of Indo-European languages emerge into history.

- Genetic evidence supports the Copper Age steppe homeland of PIE:

  - Y-DNA haplogroup R1 predominates in Europe today. It arrived on the eastern fringes of Europe with hunter-gatherers, but spread more widely in the Copper Age.

  - Present-day Europeans are mixtures from three source populations: ancient European hunters; farmers from the Near East; and ancient Siberian hunters arriving later in Europe, associated with Y-DNA haplogroup R.

CHAPTER FIVE

Stelae to Bell Beaker

> The Nasamones consult private oracles by frequent and lengthened
> visits to the sepulchres of their relatives ... and the Celts, for the
> same purpose, stay away all night at the tombs of their brave
> chieftains.[1]

This description of the Celts communing with their ancestral chiefs
comes from the 2nd century BC. Naturally, the Greeks had a word for
it. In the Greek world a *herōon* was a shrine dedicated to the cult of a hero.
Celtic sanctuaries that seem designed for just such a purpose are known
from the Iron Age (see pp. 110–11). In this chapter we delve to the roots of
the tradition.

Keen-eyed readers may have picked up a small clue to the Yamnaya
ancestry of Bell Beaker. Hair binders in precious metals are found on the
steppe (p. 75) and in Bell Beaker graves (p. 53). The characteristic Yamnaya
type are spirals, and similar ones are found in the Bell Beaker of Portugal.[2]
How did Yamnaya elements travel right across Europe? Anthropomorphic
stelae provide the missing link. Stylized human images can be found all the
way from the European steppe to the Atlantic coast of Iberia.[3] These stelae
can be linked to confident and experienced copper-working of the Yamnaya
type. A new way of life was transported to the far west of Europe, which
developed into the first stage of the Bell Beaker culture.[4]

People of stone

Some Yamnaya burials were individualized by a stone stela. The beginning of the tradition can dimly be seen at the western end of the European
steppe. A culture named after the site of Mikhailovka on the Lower Dnieper
seems to be a cross between farming and steppe influences in its first phase
(3700–3400 BC). Its people adopted the steppe habit of burial mounds. The
graves under the kurgans were often stone-lined cists. In a few, the covering

slab was roughly shaped at the top to indicate a head and shoulders. This seems to be the tentative start of what became a long steppe tradition of anthropomorphic stelae. Mikhailovka I kurgans with stelae were scattered as far west as the Danube delta and as far south as Crimea. From there the fashion spread to the central Caucasus. The custom of creating stelae flowered in the western steppe, where successor cultures to Mikhailovka I gradually came under the influence of Yamnaya.[5]

Such stelae could be carved on both back and front, and in exceptionally massive cases, on all four sides [32], and were unworked at the base, so it is clear that they were intended to stand upright. Beneath one kurgan of the Mikhailovka group the fractured remains of an anthropomorphic stone stela were found together with traces of ochre, potsherds and animal bones. It would seem that sacrifices were made at the stela.[6]

32 A stela 1.2 m (almost 4 ft) tall found at Kernosovka, Ukraine, is carved on all four sides. On the front is a face with a drooping moustache. The arms are indicated together with an array of weapons. A belt is marked with incised lines around all four sides. On the rear (not shown) a pair of footprints cross the belt.

This does not necessarily mean that the ancestors were treated as gods. A monument from a literate era provides the clue to purpose. An 8th-century BC stela from Zincirli in southeastern Turkey depicts a royal official named Kuttamuwa at his funerary banquet. Kuttamuwa himself tells us so. The text on the stela explains that Kuttamuwa commissioned it during his lifetime, and that at its inauguration in the mortuary chapel offerings were made to various gods. The most enlightening line explains that one of the offerings was 'a ram for my soul that will be in this stela'. Ancient people could visualize their soul being transferred to a memorial stone after death.[7] Human flesh is mortal, but stone may stand eternal as a symbol of the departed.

Hundreds of Yamnaya stelae have been recovered. No two are exactly alike. The overwhelming majority are simple slabs, shaped slightly to hint at a head and rounded shoulders, with little or nothing in the way of orna-ment, though many have a belt incised or painted on. Another feature that can appear is a pair of footprints. Both belt and footprints are common on the more interesting rarities, sometimes called statue-menhirs. These not only indicate arms and facial features, but also objects, which have been eagerly examined for clues to the status of the figure, such as weapons or a shepherd's crook.[8] That footprints are so prevalent suggests they have some importance. It has been argued that they are one of the symbols of a divine guide of souls, a psychopomp, who escorts the newly deceased to the afterlife.[9]

The stelae trail

Funeral stelae radiate out from the European steppe in several directions. We have already noted the trail through Bulgaria to Greece (pp. 77–78). Here we focus on the route that links Yamnaya to Bell Beaker. [33] In Romania anthropomorphic stelae have been found at Hamangia-Baia [34] and Ceamurlia de Jos, both sites on the coastal plain leading to the Danube delta.[10] Migration up the Danube brought the concept of stelae into the Carpathian Basin. Within Romania a site at Baia de Cris had two – a broken one with decorated girdle and necklace was discovered there in 1881, and a similar one in 2000.[11]

A connection with metals can be seen in the stelae trail westwards along the Mediterranean. The first attraction was the Alps. The rich copper deposits of the Alps had been discovered by metalworkers *c.* 4500–4000 BC. Experiments were made in smelting the local ore at Brixlegg above the Middle Inn Valley in the Austrian Tyrol.[12] There are similar dates for a fragmentary crucible and copper slag at Botteghino (Parma), northern Italy, on a site otherwise comparable to Neolithic sites in France.[13] One can imagine

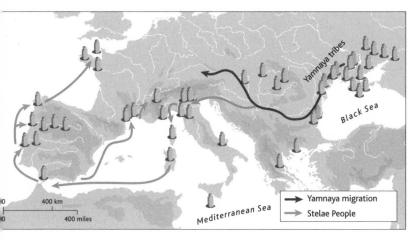

33 (above) From a starting point north of the Black Sea, Yamnaya anthropomorphic stelae radiated in several directions. One route led to Iberia and on to what is now Brittany.

34 (right) This Copper Age anthropomorphic stela from Hamangia-Baia, Romania, has a belt with a sporran-like purse hanging from it in the centre and long pockets at each side. On the rear are carved five axes and two footprints.

83

a visiting metalworker or two at that stage. At first surface ores were collected. Mining began once such easily available sources ran out. The earliest known copper mines in western Europe (c. 3500 BC) are at Monte Loreto (Castiglione Chiavarese, Liguria) in northern Italy.[14] Tuscany too has deposits of copper ore.

Copper Age cultures sprang up in Italy: Remedello in the north, Rinaldone in the west and Gaudo in the south.[15] The dating of these cultures has been an academic battleground. That is unfortunate, since the chronology is crucial to our understanding of how metallurgy spread, and who spread it. We can attribute the discovery of the Brixlegg ores to Balkan copperworkers turning their sights westwards. It dates to before the collapse of the rich Balkan towns of the 5th millennium BC. In Sardinia the arrival of metallurgy around 4000 BC suggests a flight direct from that collapse.[16] The most recent dates for Rinaldone burials centre around 3500 BC, too late for the Balkan exodus, yet too early for Yamnaya wanderings.[17] Knowledge of metallurgy could have spread down from the Alps into central Italy. So it had been suggested that Remedello was probably at least as old as Rinaldone.[18] Radiocarbon dating proves otherwise. The dates for Remedello graves centre around 2900 BC. They have been divided into phases: Remedello I (3300–2900 BC) and Remedello II (2900/2800–2400 BC).[19] That is compatible with arrivals from the Yamnaya stream, which would explain the Yamnaya elements in the Remedello culture, such as single graves and copper-arsenic alloys. The distinctive Remedello II daggers are depicted on anthropomorphic stelae of northern Italy and the western Alps.[20] [35]

So copper sources in the eastern Alps were already known in the days when the Balkans were the centre of European metallurgy, and continued to attract attention long afterwards. A group of copper prospectors seems to have left the Carpathian Basin to wend its way into northern Italy. The easiest route would be to follow the River Sava, a tributary of the Danube, to the area of present-day Ljubljana, capital of Slovenia, and then wind around the southeastern Alps to the Adriatic coast. That would mean passing through the Ljubljana Marshes. In the 4th millennium BC copper-workers settled in pile dwellings in these marshes. Their copper came from the Alps. A fragment of ray bone found amid their detritus shows contacts also with the Adriatic coast 100 km (62 miles) away. The oxygen-free bog around the pile dwellings preserved an ancient solid wooden wheel in amazingly good condition, and nearby a wooden axle, radiocarbon-dated to between

35 *Stela no. 2 from Petit-Chasseur, Sion, Switzerland, has a double spiral pendant and a dagger of the Remedello II type, with a triangular blade and half-moon pommel.*

3160 and 3100 BC. The square-cut axle would have rotated with the wheel. Early wheels of the same revolving-axle design have been found only in Switzerland and southwest Germany. It was presumably intended for a two-wheeled cart, suitable for the rolling foothills of the Alps.[21] So we have a trail of technology that leads to the Alps, where a profusion of stelae is found. Copper deposits in Sardinia were discovered much earlier, but also attracted stelae makers.

The search for copper had spread westwards along the Mediterranean by the end of the 4th millennium BC, taking stelae with it. The earliest copper mine and metallurgical complex in France is in the mountains of Languedoc at Cabrières and Péret, dating from the late 3rd millennium BC.[22] Remedello daggers are depicted in rock art of both northern Italy and southern France. The daggers appear in engravings in the French Alpine foothills at Chastel-Arnaud, Drôme, amid the interconnecting valleys between the south Alps and the Rhône Valley, a clue to the route westwards of copper metallurgy.[23] There is a concentration of Copper Age anthropomorphic stelae in the south of France. [36]

36 'La Dame de Saint Sernin' is one of a number of stelae from the south of France. The lines on the face of this female image are thought to represent scarifications. Legs are shown here and on several other stelae from this region.

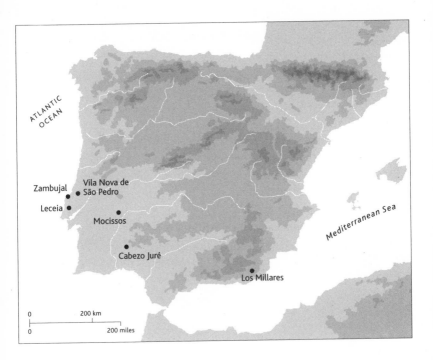

37 *Key sites in the early Copper Age of Iberia. Zambujal and Los Millares had the sea and sources of gold close at hand. Copper was mined inland at Mocissos and Cabezo Juré.*

Another rich Copper Age culture appeared in Iberia. [37] The earliest dates of copper-working there (*c.* 3100 BC) are for mining-metallurgical complexes in southwestern Iberia, such as Cabezo Juré. It is revealing that this site was colonized by a community already specialized in copper production. These incomers lived within a fortified centre, dining well and importing luxuries, while in a village outside lived the lower-status workers. The well-protected elite controlled access to horses, used probably in the transport of copper ore.[24] At this time Iberia had wild horses. Some of their DNA made its way into modern Iberian breeds.[25] Horse bones are found together with Bell Beaker pottery throughout its range, so the idea that domesticated horses spread from Iberia with Bell Beaker has enjoyed a certain popularity,[26] but sites such as Cabezo Juré, which precede Bell Beaker, suggest that the knowledge of horse-taming and copper-working arrived in Iberia together from the European steppe.

The two foci for Copper Age Iberia became the lofty, fortified settlements of Zambujal (Torres Vedras, Portugal) and Los Millares (Almería, Spain). Both were set on promontories commanding approaches by river or sea. Both began as small strongholds and expanded with the creation of new walls enclosing greater areas.[27] Zambujal had the most easily defended position. It was set on a peninsula carved out by the great River Tagus where it meets the sea. On the same peninsula other fortified sites include Vila Nova de São Pedro (Azambuja) and Leceia (Oeiras). The fort at Leceia was built around 2900–2800 BC. Like Zambujal, pottery of different styles was in use there at different periods, ending with Bell Beaker.[28] At these sites ease of defence was combined with ease of access by sea. Today Zambujal

38 This stela from Tapada, Guarda, Portugal, can be compared with 'La Dame de Saint Sernin' (p. 86) in the position of the arms and the depiction of a belt and complex necklace. It is one of a group in Iberia with a headdress.

lies 14 km (almost 9 miles) from the Atlantic coast, but in the Copper Age the nearby River Sizandro was a tidal estuary. Zambujal imported ivory from afar. Alluvial gold from the Tagus could have been traded in exchange, along with copper ware. Copper was imported from the mining-metallurgical complex at Mocissos for the workshops of Zambujal. As in the Remedello culture of northern Italy, copper-arsenic alloys were deliberately used for daggers, saws and other artifacts that required a harder metal than pure copper.[29]

Iberia has a rich variety of decorated stelae, ranging in date from the Neolithic to the Iron Age. Here we look only at the anthropomorphic type. [38] These are generally found in a prominent position within megalithic burial mounds. In Iberia some Neolithic burial chambers were re-used in the Bell Beaker period. Dating is easier where a communal burial chamber was both built and closed in the 3rd millennium. Sometimes the stelae themselves provide a clue to chronology. Obviously those depicting metal objects must be later than the Neolithic. For example, one from Longroiva in northern Portugal carries an image of a halberd of Copper Age type, together with a bow and dagger. Most are much less informative. As with Yamnaya stelae, many barely hint at a human figure, with either no objects depicted or only a shepherd's crook.[30]

Anthropomorphic stelae continue up the Atlantic coast from Iberia to Brittany, where there is a notable cluster, and even as far as the Channel Isles. [see 33] Crucially, Copper Age anthropomorphic stelae along the Mediterranean and Atlantic route herald the earliest Bell Beaker pottery, that which falls into the southern sphere. [see 19]

Linking stelae to Bell Beaker

The fascinating complex at Petit-Chasseur, Sion (Valais), in western Switzerland, has been much studied. A necropolis there continued in use from the Late Neolithic through the Bell Beaker period to the Early Bronze Age. Swiss archaeologist Alain Gallay spent years on its excavation and identified 28 decorated stelae, which he sorted into two types: early and Bell Beaker period.[31] So a link was made here between stelae and Bell Beaker. The wider meaning was explored when Richard Harrison and Volker Heyd reassessed this important site, together with a remarkably similar one at Aosta in the Alps to the south of Sion.[32]

39 Anthropomorphic stela no. 25 from the necropolis at Petit-Chasseur, Sion, Switzerland, belongs to the Bell Beaker period and is decorated with patterns reminiscent of Bell Beaker pottery.

Aosta was much better preserved, with most stelae found still in situ, so comparison between the two sites made it easier to reconstruct the original appearance of Sion. Around 2700 BC a necropolis was laid out on a solar orientation. Two communal burial chambers were built on this axis. The first anthropomorphic stelae stood before them in a line facing southeast, creating a parade of sun-blessed ancestors. At both Sion and Aosta, stelae with Bell Beaker motifs were added to the parade, indicating continuity in these communities from the first arrivals through to Bell Beaker. Then came a dramatic change, still within the Bell Beaker period. All the stelae at Sion were broken and then re-used, when needed, to create individual cist burials.[33] The political implications of this upheaval will be considered later (p. 97).

The early stelae at Sion are therefore much damaged, but enough remains to pick out features and reconstruct the whole. No. 2 has the belt and stick-like arms we have seen on Yamnaya stelae, together with a double spiral pendant and a dagger of the Remedello II type. [see 35] Three other early stelae depict Remedello II daggers.[34] So the first creators of the necropolis were connected to the Remedello phase of copper-working (see p. 84).

Then the new style of stelae decoration, linked to the Bell Beaker culture, appeared. As we saw earlier, the classic weapon of Yamnaya stelae was the axe. It is not unknown for the bow and arrow to be depicted, but almost invariably together with an axe.[35] With the Bell Beaker culture came a new emphasis on the bow in grave goods, which is reflected in the stelae of this period. A symbolic bow and arrow appears on four stelae.[36]

The detail of the clothing shown is extraordinary. [39] These stylized bodies wear highly patterned garments and decorated belts. The geometric patterns are reminiscent of those on Beaker pots. A few stelae have small sporran-like purses hanging from the centre of their belts, together with longer pockets at either side.[37] The greater detail of these depictions enables us to make sense of the belt features of the Yamnaya statue from Hamangia-Baia. [see 34]

The origins of Bell Beaker pottery

The Bell Beaker culture was identified over a century ago. There has been lively debate ever since over its origins, with homelands suggested in Iberia, southeastern France, Sicily, Central Europe and the Low Countries. Since the key object that appears over the whole Bell Beaker range is the distinctive inverted-bell pot, there was a strong focus on ceramics in these searches for an origin point. Several different styles of Bell Beaker have been defined by the type of ornamentation. Most are local or regional in distribution. The two international types have attracted most attention. One widespread type, known as All Over Corded (AOC), is entirely decorated with impressions made with cord. The Corded Ware culture in central and eastern Europe (see p. 76) did not have a monopoly on the simple and effective technique of winding a twisted cord around a wet clay pot. The other type is labelled Maritime, since it is found predominantly along the Atlantic seaboard from Portugal to Brittany via Galicia. In the 1970s Dutch archaeologists presented a case in favour of the Netherlands as the home of Bell Beaker. The 'Dutch Model' was the most widely accepted for the rest of the century. In the lowlands around the mouth of the Rhine both AOC and Maritime Bell Beakers have been unearthed. This region is on the western edge of the distribution of the Corded Ware culture and a type of Corded Ware pottery is found there, with similarities to AOC, called the Protruding Foot Beaker (PFB). A sequence was proposed from PFB through AOC to Maritime.[38]

Radiocarbon dates put paid to this idea. Carbon-14 has dated the earliest Bell Beaker pottery to the 2700s BC and the earliest Corded Ware to c. 2750 BC. These two widespread cultures were contemporary. Moreover the earliest dates for Bell Beaker come from southern Europe.[39] Bell Beaker did indeed follow Corded Ware in central and eastern Europe, but these were different communities.[40] Their similarities reflect a shared cultural parent in Yamnaya: cord-impressed pottery was part of the Yamnaya assemblage.

So it seems that copper-working descendants of Yamnaya developed bell-shaped pottery in southern Europe. Though Bell Beaker pottery was generally made in the home (p. 51), there were some specialist potters. Expertise can be detected by regularity of form and decoration. French archaeologist Laure Salanova perceives the Maritime Bell Beaker as the classic form, made to a strict standard, identical wherever it is found. [40] The vessel has a uniform S-shaped profile, and is tall with a flat base. It is decorated with neat horizontal bands from top to bottom, edged by incised lines or cord impressions, and filled with simple patterns, commonly of hatched lines, incised using a shell or comb. Maritime was the model that inspired a variety of styles that spread across Europe. For example

40 A Maritime type
of Bell Beaker from
Zambujal, Portugal.

the banded decoration of the Ciempozuelos style of Spain [see 20] is more irregular than the classic Maritime style, but is clearly heir to it. So Salanova argues that we should look west for the source of Bell Beaker pottery, especially to the Tagus estuary in Portugal, which has the highest density of these classical vases.[41] At one time it was thought that Iberia had no AOC pottery, which seemed a point against it as the Bell Beaker homeland. Now corded Bell Beaker is known from four Copper Age fortified sites in Portugal and a scattering of sites in Spain, though it remains rare in Iberia in comparison with Maritime.[42]

The people who made the earliest Bell Beakers were copper-workers and could only be a few generations away from immigrants. At Zambujal there is a clear continuity from the earliest copper-workers to the beginnings of Bell Beaker.[43] A problem lies in a lack of obvious local antecedents. Several authors have argued that local Copper Age *copos* (cups) with a gently waisted outline and horizontal grooves as decoration developed into Bell Beaker.[44] This fails to convince. It is more likely that the Bell Beaker style was a synthesis of influences from more distant connections, as Jan Turek has proposed. He puts forward certain curvaceous pots with impressed decoration from Late Neolithic Morocco as a possible inspiration.[45] Yet key ingredients of the Bell Beaker design have precise predecessors on the stelae route from Ukraine to the Carpathian Basin. Inverted bell-shaped pots were made before 4000 BC north of the Black Sea.[46] [41] Cord impressions have a long history in the same region. Bell Beaker ware commonly had its decoration picked out with white paste made of crushed bone.[47] [see 20] This technique was used earlier in the Carpathian Basin.[48]

41 A *curvaceous pot of the Cucuteni culture, from Draguseni, Romania. Its decoration is very different from that of Bell Beaker, but was the shape an inspiration for the later pottery?*

So the influences that culminated in this pottery could have travelled over time along the same route that brought copper-working to Iberia. A common pattern of migration is repeated movements along the same route. We can imagine pioneers scouting out metal sources and then returning home to trade or collect family members. If so they would spread the knowledge of opportunities, which could attract more migrants. At Leceia in Portugal we see new arrivals expanding the settlement. Nestling just outside the fortifications were two huts with radiocarbon dates centring in the 2700s BC in which the pottery was exclusively Bell Beaker, while within the walls earlier local pottery gradually mixed with Maritime Bell Beaker material, after the new styles were introduced.[49]

Though huge efforts have gone into tracing the origin of Bell Beaker pottery, there is much more to the culture. The German prehistorian Edward Sangmeister deserves credit for his insight into the Bell Beaker phenomenon. He worked at the German Archaeological Institute in Madrid in the 1950s and excavated Zambujal from 1964 to 1973. Recognizing the differences between the early Bell Beaker of Zambujal and the later Bell Beaker of more easterly Iberia, he argued that the pottery spread from Iberia into Central Europe and then returned to Iberia together with new cultural influences. His 'reflux' model is followed below in spirit, if not in all its details.

Bell Beaker routes and the development of Celtic

It has long been supposed that Proto-Celtic developed around the heads of the Danube and Rhine. That fitted the identification of the Hallstatt and La Tène cultures as Celtic. Now that attention is turning to the Bell Beaker culture as the vector for Celtic, Celtic specialists John Koch and Barry Cunliffe have teamed up to propose that Celtic spread from Iberia.[50] The evidence in Iberia of both Celtic and related Indo-European languages makes this a tempting thesis, but there are insuperable difficulties. Proto-Celtic developed in contact with an early precursor to Germanic.[51] That presents no problems if we site Proto-Celtic north of the Alps, but does not fit an Iberian homeland. Later contact between Proto-Celtic and Iranian, discussed in the next chapter (p. 104), can also be explained by the traditional homeland, but not an Iberian alternative. [42]

Koch has put forward two linguistic contact arguments as a counterweight. He suggests that the key change which defines early Celtic, the

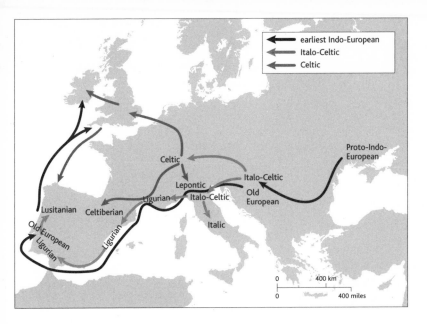

42 *Routes proposed in the present work for Old European* (Alteuropäisch) *and its descendants in the Copper and Bronze Ages. Old European, the oldest linguistic layer of Indo-European origin, was overlaid by various languages developing from Italo-Celtic.*

weakening of the Indo-European 'p' sound (see p. 62), could have occurred in contact with p-less Iberian. It is a common assumption that Iberian was the pre-Indo-European language of Iberia, but it appears actually to be a relatively late arrival, intruding into the band of Ligurian along the Mediterranean coast.[52] This seems too late and limited a contact to account for Celtic.

Koch's other suggestion suffers similarly from a chronological problem, but also a geographical one. Some linguists argue for an Afro-Asiatic influence, specifically Berber, Coptic or Semitic, on the Celtic languages of the British Isles. Its most obvious expression is seen as a change in the standard word order from the original Indo-European subject-object-verb (SOV) and the mixture of SVO and SOV which has been reconstructed for continental Celtic, to the rare VSO order.[53] The Phoenicians spoke an Afro-Asiatic language of the Semitic branch and were present in Iberia by the 8th century BC, so for Koch they could represent the supposed link, but if this affected the development of Proto-Celtic, VSO should appear in all the Celtic languages, not just those in the British Isles. It is logical to suppose that VSO in the British Isles arose from contact with a language present in the islands when Celtic speakers arrived. This need not be any member of the Afro-Asiatic family, but simply a now lost language of Neolithic farmers among the many in Europe that we can guess disappeared under the wave of Indo-European.[54] The farming languages Berber and Coptic survived because Indo-European languages did not significantly penetrate North Africa until colonial times.

Nevertheless, Koch and Cunliffe have usefully drawn attention to Iberia, a region often neglected in Celtic studies. Any model of the spread of Celtic needs to explain the Iberian linguistic mosaic. The proposal here is that the language which spread from Italy to Iberia with the Stelae People was an Indo-European dialect too early to be Celtic, and that Proto-Celtic developed where traditionally supposed, around the heads of the Danube and the Rhine, beginning during the Bell Beaker period. Thus the Late Bell Beaker movements described below could have carried early forms of Celtic into northeastern Iberia, the British Isles and the southern Alps.

The Bell Beaker communities of Iberia were in crisis from c. 2500/2400 BC. Violence and disorder may have encouraged migration. Some large Copper Age settlements such as Zambujal were abandoned. Maritime Bell Beaker travelled eastwards to southern France c. 2500 BC and also appears on the southern coast of Brittany.[55] The distinctive copper spearheads named Palmela points which seem to originate with Bell Beaker in Portugal are also found in Brittany and southern France.[56] [43]

Bell Beaker also arrived at Csepel Island in the Danube around 2500 BC. Among the finds here was a gold disc embellished with concentric circles, similar to the gold discs found on western Bell Beaker sites and interpreted as solar symbols.[57] Csepel Island has given its name to sites of the Bell Beaker Csepel group, clustered around Budapest. One attraction of the Danube Basin was access to steppe horses. Indeed the dominance of horse bones on the sites of the Csepel group suggests that they were horse-breeders.[58] Hungary has no other Bell Beaker. Anthropologically and culturally the isolated Csepel group appears an intrusion. Isotope tests showed that Bell Beaker people on Csepel Island were migrants.[59] A study of inherited tooth characteristics links the Bell Beaker folk of Csepel to those of western Switzerland, while the latter in their turn cluster with the southern Bell Beaker group in Iberia and southern France.[60] So it seems that some descendants of the Stelae People returned to their ancestral home in the Carpathian Basin.

43 *Palmela points were so named because they were first found at Palmela in Portugal. These are from a Bell Beaker burial at San Román de Hornija (Valladolid, Spain) dated to 1800 BC.*

The Bell Beaker culture took on a different configuration in the eastern Beaker sphere. Boar's tusks were worn as pendants or garment fasteners, a fashion which can be traced back to the steppe.[61] This suggests that the incomers mixed with distant relatives who had remained in the Carpathian Basin. *Begleitkeramik* (accompanying pottery) is typical of the eastern Bell Beaker group; it reflects local pottery styles. The handled pitcher and pedestalled and polypod (multi-footed) cups or bowls appear in pre-Beaker groups in Hungary and Slovakia, were absorbed into eastern Bell Beaker and then spread out of the Carpathian Basin with it. This helps us to track the influence of the eastern Beaker tradition west into northern Italy and southern France, south to Sardinia and north down the Rhine.[62] Around the mouth of the Rhine, the Rhenish style of Bell Beaker decoration developed, which spread into Britain.[63] Lastly, islands of Bell Beaker appear across a northern sphere including Jutland, northern Germany and Poland.[64] [see 19]

Some of the eastern group entered territory that had previously belonged to the southern Bell Beaker sphere. There was an abrupt change at the Alpine sites of Sion and Aosta around 2425 BC. The former Bell Beaker stelae were smashed. Objects distinctive of the eastern Bell Beaker group appear, such as boar's tusks.[65] Isotopes reveal a distant origin for one man, who had the type of cranium typical of the eastern Bell Beaker group.[66] The evidence adds up to a power shift in the middle of the Bell Beaker period from the mouth of the Tagus to the head of the Rhine. The Bell Beaker communities of the Rhône corridor who had previously looked to Iberia shifted their gaze eastwards and northwards. Bow-shaped pendants appear, along with pottery designs from the eastern Bell Beaker group.[67]

An echo of eastern Bell Beaker even reached Iberia. Around 2200 BC a new phase of Bell Beaker began in central Spain, the Ciempozuelos horizon. The predominant pottery is influenced by Maritime Bell Beaker, yet from one site came a type of pedestalled cup or bowl derived from those in the Carpathian Basin.[68] An ancient language of the Iberian *meseta* may reflect an influx at this time of speakers of the developing Proto-Celtic. Celtiberian is the most archaic form of Celtic.[69] If indeed it arrived *c.* 2200 BC, then it becomes plausible that Proto-Celtic developed during the Bell Beaker period. If the very earliest Bell Beaker arrivals in the British Isles spoke a pre-Celtic Indo-European language, later ones arriving down the Rhine would bring the earliest Celtic.

It is intriguing that around 2400 BC anthropomorphic stelae were sometimes used to close up megalithic monuments in Iberia and Brittany. This is just the period when Bell Beaker makers first entered Ireland.[70] Did migrating families say farewell to their ancestors in a ceremony of closure? There are clues that the first Bell Beaker makers in Ireland arrived from Brittany or Portugal. An earring or pendant found at Benraw may be an early import, for it is not made of Irish gold, and it is very similar to a pair of earrings found at Estremoz in Portugal.[71] Wrist-guards or bracers for archers are part of the Bell Beaker assemblage. The only type found among the southern Bell Beakers is narrow with two holes, one at each end. Broader, four-holed types predominate in Central Europe. Ireland has almost exclusively two-holed types.[72]

According to the model proposed here, that would mean that the first Bell Beaker arrivals in the British Isles spoke some form of Old European or *Alteuropäisch*. Certain river-names have been taken to support a very old stage of Western Indo-European in Ireland and Britain (see p. 61).[73] Then from about 2200 BC the earliest Celtic would start to appear with new arrivals drawn to Cornish tin and perhaps Irish gold.

It has been argued that the Celtic languages of the British Isles and Gaul are too similar to have diverged this early.[74] This case depends on them actually diverging at this point, never to meet again. The archaeological record suggests continuing contact, with recurrent bursts of migration right up to the Roman period, giving ample opportunity for new linguistic developments to pass from Gaul into the Isles. For example iron-working

Genetics: R1b flows into the British Isles

If the pattern of Y-DNA haplogroups seen in Continental Europe (box pp. 44–45) is matched in the British Isles, the haplogroup G2a probably predominated in the first farmers, while the R1b that dominates Europe today arrived in the Copper Age. G2a is rare today, but there is no need to picture genocide. The first farmers in the British Isles thrived initially, but then encountered problems. Populations seem to have fallen before they were boosted by Bell Beaker arrivals.[75] The latter brought new technologies, giving them an economic advantage, which could ensure the better survival of offspring.

Today two subclades of R1b1a2a1a2 (P312) seem to echo the two Bell Beaker routes into the Isles that we see in the archaeology, though this can only be speculation in the absence of early Bell Beaker DNA from the British Isles. The predominant one is R1b1a2a1a2c (L21) [see 9], which probably moved up the Rhine, across the Channel and from Britain to Ireland.

R1b1a2a1a2a (DF27) is common in Iberia.[76] So the rare cases of R1b-DF27* (the basal form of DF27) in Ireland today may be a remnant of Bell Beaker movements up the Atlantic. If R1b-DF27 also travelled with Bell Beaker from Iberia into the Carpathian Basin, that would explain its present wide range. It has some subclades whose bearers cluster in southwestern Europe, but others which are almost exclusive to northern Europeans and their descendants. Scandinavian branches of R1b-DF27 could have arrived in the Isles as late as Viking or Norman times.

technology arriving in the British Isles from its Celtic Continental centres was no doubt accompanied by the appropriate vocabulary. That would help to explain the complexity of the relationships between the recorded Celtic languages. [see 54]

Bronze Age mobility

Language contacts between wide-spaced Celtic-speakers would have continued throughout the Bronze Age, an era remarkable for its long-distance trade networks across Europe. However, the traffic along the Atlantic littoral petered out, becoming patchy and light c. 2100 to 1300 BC. In this period Iberia developed largely in isolation from lands to the north. Britain and Ireland had more contact with northwestern France and the Low Countries.[77]

Then came the Atlantic Bronze Age (c. 1300–700 BC), which saw prestigious items exchanged via the Atlantic seaways. The major centres were southern England and Ireland, northwestern France and northwestern Iberia.[78] This was precisely the period in which northwestern Europe suffered an increasingly wet and cold climate.[79] Relocation to the sunnier south would offer attractions. This might help to account for the Celtification of northwest Iberia.

The *Castro* (castle) culture of this region has its origins in the Late Bronze Age and continued into the Iron Age. Rather than starting in the far north of the peninsula, as we might expect if it was the product of Atlantic arrivals, it seems to begin in northwest Portugal. Yet it absorbed influences from both the Atlantic and the Mediterranean.[80] In the Late Bronze Age, cremation became the standard treatment for the dead over a large stretch of Central Europe. The ashes were buried in urns, hence the name Urnfield culture (c. 1300–750 BC). The cremation habit edged into Iberia from what is now southern France. It has often been assumed that Urnfield was solidly Celtic-speaking. Yet early Greek travellers found Ligurians along the coast of both France and Iberia.[81] [see 42] So did seafaring colonists spread an Italo-Celtic tongue? It seems that both the Lusitanians south of the Douro and their northern neighbours the Callaeci or Gallaeci arrived in the Late Bronze Age. There is no sign of a local origin for them. There are differences between the two peoples, yet they shared three deities, suggesting some joint ancestry.[82]

This does not rule out an Atlantic component in the Gallaecian mix. By the time that records appear of place- and personal names, Gallaecia was divided into two regions: in the north the Lucensis, with a centre at what is now Lugo, Spain, and in the south the Bracarensis, with a centre at what is now Braga, Portugal. [see 64] They were divided by the river Minho/Miño, which forms the northern border of Portugal. Gallaecia Lucensis appears to have been mainly Celtic-speaking, in contrast to the more Lusitanian affinities of Gallaecia Bracarensis.[83] So trade contacts during the Atlantic Bronze Age may have spread Celtic to northwestern Iberia.

Overview

- Standing stones – stelae – with hints of the humanoid link Yamnaya to Bell Beaker, accounting for the spread of Indo-European to the far west of Europe.

- Stelae of this series started at the western end of the European steppe. The tradition was taken up by the Yamnaya horizon from 3300 BC.

- There is a Yamnaya stelae trail up the Danube to the Carpathian Basin. Similar stelae appear in northern Italy, southern France and western Iberia.

- A connection with Bell Beaker is made at Sion, Switzerland, where earlier stelae continue to be supplemented in the early Bell Beaker period.

- Bell Beaker pottery first appeared in Portugal in the 2700s BC, but its influences seem to be from the European steppe and Carpathian Basin.

- The first language to travel with Bell Beaker was probably Old European IE (*Alteuropäisch*). Proto-Celtic probably developed around the Upper Danube in the Late Bell Beaker period, spreading *c.* 2200 BC to Iberia and the British Isles.

- Movement during the Atlantic Bronze Age (*c.* 1300–700 BC) may have spread Celtic to northwestern Iberia.

CHAPTER SIX
The Iron Sword

We should call a man mad, or else insensitive to pain, if he feared nothing, neither earthquake nor billows, as they say of the Kelts.[1]

Thus Aristotle cast a disapproving eye upon the fearless Celts in the 4th century BC. Courage for its own sake he deemed irrational. Yet the warrior ethos was far from unknown to the Greeks. The *Iliad* and *Odyssey* are songs in praise of heroes and battle glory. Swords, shields and armour not only feature in these tales, but also turn up in Greek tombs from many centuries earlier.[2]

Swords were first made in the Bronze Age. Unlike bows and axes, initially devised for hunting and chopping, swords had no other function but to fight other human beings. Likewise, shields and armour would only be made by communities who foresaw combat. Though helmets and body-armour could be of leather and shields of wood, metal gave better protection. For these bronze was first poured into a flat cast to create a metal sheet, and the sheet was then hammered into the required shape, using annealing (re-heating) to keep it malleable. In Central Europe the first armour appears *c.* 1300 BC at the beginning of the Urnfield culture. Approximately 120 helmets, 95 shields, 55 greaves and 30 cuirasses are known from the European Bronze Age. The distribution area of each type of armour is different; only in the Carpathian Basin and a little further to the north do we find all of them.[3]

44 *This magnificent Hallstatt C iron sword comes from a cremation grave in Gomadingen, Germany. It is of the Mindelheim type, with a long, leaf-shaped blade and hat-shaped pommel. The hilt is decorated with sheet gold.*

With the appearance of iron, the paraphernalia of war began to take on the shape familiar right up to the Middle Ages: the mounted fighter with an iron sword. [44] The transformation of warfare began with nomads of the steppe.

Steppe nomads

About the 11th century BC a long arid period began on the steppes of Europe and Kazakhstan. The Black and Caspian seas shrank. Zones of vegetation shifted. The population of the steppe faced ecological crisis. Economies reliant on a mixture of agriculture and cattle-breeding collapsed and a fully nomadic lifestyle took their place. Mobile herders could avoid over-grazing any area, moving on periodically to greener pastures. A culture sprang up on the European steppe which lasted long enough to be known to ancient writers as Cimmerian. [45] Its origins were mixed. Influences from the Asian steppe blended with those from North Caucasus and the remnants of the dying cultures of the western steppe.[4]

45 *The Cimmerians fled west and south under the pressure of Scythian advances. Both peoples were Indo-European steppe nomads.*

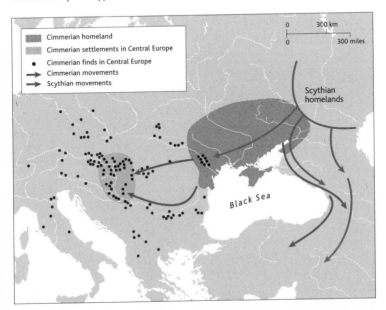

For these nomads horse riding was crucial. They developed a new bridle. The Cimmerian bits had two movable parts, meant for riding, unlike the rigid bits of the Urnfield culture, which were more suitable for traction. From 900 BC weaponry and horse harness that we can trace to the Cimmerians appear in the Late Urnfield and related cultures of the Upper and Middle Danube region. The characteristic weapons were swords and daggers with iron blades and bronze hilts. Iron-working had begun early on the Pontic steppe. From about 800 to 700 BC ceramics and ornaments from the same source are found in the graves and hoards of the Early Hallstatt in Central Europe. Cimmerians had settled in the Carpathian Basin with their steppe-bred horses and the habit of wagon burial. Their influence on the developing Hallstatt culture was profound.[5] Meanwhile metal-smiths in the Late Urnfield tradition of the Carpathian Basin seem to have taken their skills to Etruria, creating new centres of metal production for local elites and foreign exchange.[6] This placed the Hallstatt culture on a trade crossroads.

Could the Cimmerians understand the Celts? The effort to communicate may have had a linguistic result. Celtic shares one linguistic feature with Iranian (the syncretism of plain-voiced and 'voiced aspirated' stops) that is not shared with Proto-Indo-Iranian or Proto-Italo-Celtic. This points to a meeting between Celtic- and Iranian-speakers sometime after 2000 BC. The feature is also shared by Baltic, Slavic and Albanian.[7] Cimmerian contacts on the steppe and up the Danube might explain this, though there is so little evidence of the language spoken by the Cimmerians that we can only guess that it was a member of the Iranian family, if we recall the contribution to the Cimmerian culture from the Asian steppe.

Hallstatt aristocrats

Richly furnished wagon burials of the Hallstatt culture are found in southern Germany, eastern France, Switzerland, Bohemia and Upper Austria. They conjure up a society dominated by an elite. Wealth and power were concentrated in the hands of warriors entrenched on fortified hilltops.

Their wealth came from control of trade routes. Amber was prized far and wide. Its look of translucent honey trapped in time has long fascinated people. Its use for jewelry dates back deep into the past. Although it occurs in various places in Europe, the Baltic is by far the leading source of amber.

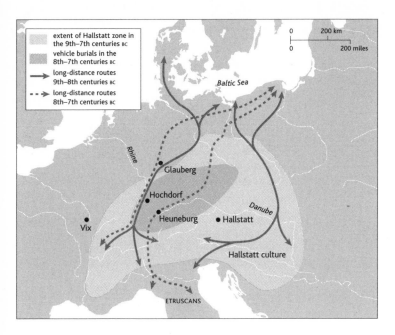

46 *The key to understanding the rise of Celtic chiefdoms is control over trading routes. Here we see the Hallstatt culture and its trade connections.*

Chemical testing can identify Baltic amber, so we can follow its progress from source to destination. In the early stages of the Hallstatt culture, it crossed the Hallstatt zone from the Danish island of Funen (Fyn) to Etruria. Sometime in the 8th century a more easterly route was established from the amber-rich Pomeranian coast to Italy and the Balkans.[8] [46] In return the Hallstatt chieftains craved the best that Mediterranean civilizations could supply. To judge by imported wares designed for drinking or transporting wine, the Hallstatt elite fully appreciated this particular grape derivative.[9]

One item seldom traded from the early Hallstatt culture was the iron sword. This new weapon was taken up with enthusiasm by Hallstatt chiefs and is the standard type in their wagon burials, but it did not travel far from the Hallstatt zone initially. The Hallstatt people had adopted iron-working in the 8th century BC as an addition to bronze-making, rather than an immediate replacement. Some other parts of Europe were even slower to switch to the new metal. So instead of a sharp transition between the Age of Bronze and that of Iron in Europe, there was a gradual shift over centuries. Iron had the advantage of being readily available, but the technology for working it was complex and labour-intensive. Rather than being cast, iron was forged and hammered on an anvil at red-heat. This process was not totally unfamiliar to bronze-smiths accustomed to hammering objects from sheet metal. So now to armour could be added the iron sword.[10]

The best-studied Hallstatt hillfort is the Heuneburg in southern Germany. [47] It is superbly sited. [see 46] The hill overlooks the Upper Danube, thus controlling east–west trade from the Danube to the Rhône Valley, and also a route south from Pomerania to Italy. Extensive excavations have revealed a major political and commercial centre. Extraordinary power required extraordinary protection. When it was first laid out the Heuneburg had houses and a defensive wall of traditional type for the region, but around 600 BC this first wall was replaced by a Mediterranean-style defence with bastions made of sun-dried bricks, unique in Central Europe. Was a southern architect enticed north by a prudent prince?[11]

Recent work has uncovered more of a fortified lower town, and in the process overturned the prevailing view of it. Scholars had long thought that these secondary fortifications were medieval. The research project 'Early Celtic Princely Centres' (2004–2010) made the startling discovery that they were in fact constructed in the Final Hallstatt period. Remains of a timber bridge crossing the outer ditch could be dendro-dated to 590 BC. Also uncovered was a massive gatehouse of around the same date guarding the entrance to the lower town. Outside the lower town, closely spaced farmsteads were protected by palisades. They presumably supplied food to the denser population within the walls. This concentration of people gives the Heuneburg an urban flavour. A town has its own economy. It may provide a market for agricultural produce, but it is more than a farm or estate centre. Goods are made and traded there. Local authority may be centred there. Pottery, jewelry and textiles were certainly made at the Heuneburg, but territorial and trade power was probably more significant than local craft. Heuneburg's impressive defences and the sumptuous burials around the settlement proclaim its status as a political capital.[12]

Not all the rich burials nearby are of warrior chiefs. Mound 4 of the Bettelbühl necropolis, 2.5 km (roughly 1½ miles) southeast of the Heuneburg, has been yielding wondrously rich grave goods. The main burial was that of a wealthy woman, dubbed a Celtic princess by her discoverers. She lay in a

47 *The flat top of the Heuneburg was ideal for a hillfort. Below it lay a fortified lower town, with farms outside it.*

chamber constructed of timber from a tree cut in the year 583 BC; it proved to be a treasure-house of high-quality craftwork in gold, amber and bronze. A secondary burial of a two- to four-year-old girl was also furnished with golden jewelry. So young a child could not have acquired status by her own actions. Here, then, is a hint that the Celts were developing the idea of inherited status, the foundation of aristocracy.[13]

Of the 100 or so Hallstatt wagon graves, the one at Hochdorf stands out for its conspicuous consumption. [49] The contents of the burial chamber were exceptionally well preserved, so we know that a tall man of about 40 had been buried in colourful textiles and a conical hat made of birch bark. A similar hat (and little else) is worn by the Warrior of Hirschlanden, the earliest life-size and lifelike statue known from a Celtic sculptor. [48] It is what the Hochdorf chief wore on his feet, though, that has attracted most attention. His pointed, slightly upturned leather shoes had lavish gold leaf decoration. A BBC television programme in 1987 christened him 'The Man with the Golden Shoes'. Gold was not spared elsewhere about his person either. He wore a gold collar and bracelet. His belt was decorated in gold, and the bronze dagger beside it was completely covered in gold leaf. If this gold-laden costume strikes you as impractical day-to-day wear, you would be right. All the gold leaf was added specifically for the burial.

This glittering figure had been tenderly laid on blankets spread on a bronze couch, unique for its place and time. It is decorated with warrior scenes and supported on wheeled female figures. At the foot of his couch was a massive bronze cauldron which had held about 450 litres (100 gallons) of mead. It is decorated around the brim with three lions, beasts unknown to the Celts of this era. That alone should tell us that this magnificent object was imported. Indeed it is Greek in style and its copper has a high bismuth level, which suggests a Greek ore. It was probably made by Greeks in southern Italy. On the other side of the chamber was an impressive iron-bound four-wheeled wagon.[14] The iron tyres had been nailed in place, which must have made for a bumpy ride. (From around the 2nd century BC such iron tyres were heated and then allowed to cool on the wooden wheel, shrinking them into place.[15])

The gold collar worn by the Hochdorf chieftain is sometimes described as a torc, but that is misleading. It was made of sheet gold which had not been rolled into the circular cross-section of a torc. It had no opening. It was large enough to slip over the head of its wearer and sit on the shoulders. The classic torc is a ring close around the

48 (left) *The Warrior of Hirschlanden is the earliest life-size and reasonably lifelike stone statue known from a Celtic sculptor. He wears a torc around his neck and a belt with a typical late Hallstatt dagger. His pointed hat was perhaps made of birch bark, like that found in the princely grave of Hochdorf, approximately 5 km (3 miles) from Hirschlanden. The sculptor gave him legs thick enough to provide solid support and avoided the arms breaking off by portraying them clasped to the body.*

49 (opposite) *Reconstruction in the Keltenmuseum Hochdorf/Enz of the chieftain's wagon burial discovered at Hochdorf in Baden-Württemberg, Germany. The chieftain was laid on a couch made of sheet bronze, with a huge bronze cauldron at its foot which had been filled with mead. The wagon in the foreground is heaped with bronze dishes and horse harness.*

throat, which opens at the front. The Warrior of Hirschlanden wears one. So did a man buried in some state at Hochmichele, 3.5 km (2 miles) west of the Heuneburg, in the Final Hallstatt period.[16] Particularly interesting is the burial of a torc-wearing warrior at Saint-Romain-de-Jalionas (France) in the 8th century BC,[17] since that takes us back to the start of the Hallstatt culture. With these Hallstatt-era burials, we have solid evidence that torcs were not simply an item of jewelry for women, but were also worn by high-status men.

Rivalling the Hochdorf chief in magnificence is the Lady of Vix. She is named for the French village where she was found. The Vix area is dominated by Mont Lassois, a steep, flat-topped hill overlooking the upper reaches of the Seine. Today the church of St Marcel of Vix stands upon it, while the village itself lies in the valley by the Seine. Southeast of the village, within a curve of the river, is a necropolis first used in the late Bronze Age. Here was found the wagon tomb of the Lady of Vix, the contents of which remain unparalleled. Her wealth can be explained by someone's shrewd grasp of geography. The top of Mont Lassois was ideal for fortification and it stood at a route axis. [see 46] Diodorus Siculus describes tin being transported from Cornwall to Gaul and then south to the mouth of the Rhône.[18] Tin travelling up the Seine could have been disembarked near Mont Lassois, where the Seine ceased to be navigable, and transported by land to the Saône Valley, leading to the river Rhône.

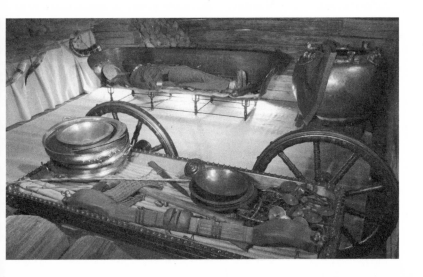

Luxury goods from the Mediterranean are lavishly displayed in the tomb of the Lady of Vix. So rich a female burial has fascinated generations of scholars. How could she fit into a society of warrior princes? Some even wondered if the body could be that of a male transvestite, until its gender was finally determined by DNA. This was indeed a woman who died at the age of about 30 and was buried between 500 and 450 BC.[19] She lay on the body of a wagon, the four wheels of which were placed against the walls of the chamber. She wore a hollow gold torc unlike any other. Ball terminals are found on many later examples, but these are unusual, being at right-angles to the ring. The junction between ring and terminal is decorated with a lion paw on the inside and a winged horse on the outside. [50] Pegasus leaps to mind when we think of winged horses. On the Vix torc he stands on an intricate filigree pedestal. Could that depict the Hippocrene ('horse-fountain') spring on Mount Helicon, which Greek myth-makers declared had been created by Pegasus stamping his hoof?[20] The idea that those who drank of the Hippocrene were granted poetical inspiration is not recorded until long after the burial of the Lady of Vix. Since eloquence was so highly valued by the Celts, it is tempting to think that we see here a symbol of the flight of imagination, but perhaps that would be a flight of imagination itself.

The Lady of Vix was amply supplied with other jewelry too, in gold, lignite, coral, amber and bronze. The most spectacular feature of her tomb, though, was a gigantic bronze krater, dwarfing even the Hochdorf cauldron. The Greek krater was a vessel wherein water and wine were blended. This particular krater is 1.64 m (5 ft 5 in) high and has a capacity of 1,100 litres (roughly 240 gallons). Around the neck is a parade of Greek warriors, some on foot, others driving four-horse chariots. Most authorities agree that it came from the same Greek workshop as the cauldron at Hochdorf.[21]

The Lady of Vix was evidently an important person, but what exactly was her role? Was she a priestess or a political leader? Even within patriarchal societies, women may sometimes inherit a powerful role from father or husband, in default of a male heir. Boudica is a famous example among the British Celts. She led her people after her husband died leaving only daughters.[22] Clues emerged nearly 40 years after the excavation of the tomb of the Lady of Vix. In 1991 aerial photographs revealed a square feature nearby. Excavation brought to light two headless, seated statues, one depicting a warrior and the other a woman wearing the distinctive torc of the Lady of Vix. This was a significant discovery. These figures were placed within

50 *The unique gold torc worn by the Lady of Vix, with a detail showing one of the winged horses decorating its ball terminals.*

a ditched enclosure at the heart of the necropolis, interpreted as a sanctuary.[23] The pairing of the Lady of Vix with a warrior suggests that they were man and wife, or closely related. They could be the founders of a dynastic lineage. Some political upheaval around 450 BC led to the beheading of these powerful images at Vix. At the same time, Mont Lassois lost its dominant position.[24]

Glauberg (Hesse, Germany) is a fine example of a late Hallstatt/early La Tène (6th–4th century BC) princely seat. Like the Heuneburg, it is a fortified hilltop with farms and burials on the slopes below it. In July 1996 archaeologists were excited to discover beside one of the burial mounds the almost complete statue of a man soon dubbed the 'Glauberg prince'.[25] [51] Intriguingly, the statue is crowned with something akin to the laurel wreaths bestowed upon Roman emperors. A similar headdress appears on several roughly contemporary statues and other depictions from the Hallstatt zone.[26]

The mound beside this striking statue had already been excavated. It contained the princely inhumation of a man in his 20s, which had escaped the attention of tomb robbers. It was so well preserved that it has yielded a mass of information. There can be no doubt that the statue portrays this young lord, for the burial contained a magnificent gold torc which matched that on the statue. [52] Other jewelry included arm-rings and a finger-ring, also as seen on the statue. It was even possible to detect the remains of his leaf crown.[27]

The buried prince was equipped as a warrior with an iron sword, spearheads, arrowheads in a quiver and a shield. Bioarchaeological tests revealed that he had enjoyed a high-quality diet with plenty of animal protein. By contrast, individuals buried in pits nearby had numerous joint lesions, indicating a strenuous lifestyle. Their diet was much poorer than that of the prince. They ate a lot of millet and less animal protein. Their burials were so informal that it even crossed the minds of their excavators that they might be slaves. We cannot be sure. What stands out is the contrast between prince and pauper.[28]

Like the Warrior of Hirschlanden, the Glauberg prince is not as confidently representational as Greek sculpture of the same period. While the legs are lifelike, the sculptor avoided piercing the upper section. Leaving gaps between body and arms

51 *This sandstone statue from Glauberg in Hesse, Germany, is a rare depiction by Celts of a Celtic warrior. He wears a three-pronged torc like one from the adjacent burial mound (opposite). On his head is a curious crown of leaves, remains of which were found in the same grave.*

52 *This magnificent and unique gold torc comes from the princely burial of a young man at Glauberg. Most torcs were simply rings around the neck, plain or twisted. The front half of this ring is decorated with ten human face masks, and from it protrude decorative finials flanked by two grotesque figures with enlarged heads.*

would risk broken arms. That solidity gives the upper body a similarity to the anthropomorphic stelae of the Copper Age, but the considerable gap in time makes it impossible to claim a continuous tradition from the earlier stelae to these Iron Age statues.

Celtic caught in transition

The Golasecca culture of the north Italian lake region acted as a trade gateway between Hallstatt and the Etruscans. Here Celtic-speakers were in contact with literacy. They adapted an Etruscan script to write in their own language, and so left us the first inscriptions that are generally agreed to be Celtic. There are about 140 such inscriptions, beginning c. 600 BC and ending around 1 BC.[29]

Their language was labelled Lepontic by modern scholars, knowing that a people called Lepontii lived within the area in Roman times. In 55 BC Julius Caesar noted that the Rhine rose in the country of the Lepontii in the Alps.[30] In the 1st century AD Pliny the Elder wrote that one group of the Lepontii lived around the source of the Rhône.[31] A century later Ptolemy mentions the Lepontii living in the Alps and their town of Oscela.[32] This town (now Domodossola) has given its name to the valley (Val d'Ossola) in which the Toce River runs. The upper reaches of the River Ticino run through the Valle

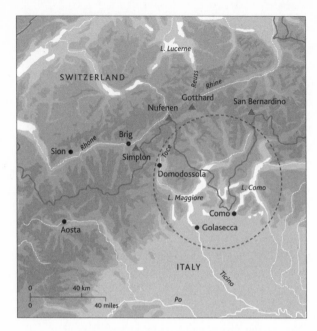

53 *The region in which Lepontic inscriptions are found is circled. Golasecca culture finds are scattered over the same area and as far south as the River Po. Important Alpine passes are marked by red triangles.*

Leventina, which preserves the name of the Lepontii. What all these locations have in common is rivers with their source in or close to the Gotthard massif. [53]

Today traffic hums daily through the high Gotthard Pass. It crosses the saddle between the sources of two rivers: the turbulent Reuss, running north into Lake Lucerne (Switzerland), and the Ticino flowing south through Lake Maggiore (Italy) to join the Po. To the west the Simplon railway tunnel connects Brig in Switzerland to Domodossola in Italy. Before its construction the connection was via the Simplon Pass. Both these passes were far more dangerous before modern roads and bridges. Yet the Golasecca culture clearly thrived on trade through these and other Alpine passes. Objects of Golasecca manufacture are found north of the Alps, along with Etruscan luxury goods, while Hallstatt influences trickled south.[33]

Naturally, scholars have wondered how Celts came to be in northern Italy before the well-known expansions of the Gauls in the 4th century BC (discussed in Chapter 7). The Golasecca culture began in the 8th century BC, developing from the local Bronze Age culture. This can be traced back to a variety of Urnfield that arrived in the 13th century BC. Given its wide cultural connections north of the Alps, and its seemingly abrupt arrival, this brand of Urnfield has been generally favoured by scholars as the vector of the first Celtic language south of the Alps.[34]

Yet if we go further back in time we reach the Bell Beaker sites of Sion on the upper Rhône and Aosta in the southern Alps. [53] It will be remembered that they received a sudden influx of new, eastern Bell Beaker material c. 2425 BC (see p. 97). So here we have an earlier wave that could have brought Celtic to the southern Alps. If so, the continued use of trans-Alpine trade routes would keep those Celts of the southern Alps in touch linguistically with the developing core of Proto-Celtic north of the Alps as it gradually turned into Gaulish. Yet Lepontic seems best classified as a separate language from Gaulish.[35]

The relationship between the various Celtic languages is complex. [54] One sound change is well known: the shift from k^w to p in some Celtic languages. The Proto-Indo-European and Proto-Celtic k^w sound can be seen in the PIE word for horse, *ek^wos, which became *equus* in Latin and *equos* in early Celtic, and passed down into Old Irish as *ech*. *Equos* appears as a month on the lunar calendar inscribed on bronze which was discovered near Coligny in France. The Coligny calendar uses the Latin alphabet,

54 *This conjectural tree of the Celtic languages attempts to take into account the complexities caused by wave after wave of Celtic dialects entering the British Isles and interactions between speakers of the different languages.*

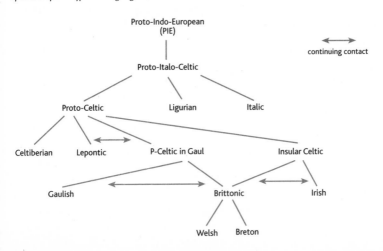

which dates it to the Gallo-Roman period.[36] By that time the *qu* sound had been generally replaced in Gaulish by *p*, as we see in the many dedications to the horse goddess Epona.[37] Indeed this sound change had taken place centuries earlier, for it appears in the earliest name known for Britain (see pp. 169–70). Ptolemy's *Geography* records 'p' forms of tribes in Britain and Gaul: the Epidii (people of the horse) in Kintyre, and the Menapi of Belgic Gaul. Yet the archaic form Sequana was retained for the Seine.[38] The occasional archaism helps to uncover the process of change.

So it has been customary to label the Brittonic group of Celtic languages together with Gaulish, as P-Celtic [see 54], while the Gaelic group is labelled Q-Celtic. Language trees have often simply split Celtic into those two familiar categories. Linguist Kim McCone protested against this, arguing that the important division is between Insular and Continental Celtic. Insular in this context includes Breton (as a descendant of Brittonic). There is certainly a major difference between Insular and Continental Celtic. The latter was dead by the end of the Roman period. Welsh, Breton and Gaelic have gone on developing since. This means that they have had centuries to develop differences from the Continental group. So comparing ancient with modern could be misleading.[39]

The earliest form of Celtic to enter the British Isles was probably Proto-Celtic, which would gradually diverge from its parent. La Tène movements from Gaul to Britain would explain the similarities between Gaulish and Brittonic. Continuing interaction between Celtic-speakers in Britain and Ireland would blur the distinctions between languages. So we can understand the similarities between Brittonic and Irish, without ascribing them all to a very early date.[40]

La Tène warriors

There is no abrupt break between the Hallstatt and La Tène cultures. The one flows into the other. We have already seen that the important site at Glauberg flourished from Late Hallstatt to Early La Tène (see p. 111). At Hallstatt itself there is a notable tomb of the early La Tène era. Continuity seems quite common.[41] Yet signs of power struggles around 450 BC crop up here and there. The abandonment of Mont Lassois has already been mentioned (p. 111). The Heuneburg was abandoned around 450 BC, with no obvious explanation.[42]

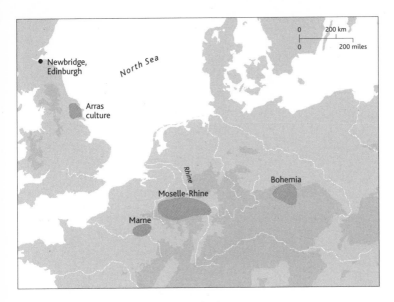

55 *Map of early La Tène chariot burials, 5th–early 4th century BC.*

Around the same period new centres of power appear along the northern fringe of the Hallstatt zone [see 11], concentrated particularly around the rivers Moselle and Marne and in Bohemia.[43] [55] All these areas not only had navigable rivers, but also access to iron ore, and forest to provide the charcoal for iron-working. The Moselle was a tributary of the Rhine already well known to the Celts. There are Hallstatt wagon burials at sites along it from Trier to Koblenz (Germany). In the La Tène period the wagon gave way to the chariot. Chariot tombs cluster along the Moselle and the adjoining middle Rhine, and even more densely between the rivers Marne and Oise, around present-day Reims (France). In Bohemia they are mainly found along the River Vltava and its tributaries. The Vltava is the longest river in present-day Czech Republic and was a trade-route for the Celts.[44]

The chariot had become one of the key symbols of the Celtic warrior aristocracy, along with the gold torc, wine and weaponry (see also pp. 34–38). Instead of burial under an impressive mound, we find flat graves of this period in which males were buried with weaponry and females with jewelry. The chariot itself became a fearsome thing in battle as the Celts learned how to deploy it to great effect against their foes.

The Celts came late to chariot-building. Greek chariots are pictured on the Vix krater, with their typical four-spoke wheels, while the Celts still favoured wagons. Celtic chariot burials start in the 5th century BC. Generally the wooden parts of Celtic chariots have decayed and all that is left is metal, but the lake mud of the La Tène site preserved yokes and a wheel [see 13], as well as metal parts of a chariot including cotters. A cotter is a bolt or pin used to secure two other parts, a clue that the chariot had some form of suspension. So Andres Furger-Gunti of the Swiss National Museum in Zurich engaged craftsmen to reconstruct the La Tène chariot as an exercise in experimental archaeology. He was particularly interested in solving the problem of the suspension. He opted for a longitudinal type, with two sidearms curved up and back from the pole, to provide rests for the double cotters supplying the suspension for the platform. The end result was fully functional. Only then was he told that Irish literature supported him.[45] A more recent analysis of early Irish chariot terminology drew the same conclusion.[46]

Shape-shifting art

There is more to the Celts than warfare and chariots. This is not a book about Celtic art, yet we cannot pass over the artistic flowering in the La Tène period. Contact with Mediterranean civilizations brought Classical motifs into the Celtic repertoire. Even the earliest Celtic coins copied Greek coins (see p. 129). The fantastic beasts of Scythian goldwork may have been another influence on the Celtic aesthetic, though the parallels are not close.[47]

What lifted Celtic art above imitation was the La Tène confidence to innovate. A Celtic preference for curvilinear rather than angular design can be seen in the Hallstatt period, but these patterns were regular and could be drawn with compasses. Such work continues into La Tène, but we also see a new freedom. Gradually the full glory of the Celtic visual imagination emerged. Curving plant tendrils could sprout a sleek animal head or melt into abstract twists and turns. A horse could be evoked in fluid curves that make it look half seahorse. [56] Celtic art had parted company from the drive towards ever greater naturalism within the Classical world. The famous head from Bohemia [57] makes a perfect contrast with the equally famous sculpture of the Dying Gaul.[48] [see 63] Both have the Celtic insignia of torcs and moustaches, but how different they look. With the Dying Gaul a gifted

56 (left) Gold stater of the Parisii in Gaul, c. 70–60 BC.

57 (right) Was this a leader of the Boii or a sacred figure? This stone head from the shrine at Mšecké Žehrovice, Czech Republic, has all the hallmarks of the La Tène style, with curvilinear shapes favoured over naturalism.

Greek sculptor imagines reality, or an idealized version of it. We feel that this man could have breathed and hurt and died. The head from Bohemia is more of a mask. It conjures up the haughty pride of an individual, yet sets that person apart from the human realm, with his bulging almond eyes, twirling eyebrows, and ears in the shape of a lotus flower.

Oppida

By the 2nd century BC Celts were developing their own towns. Caesar used the word oppidum (plural oppida) to describe the major Celtic settlements that he encountered on his campaign of conquest. This Latin word was used in Italy for the civic centre of a territory and its people. No doubt Caesar perceived a similar status for settlements functioning as tribal centres in Gaul. Much ink has been spilled debating whether oppida were truly towns. Part of the confusion arises from modern archaeological usage of the term. It has sometimes been so loose as to include all fortified Celtic sites of the late La Tène period. A fort is not always a town and vice versa. While most of the oppida Caesar knew were indeed walled towns, a town of this date was not invariably walled. Nor were early towns necessarily grid-planned, though they could be. The key factors that point to urban life are trade, manufacture and administration. Clues in the archaeology could be public buildings or coin minting.

Some of these Celtic towns were the predecessors of Roman and modern towns or cities. Others faded away before the Roman conquest. Some were developments of earlier hillforts. Others were laid out in lowlands. Generalization therefore would be folly. One common factor though is a location on a trade route, usually riverine or coastal.

Zavist, now on the southern fringe of Prague (Czech Republic) was an excellent choice of site: a large and easily defended hilltop, overlooking the Vltava near its confluence with the Berounka. A town with massive ramparts was built there in the 2nd century BC. The Celtic name of Zavist is unknown, but it seems to have been the capital of the Boii tribe, who gave their name to Bohemia. Zavist flourished long enough to see several phases of rebuilding, growing to around 118 ha (290 acres) in size, but was abandoned in the late 1st century BC, as the Boii came under pressure from expanding Germani. The Boii left a trail westwards. An inscription mentioning a member of the tribe was found in Manching in Bavaria (Germany). The Boii settled a short distance to the east at Boioduron (fortified settlement of the Boii), modern Passau.[49]

By comparison with Zavist, the oppidum of Manching was a giant, at a final 380 ha (938 acres). It sprawled on a flood-free low terrace beside the River Paar, which at that time flowed into an arm of the Danube nearby. So it was well placed for trade. Iron-smelting sites dotted its hinterland, and metal waste within the town attests to a plentiful production of iron objects, but Manching did not depend on a single industry. Tools for leather- and textile-working have been found within the oppidum. The town was laid out with streets, squares, cult structures, commercial districts and workshops. Defence was evidently not the first consideration. When the settlement began around 300 BC it had no surrounding walls. It acquired ramparts c. 120 BC. Despite all the effort that must have gone into the creation of a 7-km (over 4-mile) long fortification, Manching was abandoned c. 50 BC, before the Roman conquest of the region.[50]

Was it the success of the La Tène culture that generated the will to expand into new territories? Or was Late La Tène a culture in decline and under threat, jettisoning streams of migrants to find a life elsewhere? These are questions tackled in Chapter 7, as we focus on the wanderlust of the Gauls.

Overview

- In the Iron Age, the paraphernalia of war began to take on the shape familiar right up to the Middle Ages: the mounted fighter with an iron sword.

- The transformation of warfare began with nomads of the steppe. By moving up the Danube into the Carpathian Basin, they introduced iron-working, swords, horse gear and wagon burial to the developing Hallstatt culture.

- The Hallstatt culture was dominated by a warrior elite, entrenched on fortified hilltops and buried often with wagons. Such burials are found in southern Germany, eastern France, Switzerland, Bohemia and Upper Austria.

- The Golasecca culture of the north Italian lake region acted as a trade gateway between Hallstatt and the Etruscans. Celtic-speakers adapted an Etruscan script to write in their own language, called Lepontic by modern scholars. Inscriptions in Lepontic start from c. 600 BC.

- Some Hallstatt sites were abandoned around 450 BC. Around the same period new centres of power appear around the rivers Moselle and Marne and in Bohemia, which represent the start of the La Tène culture.

- Key features that distinguish La Tène from Hallstatt are chariots and greater artistic freedom and confidence.

- By the 2nd century BC Celts were developing their own towns, which the Romans called oppida. The word has remained in the archaeological vocabulary.

CHAPTER SEVEN

On the Move

The Gauls, when the land that had produced them was unable, from their excessive increase of population, to contain them, sent out three hundred thousand men, as a sacred spring, to seek new settlements. Of these adventurers part settled in Italy, and took and burnt the city of Rome; and part penetrated into the remotest parts of Illyricum under the direction of a flight of birds (for the Gauls are skilled in augury beyond other nations) making their way amidst great slaughter of the barbarous tribes, and fixed their abode in Pannonia. They were a savage, bold and warlike nation, and were the first after Hercules ... to pass the unconquered heights of the Alps.[1]

So wrote Pompeius Trogus, himself a Romanized Gaul, in the 1st century BC. These events were centuries earlier, but still fresh in the minds of both Romans and Greeks. Where the Celts thrust into the civilizations of the Mediterranean, their onslaughts were recorded for posterity. We hear of their exploits from their enemies. The attack on Rome in 390 BC burnt its brutal message into the collective consciousness of an emerging power, and spurred the Romans to ever more conquests to bolster their security. The Romans neither forgot nor forgave and were to turn the tables centuries later.

58 Birds were a popular emblem in Celtic art. Here they decorate a bronze flesh-fork, used in feasting, from Dunaverney, Co. Antrim (950 BC–750 BC). Two swans and three cygnets face two ravens. Both swans and ravens appear in Irish myth.

Other Gauls marched southeast in the 3rd century BC even as far as Greece and Anatolia. Their attack on the sacred site at Delphi deeply shocked the proud Greeks and was likewise never forgotten. By contrast Celtic movements into prehistoric Britain and Iberia have to be traced mainly by the objects and place-names they left behind.

The forces driving expansion

What were the reasons for this burst of mobility? As mentioned in the last chapter (p. 120), the advance of the Germani into what had been Celtic territory put such pressure on the Boii that Zavist was abandoned in the late 1st century BC. Germanic expansion had started centuries earlier, bearing hard on Celtic-speakers east of the Rhine. Gaulish druids knew that their land was partly inhabited by the descendants of refugees. Fortunately, Roman historian Ammianus Marcellinus preserved their account. People had 'poured in from the islands on the coast, and from the districts across the Rhine, having been driven from their former abodes by frequent wars, and sometimes by inroads of the tempestuous sea'.[2] Caesar puts a name to these incomers. They were Belgae. He says that their ancestors had long ago come across the Rhine from Germany, expelling the former inhabitants from northeast Gaul.[3] Their recorded tribal, personal and place-names are Celtic (with very few exceptions). They had a late La Tène culture. Thus their ancestry was from what the Romans called Germania, but they were Celts.[4]

The reference by Gaulish druids to islands and the tempestuous sea is significant. The North Sea coast of what is now the Netherlands and Germany has been gradually subsiding for millennia, creating the Wadden Sea, with its chain of islands separating it from the North Sea. Periodic floods would have been catastrophic for Germani spreading out from a homeland in north Germany and Poland. So in addition to floods directly affecting Celts east of the Rhine, there would also have been pressure from Germani trying to escape these disasters.

As the Belgae were displaced into Gaul, they in turn displaced Gauls. The Parisii are a case in point. The Marne territory was thick with early chariot burials. Yet in the later La Tène period chariot burials of the same type cluster around Paris, territory of the Gaulish Parisii.[5] We have already seen the remarkable example at Roissy c. 300 BC (p. 37). It seems that the Parisii were pushed westwards by the Remi, a Belgic tribe who in Caesar's day had an oppidum at Durocortorum,[6] the site of modern-day Reims. Such a crisis might explain why Ptolemy recorded Parisi in Britain. The chariot burial at Ferry Fryston which seemed so similar to Continental types was dated c. 355 BC (see p. 38). Why choose East Yorkshire? There was easy access to iron ore and woodland for charcoal. A concentration of iron-working in the area is contemporaneous with the chariot burials and close to them.[7]

The chariot at Newbridge in Scotland (5th century BC) seems too early to be part of this domino effect. Indeed, La Tène influences generally started seeping across the Channel around 450 BC. Even before that, Hallstatt material is found in Lowland Britain; it reached as far north as the Forth–Clyde line. Then there is the surge southwards across the Alps around 400 BC. Pompeius Trogus, as we saw in the quotation at the head of this chapter, blamed overpopulation. He also mentions 'civil discords and perpetual contentions at home'.[8] His contemporary Livy knew of two entirely different colourful traditions about the coming of the Gauls to Italy. He separated the two in time. One, which he set around 600 BC, tells of an otherwise unknown Gallic king, Ambigatus, under whose sway 'the harvests were so abundant and the population increased so rapidly in Gaul' that he was 'anxious to relieve his realm from the burden of overpopulation'. So he sent his nephews to lead the adventurous to distant lands, including Italy.[9] Overpopulation from agricultural surplus is entirely credible for the period 650–450 BC, when the climate was warm and dry. However, the major onrush of Gauls to Italy came around 400 BC, when there was a climate crisis and land marginal for cereal production was abandoned.[10]

The other tradition Livy knew related to this later period. It claimed that the Gauls were lured into Italy by its delicious fruits and wine, introduced to them by a trader from Clusium (Chiusi) who wanted revenge on the city. This story was told to explain the siege of Clusium in 391 BC.[11] Livy seems to have taken it from the works of Dionysius of Halicarnassus, who goes into more detail, some of it seriously uncomplimentary to Gallic cuisine:

> The Gauls at that time had no knowledge either of wine made
> from grapes or of oils such as is produced by our olive trees, but
> used for wine a foul-smelling liquor made from barley rotted in
> water, and for oil, stale lard, disgusting both in smell and taste.[12]

Pliny the Elder in the 1st century AD gives another tale of gastronomic temptation:

It is related that the Gauls, separated from us as they were by the Alps, which then formed an almost insurmountable bulwark, had, as their chief motive for invading Italy, its dried figs, its grapes, its oil, and its wine, samples of which had been brought back to them by Helico, a citizen of the Helvetii, who had been staying at Rome, to practise there as an artisan.[13]

Here Pliny captures the mechanics of migration. People often move for economic advantage, but they need to know of good opportunities. Trade is one route to hear of them. It can encourage a few migrant workers, who then communicate with the people back home, encouraging more to make the journey. So a trickle of migration can turn into a flood. Pliny condenses the process into a simple story of one man. In fact these trade goods were spreading much more widely than to just one tribe. Diodorus Siculus tells us that the Gauls were so addicted to wine that they would hand over a slave in exchange for just one jar of the intoxicating drink.[14] Wine amphoras appear in Gaul and southern Britain with increasing frequency in the generations prior to the Roman conquest. [59] (Not all the Belgae succumbed.

59 *A cremation burial of the Late Iron Age at Welwyn, southern England, was rich in feasting equipment, including five amphorae. This extravagant type of burial is uncommon in Britain and mainly restricted to the region controlled by the Catuvellauni, a Belgic tribe.*

The Nervii refused entry to traders for fear that wine and other luxuries would weaken their warriors.[15])

Wine was not the only lure of the south though. Wealthy warlords attract warriors. The capacity of fighting Celts to inspire terror and panic made them sought after as mercenaries. Celts were employed by the tyrants of Syracuse, Sicily, as early as the 4th century BC.[16]

The surge southward

Through the channel of the Golasecca culture (pp. 113–14) the Gauls had plenty of time to assess the power politics of northern Italy before they ejected the Etruscans from the Po Valley around 400 BC. [60] Indeed that is precisely the picture painted by Polybius, a Greek historian closer in time to these events than Livy and his contemporaries. Polybius was born around 200 BC. His great virtue as an historian was his preference for first-hand evidence. He began his history of the rise of Rome in the year 220/219 BC, so that he was able to interview people who lived through events before he

60 *The movements of Gauls noted in Classical sources. Celtic-place-names mark the regions that Celts actually settled, rather than raided.(Compare with* [25].) *Dates are BC.*

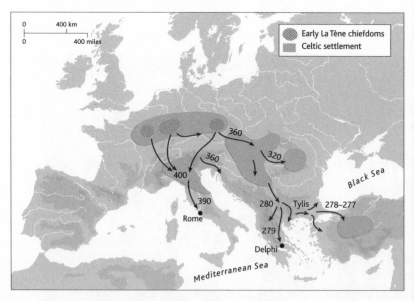

was born, and then to record an era of which he had personal knowledge, ending in the year 146 BC. Conceding that his Greek readership might not be acquainted with what modern authors call the back-story, he used his first two volumes to cover crucial earlier events. Polybius was also among the first to advocate the steely eye of the seeker after truth in historical narrative. This dispassionate voice is well worth heeding:

> Long ago ... the Po plain was home to the Etruscans. The Celts had plenty of dealings with the Etruscans, since they were near neighbours, and they cast covetous eyes on the beauty of the land. On some feeble pretext, they suddenly invaded with a huge army, drove the Etruscans out of the Po plain, and took the land for themselves. The first part of the territory, near the source of the Po, became home to the Laevi and Libicii; after them came the Insubres, the largest of the Celtic tribes; and next to the Insubres along the river were the Cenomani.... The first stretch of land on the other side of the Po, the Apennine side, became the home of the Anares, the next of the Boii; the region next closest to the Adriatic was occupied by the Lingones, and the coastal area by the Senones.[17]

Rome was peripheral to these events, rather than the prime target. According to later sources such as Livy, it was the siege of Clusium well to the south of the Po Valley and dangerously close to Rome, that drew the Romans into a battle that proved so disastrous for them. [61] The Gauls were able to plunder Rome itself in 390 BC before they were themselves defeated.[18]

The Etruscans had an urban civilization, but what the Gauls wanted was their fertile land on the plain of the Po. The towns were either left to crumble or occupied on a reduced scale.[19] Polybius tells us that the villages of these Gauls were unwalled and lacked any civilized amenities.[20] So no sophisticated city should be imagined when we read that the Insubres founded Mediolanum (Milan) and the Cenomani founded Brixia (Brescia) and Verona, all Celtic place-names.[21] Nevertheless, Italian archaeologists were quietly pleased to find that Milan, noted in modern times as an industrial centre, can boast a concentration of Iron Age metalworking sites. Some of these do indeed pre-date the Roman period and can be linked to the

La Tène culture.[22] Enough Celtic material has been found over the whole region to support the historical accounts.[23] Furthermore, the incoming Gauls adopted the alphabet used earlier for Lepontic to leave inscriptions in their own language, known as Cisalpine Gaulish.[24]

At around the same time that we find Boii among the arrivals in Italy, others of this numerous tribe were spreading eastwards into Moravia, southwestern Slovakia and northeastern Austria. They could then drift down the Danube to the Carpathian Basin.[25] Here they could find good grazing. From the southern Carpathian Basin the River Sava leads to the southeastern Alps and ways down to the Adriatic. It seems that some Celts used the Sava to join up with Celtic-speakers of the Alps, creating a trade route from the Alps and the Adriatic to the Danube. La Tène material in the northern Balkans, together with items from the lower Danube region, tell the tale. [62] Celts who appear in history as the Scordisci settled around the confluence of the Sava and the Danube. Their fortress of Singidunum (modern Belgrade) was strategically placed on a hilltop overlooking this meeting place of riverine routes.[26]

All this activity meant pushing in among Illyrians. One devious tactic was recorded by a contemporary Greek historian. The story goes that the

61 *Bronze figure of a Celtic spearman from the Rome area, 3rd century BC. His torc makes him instantly identifiable as a Celt. Otherwise he wears nothing but a belt and helmet, in keeping with Roman descriptions of the Celts fighting naked.*

62 *Detail of an iron scabbard from grave 6 at Dobova, Slovenia, dating from around 200 BC, with fine decoration in the La Tène style. Dobova is within the area of the Taurisci.*

Celts poisoned their own food and wine with noxious herbs, then left their camp by night in pretended confusion. The Illyrians took possession of their camp and gorged happily on the provisions found there. Soon they succumbed to violent diarrhoea. While they were helplessly ill, the Celts returned and slew them easily.[27]

The young Philip II of Macedon had driven Illyrians out of northwest Macedonia in 358 BC. On the principle that my enemy's enemy is my friend, the incoming Celts may have been well disposed towards Philip. There is no surviving record that Philip employed Celts as mercenaries, yet his coinage became familiar to many of them. His silver tetradrachms were copied by the Boii and Scordisci in minting the first Celtic coins. Certainly, after Philip was assassinated in 336 BC, Celts from near the Adriatic sent ambassadors to his son Alexander the Great, as he secured his northern border the following year. The story is told that Alexander welcomed them warmly, and while they were sharing a drink asked what they feared the most, expecting them to confess to an overwhelming fear of him. Instead they replied that they feared nothing except that the sky might fall on them.[28] One suspects a problem in translation. The Celts saw the divine in nature. Evidence of a sky-god is found throughout the Celtic-speaking world. So the response of the Celts to Alexander could well have been the pagan equivalent of 'We fear nothing but the Lord'. That may have been a disappointment to a young man driven by a sense of destiny, but these Celts had no reason to fear him. His eyes were on the east. Which particular Celtic tribe had sent these sky-fearing ambassadors to Alexander is not recorded, but when the northern Balkans emerged more clearly into history, the Taurisci were living in what is now central and eastern Slovenia and northwest Croatia. So they are the most likely candidates.[29]

The Celtic friendship with Macedonia lasted until the death of Alexander in 323 BC. A delegation of Gauls met him on his march to Babylon in the year of his death.[30] This brilliant commander had welded together a huge empire, but without his charismatic presence it fell apart. In its fragmented state it became vulnerable to Celtic expansions. Even the throne of Macedonia could not be secured for Alexander the Great's infant son. In 317 BC Cassander, a distant relative, declared himself regent. He shored up his own claim to the throne by marriage to Alexander's half-sister, and within a few years had executed Alexander's son. Meanwhile the Celts were making further inroads into Illyria, pushing a major Illyrian tribe into the arms of Cassander in 310 BC.[31]

Macedonia was further weakened on the death of Cassander in 297, when his sons squabbled over their inheritance. It was seized from them first by a league of Greek city-states and then by Thrace. Into this chaos of political rivalry the Celts struck in force. An army led by Bolgios in 281 BC attacked Macedonia and in 279 cut off the head of the foolish king who had not taken their threat seriously. Macedonia was only saved by a man named Sosthenes, of humble birth but with the mind of a general, who raised an army to defend the country.[32]

Furious that Bolgios had been so easily thwarted by this hero of the hour, another Celtic commander, Brennos of the Prausi or Tolistobogii, ravaged Macedonia with a huge force, and led them south into Greece, intent on plundering the oracle at Delphi. Brennos was defeated at Delphi not by armies but by natural forces. An earthquake and thunderstorm were followed by rock falls. The Gauls even fought each other in the ensuing panic. Brennos advised his men to retreat, killing their wounded to avoid delay. He led by example. Badly wounded, he drank deep of unwatered wine and then stabbed himself to death. Greeks harried the retreat all the way, gradually destroying the desecrators of Delphi until not one was left alive, or so the Greek authors closest to the period say.[33]

Centuries later the Greek historian Athenaeus of Naucratis thought that the Scordisci were a remnant of the force that attacked Delphi. Writing around AD 190, Athenaeus tells us that the leader who brought them to safety was one Bathanattus. 'From him also the road by which they retreated is called Bathanattia, and they call his descendants Bathanatti to this very day.'[34] Though this certainly sounds like reliable local knowledge of a founding hero, we may doubt that Bathanattus ever saw Delphi. The drama of Delphi so dominated Greek accounts of the Celts that it would be easy to assume that he must fit into this well-known story. The truth was probably more complex. Celts had been moving along the Danube for some time before the burst of activity around 280 BC. Their numbers may well have been swollen by an influx of newcomers in that fateful period, but the hordes of arrivals were not a single fighting force. Bands from different tribes might unite behind one leader for as long as it suited them, but split apart just as easily.

The massive army under Brennos divided before it had even reached Macedonia. Livy tells us that a quarrel arose and as many as 20,000 Celts parted company with Brennos between Thrace and Illyria. They and their descendants remained a force in southeastern Europe for over half a century and in Asia Minor until the Roman period. Moving into Thrace, they carved out a kingdom for themselves in what is now Bulgaria, from which they threatened Byzantium. This city founded by Greek colonists on the European coast of the Bosporus had grown so rich on trade that it could afford to pay massive tribute to keep the Gauls at bay. These Gauls were massacred by Thracians in 212 BC, but not before they had sent an offshoot into Asia Minor.[35]

Across the Bosporus from Byzantium was the kingdom of Bithynia, which offered an opportunity for mercenaries just as the eager horde of fighting Celts had arrived on the opposite shore. In about 280 BC Nicomedes succeeded his father Zipoetes on the throne of Bithynia. He immediately had two of his brothers put to death, but the third, Zipoetes II, escaped and challenged his rule. Nicomedes engaged a large force of these conveniently placed Celts to defeat his brother, in which they succeeded in 276 BC.[36]

In Asia Minor these Celts gained the name *Galatoi* (the Greek version of 'Gauls'), which the Romans rendered as *Galatae*.[37] On the loose after the end of their contract with Nicomedes, they terrorized the whole of Anatolia west of the Taurus Mountains into granting them tribute. None dared refuse them until Attalus I of Pergamon (241–197 BC). Attalus saw himself as the champion of the Greek cities of Asia Minor against these barbarians, and was victorious in battle against the Galatians.[38] [63] By 232 BC the Galatians were contained within an area of Anatolia roughly centred on the hillfort of the Tectosagi at what is now Ankara.[39] Strabo knew of a tribe of Tectosagi in southwest Gaul near the Pyrenees and assumed simply from the matching name that here was the origin of the Galatian Tectosagi.[40] This seems unlikely geographically. Celts moving down the Danube were probably from east of the Rhine. Since Tectosagi means 'journey-seekers', it would fit a band of migrants.

63 Detail of the sculpture of the Dying Gaul showing the face, hairstyle and torc. It is thought to be a Roman replica in marble of a lost Hellenistic original dedicated to Athena at Pergamon by Attalus I to commemorate his victories over the Galatians.

Strabo tells us that the meeting place for the annual assemblies of the Galatians was *Drunemeton* (sacred place of oaks).[41] There could be no clearer proof that they were Celtic-speakers. The element *-dru* (oak) is the basis for the word druid. *Nemeton* (sacred place) appears in a Gaulish inscription. Wherever Celts lived, *-nemet-* provided a component of tribal names, gods' names and place-names.[42]

Galatia remained an independent state until swept up into the Roman empire. As the Celtic-speakers closest to Jerusalem at the time of Christ, the Galatians lay within the scope of the earliest Christian drive to convert. St Paul visited Galatia during his second missionary journey,[43] and some years later (*c*. AD 51) wrote an impassioned letter to the churches of the Galatians, preserved in the New Testament.

St Jerome remarked that the Galatians spoke a language almost identical (apart from a Greek influence) to that of the Treveri,[44] among whom he had studied at their capital Trier (in present-day Germany). He encountered the Galatians in AD 372/3 on his travels in the Near East.[45] The Treveri were Belgae. This is interesting confirmation that the Belgae spoke Gaulish, for what remnants we have of the Galatian language appear Gaulish with a Greek overlay.[46]

Iberia: the tangled skein

The puzzle of how Celtic-speakers arrived in Iberia has occupied a series of scholars. Influences from Central Europe are limited.[47] It has been suggested above (pp. 98–100) that the oldest layer of Celtic to enter Iberia came with a late Bell Beaker influx across the Pyrenees into the eastern meseta *c*. 2200 BC, which was to emerge in written form as Celtiberian, while in what is now Galicia the initial contact with Celtic-speakers may have come through interaction with northwest Europe between 1300 and 700 BC.

By the Roman period Celtic place-names were scattered far more widely across Iberia. [see 25] Those ending in *-briga* ('hillfort', 'high place') have attracted particular attention. [64] Many fall within the region where inscriptions have been found in the Lusitanian language. That does not mean that Lusitanian must therefore be Celtic. Lusitanian and Celtic have distinctly different ways of handling what linguists call the vocalic /r/. Celtic is unique in converting it to 'ri', as in *-briga*. So it seems that Celtic had crept into what had been Lusitanian territory. Both there and in Galicia, place-names

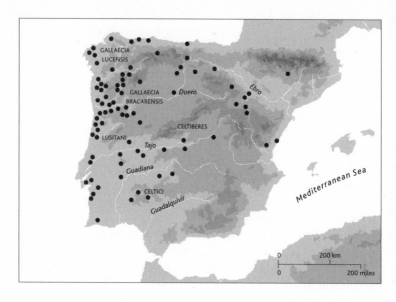

64 *Place-names in Iberia ending in -briga, the Celtic word for 'hillfort' or 'high place'. This distribution shows that Celtic speakers had spread into areas that were previously Lusitanian-speaking.*

ending in the Celtic *-briga* or *-bris* can have a non-Celtic first element, no doubt derived from a pre-existing place-name. These are no less Celtic than cases where the first element is also Celtic, such as *Nemetobriga* (Trives Viejo in modern-day Galicia). The inclusion of *-briga* tells us that Celts created the name that was recorded by the Romans.[48]

So who were the newcomers? The scatter of Celtiberian objects in western and southwest Iberia suggest that the Celtiberi had been expanding westwards for several centuries before the Romans arrived.[49] In Roman times there was a mint producing typically Celtiberian coins in Villas Viejas del Tamuja within ancient Lusitania.[50] Pliny deduced from their religious rites, their language and the names of their towns that the Celtici of the Roman province of Baetica in what is now southern Spain were descended from the Celtiberians and had come from Lusitania.[51] This slightly confusing passage seems to mean that the Celtiberians in his view had expanded first into Lusitania and then from there to Baetica. Strabo claims that the Celts living around the River Guadiana, within the Roman province of Baetica, were kinsmen to those of Gallaecia (Galicia).[52] Certainly there is at least one inscription in Galicia to Reue Ana Baraego, the god of the Guadiana and Albárregas rivers. There are also Latin inscriptions to individuals from Celtiberia, evidently arrivals in Roman times.[53]

The last wave of Celtic-speakers to arrive were Gauls, though the impact they had is hard to judge. A group of place-names in Iberia end in *-dunum* (meaning 'enclosure' or 'fort'), which is commonly found in Gaul. However, the underlying word *-duno* is Celtic rather than specifically Gaulish, so we cannot be certain that all of these mark the trail of a Gaulish influx. On the other hand some place-names ancient and modern leave no doubt of the existence of Gauls in Iberia, such as *Forum Gallorum*, located probably close to modern-day Gurrea de Gállego in Aragon. Likewise ancient *Gallicum* was probably on the Roman road near present-day San Mateo de Gállego in Aragon. *Gallica Flavia* might be modern Fraga in Aragon.[54] This cluster of names in Aragon suggests that some Gauls at least had crossed the Pyrenees.

La Tène in the British Isles

The La Tène culture spread deep into Britain soon after it arose on the Continent. [65] Many archaeologists have preferred to explain this by trade contact rather than migration, but that scarcely explains the linguistic similarity of Gaulish and Brittonic. Movement there clearly was. Climate change seems likely to have played a part in this. As already mentioned above (p. 124), 650–450 BC was a warm, dry period in Continental Europe. High crop yields could have fed a burgeoning population. Britain might have seemed inviting around 400 BC, as conditions improved there.[55]

Ireland had become a backwater. To judge from the amount of archaeological material, productivity hit a peak in 1000–900 BC and then began

65 *The pommel of a sword hilt in the form of a male head, found near Cirencester, western England, in 2006. It is in the Late La Tène style, but unique in its depiction of an elaborate hairstyle of braids forming a loop. The face has lentoid eyes and a wide moustache above a slit mouth.*

Genetics: traces of the spread of the Gauls?

The distribution of Y-DNA haplogroup R1b-U152 is similar to that of the Urnfield culture, but also has features suggestive of the Iron Age movements of the Gauls. [see 60] The density of R1b-U152 is greatest in northern Italy and Corsica and radiates out from there.[56] [66] This pattern is interesting. A radiation in all directions from a high density centre is what we would expect if a mutation occurs within a comparatively static population. With no mass movement in one particular direction, the mutation will percolate gradually outwards from its origin point.[57] R1b-U152 may have fanned out initially within Urnfield. This would not necessarily be exclusively with Celtic-speakers. A link between Ligurians and U152 has been suggested in Italy,[58] and might explain some U152 in Iberia.

If we picture a gradual seepage of this haplogroup across Gaul in the Bronze Age, then it would naturally spread with subsequent movements of Gauls. The presence of R1b-U152 in central Anatolia is interesting, since part of that region was colonized by Gauls.

Given its concentration in Italy, the same haplogroup probably spread within the Roman empire at a later date. The discovery of subclades of U152 offers promise that one day we might be able to distinguish between one hypothetical movement and another, by testing ancient DNA.

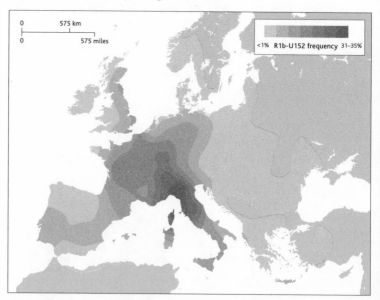

66 Y-DNA R1b-U152 radiates from a high density core in northern Italy and Corsica.

to fall. During the early Iron Age (c. 800/750–400 BC) evidence of human occupation is thin in the Irish landscape. This does not mean that the population completely disappeared. Modern archaeological methods reveal more subtle signs of activity, even if magnificent metalwork is no longer to be seen.[59] Yet the conclusion is inescapable that Ireland had sunk into a poverty that would not support large numbers. Decline began before the end of the Bronze Age, so we cannot simply blame a fall in international demand for bronze or its raw materials. Naturally, Ireland would have lost its pioneer advantage as bronze-making spread across western Europe. The same is true of Britain. It is even possible that Irish tin and gold were panned out, for the gold in objects from Iron Age Ireland does not seem to come from the Mourne Mountains.[60] Looming over the period though are the grey skies of climate shift. The change to a cooler and wetter climate around 800 BC would have had an impact on farming.

There is a sharp increase in activity in Ireland at around 400 BC, followed by stability until the end of the millennium.[61] Population growth may have begun as local farmers enjoyed a warmer, drier climate. It seems no coincidence though that the first La Tène objects appear in Ireland by around 300 BC. Migrants would find a warmer Ireland more appealing. The early metalwork imports have parallels on the Continent,[62] though this does not mean that they arrived direct from there. People entering Britain from Gaul would no doubt bring treasured objects with them, which might still be in the possession of those of their descendants who chose to move to Ireland. The fact that La Tène is largely confined to the northern two-thirds of Ireland generated the notion that it arrived from northern Britain. A seminal study of beehive quern stones in Ireland confirmed it. These querns are linked to the La Tène culture by the decoration on some of them, and match the type of beehive quern found in the region of Britain ranging from Yorkshire to southern Scotland.[63]

If an influx from Gaul had already caused the famous sound-shift to P-Celtic in Britain (see pp. 115–16), then newcomers from Britain would have taken it to Ireland. It seems that they did. By the time Ptolemy wrote his *Geography* in the 2nd century AD there were both Gaelic and Brittonic place and tribal names in Ireland. [67] Not all the Brittonic names need date as far back as 300 BC though. Ptolemy was writing after the Roman conquest of Britain, which seems to have driven some unhappy Britons across the Irish Sea (see pp. 155–56).[64]

On the face of it, Ptolemy's Ireland bears little resemblance to the pre-historic division of Ireland into five provinces (the Pentarchy) which can be deduced from native sources.[65] We can detect in Ptolemy the familiar name of only one of these. The *Ouolountioi* (in Ptolemy's original Greek) lived in northeast Ireland. They appear later as the Ulaid, who gave their name to the province of Ulster. We have already seen the archaeological evidence for this province (see p. 18). The Iwerni (*Iouerni* in Ptolemy's Greek) tribe is placed in southern Ireland, and appears in later sources as the Érainn, a group of dynasties who ruled in Munster prior to the 7th century AD. The town named after them by Ptolemy could be *Teamhair 'Erann*, which appears in the Ulster Cycle as the muster-place for the Érainn.[66] The Iwerni were once the people of all Ireland, as recorded by ancient Greek travellers centuries earlier (see p. 46). So it seems that they had been squeezed into the south by incomers from the La Tène period onwards.

67 The Celtic tribes of Ireland as noted by the geographer Ptolemy in the 2nd century AD. The Brigantes of southeast Ireland were probably an off-shoot of those in Britain.

Genetics: traces of the spread of La Tène to Ireland?

A likely genetic signature of La Tène in Ireland is Y-DNA R1b-M222 [see 102] carried by up to 44 per cent of men in parts of Northern Ireland today.[67] Given the drastic drop in population in Iron Age Ireland, it would not have taken many incomers to have made such a strong genetic impact. A study restricted to the counties forming the Republic of Ireland found 20 per cent of men in Donegal were R1b-M222, much higher than in other parts of the Republic. Northwestern Ireland was supposed to be the territory of the Northern Uí Néill, descendants of the fabled 5th-century warlord, Niall of the Nine Hostages. It also appears among the Connachta, supposed descendants of the brothers of Niall. So R1b-M222 was initially labelled as the lineage of Niall.[68]

Alas this attractive idea rested on genealogies that were tampered with around AD 730 to make the famous Niall the ancestor of unrelated kings based in Donegal, who then claimed to be the Northern Uí Néill.[69] Wider sampling subsequently showed the highest concentrations of R1b-M222 in northeastern Ireland (Belfast 44 per cent) and western Ireland (Mayo 43 per cent). Outside Ireland roughly 10 per cent of men carry M222 in northern England (Yorkshire), western Scotland (Skye) and northeastern Scotland (Moray).[70] This is not the pattern that we would expect from Irish migrants into Britain.

Recently a parent to R1b-M222 has been slotted into the 'family tree', defined by the marker Z2961. It is too new a discovery for its distribution to be known, but one carrier has the Welsh surname Powell.[71] A working theory would be that M222 arose among the Celts in Britain. Ancient DNA may one day settle the matter.

Belgae in Britain

In the two centuries before the Claudian invasion of Britain, the south of the country was subjected first to raiding and then to settlement by an earlier wave of invaders, the Belgae. Caesar learnt in 54 BC that Belgae from Gaul had settled along the coast of Britain, many retaining the same tribal names as their brethren across the Channel.[72] This is compatible with the archaeological evidence, if we are generous in our interpretation of 'the coast'. From 125 BC Gallo-Belgic coins appear over the whole of southeastern Britain. [68] New tribal centres appeared, similar to those in Gaul. These were large, fortified, lowland settlements. Among their inhabitants were craftsmen making the first British wheel-thrown pottery and minting the first British coins.

68 *The earliest Belgic coins appear on both sides of the Channel. The first and most spectacular type is shown here: dating from 125–100 BC this gold stater is identified with the Ambiani, since it is found in their Somme Valley territory.*

Tribal coin issues and their distribution add to our knowledge of the tribes of Britain.[73] [see 74] The Atrebates had a centre at Calleva (Silchester). They share a name with a tribe of the Gaulish Belgae living in the neighbourhood of Arras, northern France. The Catuvellauni lived to the north of them, with a town at Verolamion (St Albans). A minor tribe of the same name lived in Gaul in the valley of the River Marne; they gave their name to the town of Catalaunum (Châlons-sur-Marne). Archaeologically, the Aylesford-Swarling culture is common to the British Catuvellauni, their eastern neighbours the Trinovantes, with their tribal centre at Camulodunon (Colchester), and the Cantiaci of what is now Kent. It has parallels with that of the Continental Catuvellauni.[74] So we can confidently include the Trinovantes and Cantiaci among the Belgae in Britain. It was the Belgic tribes who took the first shock of Roman invasion.

Overview

- From *c.* 400 to *c.* 100 BC, the Gauls/Galatians expanded in many directions. Their reasons for this may include pressure from the Germani, overpopulation and desire for a better standard of living.

- East of the Rhine, Celts were under pressure from the expanding Germani. Belgae moved into northeastern Gaul and southern Britain. The Boii of Bohemia moved east, west and south.

- Pressure from incoming Belgae meant that some Gaulish tribes were displaced, for example the Parisii, who seem to have moved west to the region around present-day Paris and also to Britain.

- Brennos ravaged Macedonia with a huge force of Gauls and led them south into Greece, intent on plundering the oracle at Delphi.

- A group split away from Brennos before he even reached Macedonia. They and their descendants remained a force in southeastern Europe for over half a century and in Asia Minor until the Roman period.

- In Iberia the Celtiberians expanded west across much of the peninsula.

- The La Tène culture spread into Britain and from there to the northern two-thirds of Ireland.

- The expansion of the Celtic-speaking world had reached its greatest extent in around 100 BC. It was soon to be challenged by the rising power of Rome.

CHAPTER EIGHT
Celts vs Romans

Is there anyone on earth who is so narrow-minded or uninquisitive that he could fail to want to know how and thanks to what kind of political system almost the entire known world was conquered and brought under a single empire, the empire of the Romans, in less than fifty-three years?[1]

Polybius wrote this before the Roman conquest of Gaul and Britain. For him the known world surrounded the Mediterranean. At its greatest extent in the 2nd century AD, the Roman empire swallowed up all the Celtic-speaking peoples in Europe and Asia except those of Ireland and northern Britain. [69] It was indeed a wonder, even more so because it survived more or less intact for centuries.

69 *The Roman empire at its height encased the Mediterranean, making the Romans masters of most of the world known to previous Mediterranean mariners, Greek and Phoenician.*

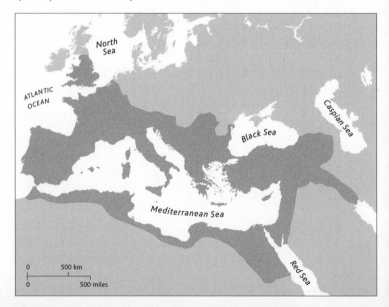

Cisalpine Gauls

The rise of the Romans first put the Cisalpine Gauls in peril. Polybius was well informed on the progress of the Roman push northwards, which was within living memory in his day. The Senones were ejected in 295 BC and lost their land to Roman colonists. The Boii, fearing a like fate, implored the aid of Etruscans to attack the Romans, but were defeated and had to come to terms. There followed 45 years of peaceful co-existence, until a new generation had arisen that had no personal memory of defeat. The Boii and the Insubres called for support from fellow-Gauls across the Alps and marched on Rome. They were subjugated in 224–226 BC. Seeing which way the wind was blowing, the Cenomani threw in their lot with the Romans.[2]

The wind seemed to veer in the opposite direction when the mighty Carthaginians challenged Rome in the Second Punic War (218–201 BC). At the time it must have seemed to the Cisalpine Gauls an excellent opportunity to rid themselves of the upstart Latins. Rome might be flexing its muscles, but Carthage was a long-established power in the Mediterranean. Founded by Phoenician traders from Tyre, Carthage had planted colonies of its own along the coast of North Africa by 550 BC,[3] and at its height headed a Punic empire encompassing North Africa and parts of Iberia, Sicily and Sardinia. Great was the fury of the Carthaginian general Hamilcar Barca when he was forced to yield Sicily to the Romans in 241 BC. Rome's seizure of Sardinia in 237 BC was a second blow. Hamilcar resolved upon retaliation and had his nine-year-old son Hannibal solemnly swear lifelong enmity with Rome. Though Hamilcar died before he could accomplish his aims, he ensured an heir just as committed to them.[4]

Hannibal cherished high hopes of the Cisalpine Gauls as allies, given their bravery in war and hatred of Rome. He secured their support, including that of the Cenomani, before setting out on his extraordinary journey with an army complete with elephants, starting from Cartagena in Iberia. From the River Rhône onwards, he had Cisalpine Gauls as guides. Surviving the crossing of the Alps, Hannibal in the spring of 217 BC crushed the Roman army in the battle of Lake Trasimene. In the months that followed he teetered on the edge of total victory.[5] The Romans meanwhile chewed at the root of Carthaginian power in Iberia and North Africa. It was the success of the Roman general Scipio Africanus in Africa that would bring Carthage to peace talks and the recall of Hannibal from Italy.

The implications for the Cisalpine Gauls were profound. It was only a matter of time before they were absorbed into Rome's nascent empire. Yet their fate was less lamentable than they might have expected. The Cenomani were defeated in 197 BC and the Insubres and Boii in 194 BC. The Boii were scattered. The Cenomani were disarmed in 187 BC. The Insubres retained their arms, but were stripped of the small empire they had acquired by their conquest of other local tribes. So the Cisalpine Gauls were humiliated, but they were not completely ejected from Italy. It was more profitable to the Romans to leave pacified tribes in charge of their own land, but in league with Rome. The surviving Cisalpine tribes enjoyed a degree of autonomy until the region became a Roman province in 81 BC. Perhaps the aggression that the Insubres once expended in battle was channelled into commerce. They developed a bustling commercial hub at Milan.[6]

The struggle for Iberia

During the Second Punic War, the Romans undermined Hannibal by attacking the base of his power in the Iberian peninsula. This starved Carthage of a source of wealth and warriors. The Roman conquest of what they called Hispania was a slow process. It began in urgent self-defence in 218 BC and ended in 19 BC as part of a policy of imperial expansion. [70]

The immediate rationale for the Romans to throw their weight behind Iberian resistance to Carthage was their friendly relationship with the walled town known to the Romans as Saguntum (now Sagunto), approximately 30 km (20 miles) north of Valencia. This town overlooked a fertile plain and was conveniently close to the coast. It had flourished on trade. Its citizens were Iberes, who spoke a non-Indo-European language. The Mediterranean coast of Iberia which had once been home to Ligurians had gradually been taken over by the literate and urban Iberes.[7] As Hannibal was advancing towards them, the citizens of Saguntum sent repeated pleas to Rome for aid. In return the Romans merely sent legates, who protested against any attack on Saguntum. Undeterred Hannibal took the town just before he left for Italy. The Romans had their *casus belli*.[8]

Roman troops arrived in Spain under the command of the brothers Gnaeus and Publius Cornelius Scipio. Hannibal had taken the sons of many leading Iberes as an assurance of their support, housing these hostages within the walls of Saguntum. A wealthy and prominent Iberian named

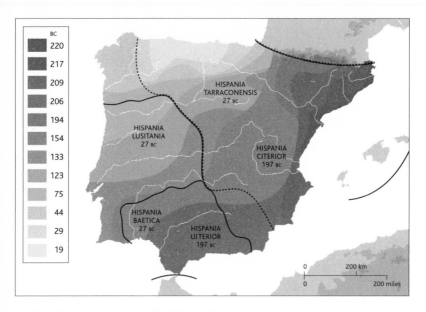

70 *The gradual Roman conquest of the Iberian peninsula, also known as Hispania. The Roman provinces of Hispania changed their borders as more territory was assimilated.*

Abilyx managed to rescue the children by deftly playing politics. As the Scipios approached, Abilyx persuaded the local Carthaginian commander that it was no longer possible for the Carthaginians to control the Iberians by fear, as the Romans might soon have their hands on the hostages. What was needed was a gesture of goodwill. Since Abilyx had previously been seen as loyal, he was allowed to whisk away the hostages under cover of darkness. He took them straight to the Roman camp. There he persuaded the Scipios that returning the children to their parents with Roman blessing would gain the friendship of the Iberes. Indeed it did make a good impression.[9]

After some successes against the Carthaginians, both Gnaeus and Publius Scipio were killed in 211 BC. The Romans laid the blame on the Celtiberian mercenaries the Scipios had recruited, who were lured away by the Carthaginians. The Roman Senate appointed another Scipio to take command in Spain, the son and namesake of Publius Cornelius Scipio, eager to avenge the deaths of his father and uncle.[10] His daring exploits in Spain and later against Carthage itself were to make him famous as Scipio Africanus or Scipio the Great.

Planning in secret, the young Scipio prepared for a surprise attack on the heart of Carthaginian power in Spain – the city of Cartagena. He took it at speed in 209 BC. In Cartagena too the Carthaginians had been holding Iberian hostages. Learning from previous experience, Scipio restored them to their homes, gaining yet more support from the Iberes.[11] By comparison with some later Roman campaigns, it was a charm offensive.

A Carthaginian general named Hanno then arrived in Spain with a fresh army and marched into Celtiberia to raise troops there. Scipio sent a commander against him who first attacked the unprotected Celtiberian camp, where the newly gathered levies were not expecting trouble so soon. The result was a resounding victory for the Romans. One such success followed another until the Carthaginians were driven from Spain and Scipio returned to Rome in triumph.[12]

This could scarcely be the end of the story. Scipio is alleged to have told his men 'Our purpose and endeavour is not that we may remain in Spain ourselves, but that the Carthaginians may not.'[13] Yet a Roman army had to be left in Spain to prevent the return of the Carthaginians. The Romans were acquiring an empire, and at the expense of the Celtic peoples.

Rome gradually extended its Hispanic territory in the 2nd century BC, and shaped a new social order. The Romans had already begun to make slaves of selected prisoners during the early campaign among the Iberes. When Scipio took Cartagena, he made a class distinction between its citizens and its working men. The former were granted their freedom. The working men were told that for the time being they were public slaves of Rome, but if they showed goodwill and industry in their crafts, they would have their freedom if the war against Carthage ended in Roman victory. Thus he ensured that even his captives would be zealous in the Roman cause.[14]

As time went on, the Romans developed a policy of taking as slaves those who resisted the Roman expansion. No doubt this was intended to encourage peaceful co-operation in Rome's imperial designs, but it also produced a supply of slave labour that became crucial to the imperial economy. Thousands of male and female slaves were shipped back to Rome for sale. Celts might find themselves tending Roman fields or dressing the hair of Roman ladies. After generations in Roman servitude their very origins might be forgotten. They were Romanized just as effectively as those chiefs coaxed to become clients of Rome by gifts and favours.

One figure stands out as a local hero of the resistance. Viriatus (or Viriato) was a Lusitanian guerrilla leader whose memory remains green in Portugal and Spain.[15] Some Roman officials were becoming rapacious in the arrogance of power. Those appointed to short-term posts had little incentive to learn about the locals or build up a good relationship with them. There was a grumbling resentment in the Roman province of Hispania, which found an outlet in 171 BC in a deputation to the Roman Senate, begging that the allies of Rome should not be treated more shamefully than their enemies.[16] The popularity of Viriatus among later generations has led to an accumulation of legend around him. What we know scarcely needs embellishment. Viriatus was remarkably strong, healthy and agile, having been a shepherd on the mountains from his childhood. For most of his life he lived under the open sky and was satisfied with nature's bedding. He was thus inured to spartan living. He always carried weapons and was famed for his deeds of arms, but it was his intelligence and tactical ability that lifted him to leadership. At first he led a group of bandits. Progressing from raider chief to warlord in the 140s BC, he was successful in battle against the Romans. In the end the Romans resorted to arranging the assassination of this charismatic figure by some of his own kinsmen.[17]

Julius Caesar served as governor of Hispania from 62 to 60 BC. He took Rome's writ into the far northwest of the peninsula by conquering the Gallaeci and Lusitani. It was here that he was first acclaimed *imperator* by his troops,[18] an honorific title for military commanders at the time, but also perhaps a poignant foreshadowing of the imperial title his heirs were to seize.

Caesar's conquest of Gaul

Both Romans and Gauls were politically in transition. Most of the Gaulish tribes were still led by kings, but some had abandoned hereditary monarchy in favour of government closer to the Roman model.[19] The Romans had replaced their monarchy by elected officials long before. It was still possible in emergencies for a dictator to be appointed for a limited period, who had absolute control, civil and military. Julius Caesar would be granted almost regal powers a few years after his Gallic campaign.[20]

Before that he was elected as one of Rome's two consuls for 59 BC. The post of consul was for one year. By this time it was usual for the consul to be rewarded at the end of his term by a lucrative post as a provincial governor. Caesar gained Roman Gaul, together with Illyricum.[21] Both Cisalpine Gaul and Gallia Narbonensis were already Roman provinces. The latter had been acquired in part to provide a land corridor for troops from Italy to Hispania.

Caesar had no brief and no immediate plan to conquer the rest of Gaul. Yet he would have been well aware of the enormous prestige and popularity that would accrue to a commander who did so. Gaul was a prize worth fighting for, with its swathes of good agricultural land blessed with sunshine to ripen corn and grapes, yet well-watered by clouds from the Atlantic and the Mediterranean. Given a suitable pretext first by the Helvetii and then by the Aedui, Caesar seized the prize. [71]

The Helvetii were a warlike Gallic tribe living in what is now Switzerland, who had been under pressure for half a century from the expansion of the Germani. They determined to migrate en masse and conquer the rest of Gaul. As it chanced, their plan matured in Caesar's first year as governor of Roman Gaul. The Helvetii were joined by several neighbouring Celtic tribes, including a remnant of the Boii who had migrated westwards across the Rhine not long before. The leaders of this swollen horde decided to take the broadest track, which was through the Roman province in southern Gaul. Learning of their intentions, Caesar raced from Rome to confront them at Geneva.[22]

Caesar's first action was to destroy the bridge across the Rhône at Geneva. The Romans have so often been credited with bringing a transport infrastructure to the Celtic lands that it needs to be said that a system of roads and bridges already existed in Gaul. Caesar encountered roads in Britain too. In Ireland, which was never engulfed by the Roman empire, the early medieval law texts made provisions for public roads.[23] What Roman civil engineers achieved was a system of stone bridges and straight, metalled roads built to withstand heavy traffic. Legions on the march could travel at speed along these imperial arteries.

In the face of Caesar's opposition, the Helvetii abandoned their plan to pass through the Roman province and took another route, but Caesar pursued them anyway and forced them to return to their former territory. There they would continue to be a useful buffer between the Germani and Roman Gaul.[24]

This demonstration of the power of Rome was not lost on other Gallic tribes. Their conquest by the Helvetii had been averted. Could Rome resolve

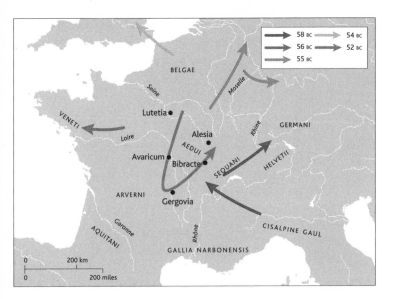

71 *Caesar's campaigns in Gaul. The southern part of the lands of the Gauls had been taken by the Romans before Caesar's day. As governor of Cisalpine Gaul and Gallia Narbonensis, Caesar was drawn into the politics of the warring Gaulish tribes and ended by taking the rest of Gaul into the Roman empire.*

another pressing problem? For many years the Aedui had been locked in a struggle for supremacy with their neighbours the Arverni and Sequani. The Aedui lived in what is now central France, between the Loire and the Saône rivers, with their capital at Bibracte. They had long been in the ascendant and in alliance with Rome. To their southwest lived the Arverni in the Auvergne mountains. To their east beyond the Saône lived the Sequani, with whom they were in conflict over tolls on traffic along the Saône. In the 60s BC the Arverni and Sequani had taken the reckless step of hiring thousands of Germanic mercenaries. This certainly achieved their aim of defeating the Aedui, who were crushed in 61 BC. Yet a worse fate befell the victorious Sequani. The Germanic mercenaries acquired a taste for the Gallic standard of living. The productive land of Gaul supported a way of life unknown in the Germania of their day. The chieftain Ariovistus settled in the territory of the Sequani and seized a third of their land. He soon invited many thousands of Germani to Gaul and demanded that more Sequani evacuate their land to make room for these new settlers.[25]

So Caesar found himself in an odd position. He received a request for aid in 58 BC from both the Aedui and their former enemies. This gave him one reason for war. The underlying threat of the encroaching Germani was a more powerful one. The Gauls themselves feared complete takeover. That would leave the way clear for the Germani to fall upon Roman Gaul and enter Italy. Thus Caesar felt justified in his campaign that same year to expel Ariovistus from Gaul.[26]

It was bound to occur to some Gauls that the price of Roman aid could be Roman domination. Reaction was not slow in coming. Rumours reached Caesar that winter that the Belgae were conspiring against him. Caesar tells us that 'They were afraid that if all the rest of Gaul was subdued, our troops would advance against them.'[27] It may be that they expected to be ejected from Gaul along with those Germani who had settled there, since they were all intruders from east of the Rhine. The Belgae were certainly willing to ally themselves in this campaign against Rome with those Germani who had managed to cross the Rhine.[28]

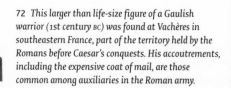

Caesar lost no time in responding. He raised another two legions in Italy and sent them into Gaul in the spring of 57 BC. This brought Caesar's forces up to eight legions, each nominally of 6,000 men. So rapid was their march that they surprised the Remi, the first Belgic tribe encountered, who promptly sided with Rome. The Remi provided Caesar with information on the Belgic fighting forces. The total number of men in the Belgic and Germanic coalition opposing Caesar was calculated at 298,000, compared to his 48,000.[29]

72 *This larger than life-size figure of a Gaulish warrior (1st century BC) was found at Vachères in southeastern France, part of the territory held by the Romans before Caesar's conquests. His accoutrements, including the expensive coat of mail, are those common among auxiliaries in the Roman army.*

There followed a master class by Caesar in military tactics. Even if the estimate of the opposing forces was exaggerated, the Romans were clearly outnumbered. On the other hand, neither the Celts nor the Germani had standing armies of full-time soldiers. The massive coalition army was a temporary alliance. Caesar kept the Belgae and their allies busy with daily skirmishes, but avoided a full-scale battle. The Belgae could not maintain a massive, hungry army in the field indefinitely. Corn supplies ran low. The decision was made for every man to return home and await events. This retreat allowed Caesar to conquer the Belgic tribes piecemeal over the course of that year. Meanwhile, the Veneti and other Gallic tribes of the Atlantic seaboard had been subjected to Roman rule by a commander sent by Caesar with just one legion. So Caesar considered Gaul to be pacified at the end of 57 BC.[30] [72]

Not all Gauls tamely accepted this. Rebellion followed rebellion. This restless mood threw up a leader in 52 BC whose name has echoed down the centuries – Vercingetorix. Caesar describes him as 'a powerful young Arvernian, whose father Celtillus had held suzerainty over all Gaul, and who had been put to death by his compatriots for seeking to make himself king'.[31] Here was a man bred to leadership and politics. Vercingetorix was determined to free Gaul. He had no trouble rousing his own retainers to action, but the Arvernian elders refused to take the risk of rebellion and expelled him from their oppidum at Gergovia. Undaunted, he raised a rag-tag band from the countryside around, expelled his opponents and was proclaimed king of the Arverni. Roman rule was unpopular enough to secure him the immediate support of other tribes of central and western Gaul.[32]

In the Asterix series of comic books set in Roman Gaul, a running joke is that all Gauls recall the battle of Gergovia (won by Vercingetorix), while no one has a clue about the siege of Alesia (where Vercingetorix capitulated). The reality is more complex. Vercingetorix has been celebrated as much in defeat as victory. As he saw his men slaughtered by the Romans at Alesia and defeat was inevitable, Vercingetorix addressed an assembly:

> I did not undertake the war for private ends, but in the cause of national liberty. And since I must now accept my fate, I place myself at your disposal. Make amends to the Romans by killing me or surrender me alive as you think best.[33]

73 Vercingetorix Throws Down His Arms at the Feet of Julius Caesar. *This painting by Lionel Noel Royer (1899) shows the scene described by Plutarch.*

Consultation with Caesar brought the request back to Alesia for the arms and chiefs of the Gauls. As Plutarch tells the tale, Vercingetorix put on his most beautiful armour and had his horse carefully groomed. He then rode out through the gates to where Caesar was seated, where he leapt from his horse, stripped off his armour and sat at Caesar's feet.[34] This was the sacrifice that turned him into a tragic hero. [73] Vercingetorix no doubt knew the Roman habit of parading captured enemies through the streets of Rome in triumphal processions, before executing them. This was indeed to be his fate. It was the end of resistance to Rome in Gaul.

Britannia

The Romans carved a province for themselves out of most of Britain, which they called Britannia. In a sense the Romans created what would become Scotland, for until their arrival there had been no division of Britain in this way. One could scarcely call it undivided though. Celtic tribes jostled each other for territory. Indeed these divisions aided the Romans in taking over southern Britain.

The powerful and pugnacious Catuvellauni were a danger to their neighbours. Their king Cassivellaunos had killed the king of the Trinovantes, whose son Mandubracios fled to Gaul and placed himself under Caesar's protection. Caesar did not use this as his excuse for the invasion of Britain, however. Instead he claimed that in almost all his Gallic campaigns, the Gauls had received reinforcements from Britain. Though that is more than likely, it scarcely warranted such a response. Caesar was thriving on the glory of conquest. In the late summer of 55 BC he set out to reconnoitre, knowing that the fighting season was too advanced for a full campaign. He was defeated as much by the weather as by the ferocity of the Britons. The following spring he set sail for Britain again. The Britons were prepared. They had appointed Cassivellaunos their war leader. Though he had previously been continually at war with other British tribes, the threat of Roman

74 *The Roman campaigns under Aulus Plautius focused on the commercially valuable southeast of Britain.*

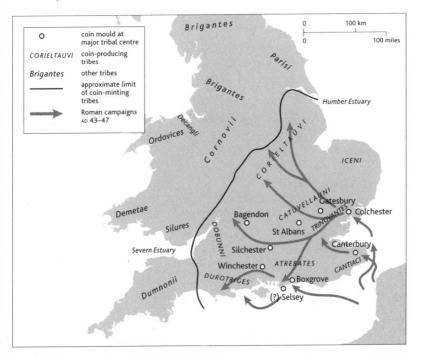

invasion had created a common cause. The Trinovantes had not forgotten their injury though. They preferred to seek the support of Caesar. Seeing that they were well treated by the Romans, several other tribes chose the same path. A Roman assault on the stronghold of Cassivellaunos brought him to terms. Caesar did not attempt to garrison the island. He was satisfied to take hostages, fix an annual tribute to be paid and sail away.[35] As Tacitus puts it, Caesar pointed Britain out, rather than handed it over, to posterity.[36]

It was Caesar's great-great-grand-nephew Claudius who conquered Britain. He was no great military commander, but he did not need to be. He selected competent men for that role. The most famous today is Vespasian, who was to become emperor himself in AD 69. When Claudius was raised to the purple in AD 41, he appointed Vespasian as legate of the 2nd Augustan legion, at that time stationed near the Rhine. It was well placed to participate in the invasion of Britain in AD 43, along with three other legions. Overall command was given to Aulus Plautius. [74]

The relentless expansionism of the Catuvellauni was still alienating other Celtic tribes to Roman advantage. By AD 43 the Catuvellauni had taken over the Trinovantes, the Atrebates and part of the Dobunni. Two British kings had taken refuge with emperor Augustus. One may have been Tincomaros, grandson of Commios of the Atrebates. His coins cluster on the south coast around Chichester. So he would have been the king who received support from a Roman military presence (arriving between 10 BC and AD 10), remains of which have been found near Fishbourne Roman palace.[37] From around AD 10 Virica, another grandson of Commios, began to issue coins. He was ousted from Calleva (Silchester) in about AD 25 by a brother of Cunobelinos, king of the Catuvellauni.[38] [75]

75 Struck bronze coin of the British ruler Cunobelinos, AD 10–41/2. The obverse has the name CVNOBELINVS with a beardless helmeted head looking right. The life story of Cunobelinos was mangled by Geoffrey of Monmouth, then further fictionalized by Shakespeare in Cymbeline.

Then Caratacos (Caratacus), son of Cunobelinos, conquered the entire kingdom of the Atrebates after AD 40, driving Virica to seek refuge and allies in Rome. It was Virica who persuaded Claudius to send a force to Britain. By this time Cunobelinos was dead, so it was his sons Caratacos and Togodumnos who led the initial resistance to the Roman invasion. Putting these kings to flight, Aulus Plautius advanced westwards. Those of the Dobunni under the Catuvellaunian yoke were willing to welcome the Romans. South of the River Avon, among the southern Dobunni and the Durotriges, Vespasian faced hard fighting.[39] This was a region worth fighting for, with sources of lead and silver in the Mendips, which the Romans went on to exploit. Further south again was the famed tin of Cornwall. Tacitus counted the gold, silver and other metals of Britain as the reward for victory.[40]

The conquest of the Celtic tribes of Britain was piecemeal. [76] To the north of the initial border of the Roman province lay the extensive territory of the Brigantes, stretching over most of what is now northern England. At the time of the Roman invasion they were led by Queen Cartimandua, who preferred the Romans to the Catuvellauni. When Caratacos sought her protection, he was put in chains and delivered up to the Romans, nine years after the start of the conquest. This was a major coup for Claudius. The fame of Caratacos had spread even to Italy. Crowds lined the streets of Rome to see the man who had defied imperial power for so long. He was paraded in triumph with his wife and brothers, who had been captured earlier. Such was the eloquence of Caratacos as he stood before Claudius that he and his family were pardoned and released from their chains.[41]

Thus Cartimandua purchased Roman favour and became a client queen. After the removal of Caratacos, her husband Venutios was regarded as the most competent British commander. So divorcing him was Cartimandua's gravest error. In his place she took Vellocatos, his former armour-bearer, not only in marriage, but also to share in governing the realm. This scandal rocked her household to its foundation. The tribe favoured Venutios.[42]

War broke out between Cartimandua and Venutios. In desperation Cartimandua called for Roman support. The Romans rescued her person, but not her throne, which was lost to Venutios, now an enemy of Rome. He was defeated by Petilius Cerialis, governor of Britain AD 71–73, who took most of the territory of the Brigantes.[43] It seems likely that some of the Brigantes fled to Ireland at this time, for the tribe was recorded by Ptolemy there. [see 67] Certainly, a group from what is now northeast England settled briefly around this time on the small island of Lambay, off the coast of Co. Dublin. In the next century a woman was buried in classic Roman style at Stonyford, Co. Kilkenny.[44] This lies not far from the Bronze Age hill fort at Freestone Hill, which in the Iron Age housed a Romano-British sanctuary.[45] Here we have evidence of a Romano-British presence in the area indicated by Ptolemy as the territory of the Brigantes.

There may have been other refugees from the Romans. The *Fir Domnann* appear in the *Lebor Gabála Érenn* as among the invaders of Ireland. (*Fir* means 'people'.) They were probably related to the Dumnonii of southwest Britain and what is now the western Scottish Lowlands. The name occurs in *Inber Domnann* (Malahide Bay, Co. Dublin), and in northwest Mayo as *Iorrais Domnann* (Erris, Co. Mayo) and the nearby *Mag Domnann* and *Dun Domnann*. An early Irish poem describes one of their leaders as the over-king of Leinster.[46]

Agricola, governor of the province from AD 77 to 84, pushed the frontier north to the Forth–Clyde line in AD 79–80. Indeed he drove deeper into Caledonia with the aim of spreading Roman rule over the whole of Britannia from shore to shore.[47] The logic is understandable. To capture the whole of an island means that nature provides its borders. On the other hand the Caledonian highlands were inhospitable, held nothing that the Romans wanted and would be a drain on manpower to keep pacified. Subsequent Roman commanders preferred a divided island with a man-made frontier. In AD 122 the emperor Hadrian ordered the construction of a wall running for 120 km (75 miles) between the Solway and the Tyne. Just 20 years later the emperor Antoninus Pius decided to move the frontier up to the Forth–Clyde line first secured by Agricola. It was fortified by a bank and ditch, known rather misleadingly as the Antonine Wall. This was abandoned in favour of Hadrian's Wall after Antoninus Pius died.

The incoming Romans imposed their rule partly through existing tribal organization. A tribe would become a Roman *civitas*. An existing oppidum could be Romanized. For example Calleva became the Romano-British town of Calleva Atrebatum (Silchester). There was some reorganization. Part of the land of the Atrebates was hived off for a new polity labelled the Regni (the people of the king). This evidently refers to the status that Togidubnos (perhaps a relative of Virica) enjoyed as a client-king after the Roman conquest, with his palace at what is now Fishbourne. Tacitus cynically saw it

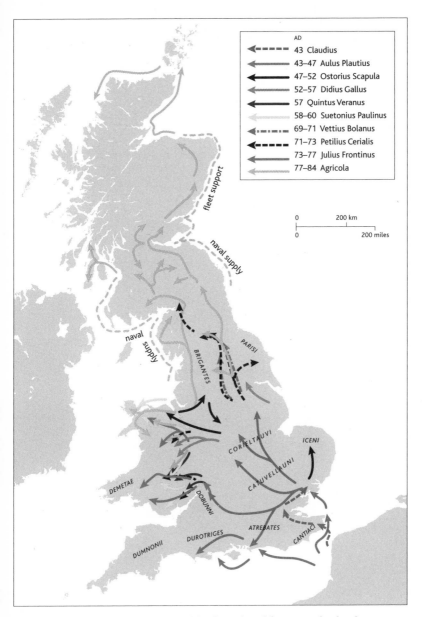

	AD	
◄======	43	Claudius
◄——	43–47	Aulus Plautius
◄——	47–52	Ostorius Scapula
◄——	52–57	Didius Gallus
◄——	57	Quintus Veranus
◄——	58–60	Suetonius Paulinus
◄—·—·	69–71	Vettius Bolanus
◄------	71–73	Petilius Cerialis
◄——	73–77	Julius Frontinus
◄——	77–84	Agricola

76 *The Roman conquest of Britain took several decades. In the end the Romans abandoned the attempt to complete it by taking the Scottish Highlands.*

as an example of the long-established Roman custom of employing even kings to make others slaves.[48]

Roman understanding of the Celtic tribes beyond Hadrian's Wall was more sketchy. Several tribal names were recorded there by Ptolemy around AD 150, but we hear no more of most of them. One tribal name that does recur is that of the Caledonii (Caledonians). If we translate Ptolemy's directions into modern terms, they lived in the Great Glen around Loch Ness and the highlands to the south of it as far as the Firth of Clyde. Their name is preserved in the place-name Dunkeld, which in the 9th century was called Dun Chaillden (fort of the Caledonii).[49] The Caledonians became so notable in fighting the Romans that the latter sometimes called the whole of north Britain beyond their border Caledonia.

In AD 208 the 'barbarians' north of the Roman border were overrunning Roman Britannia, looting and destroying. The emperor Septimius Severus arrived in person to drive them back. These Britons were described in Herodian as avoiding clothing, because it would obscure the tattoos on their bodies consisting of coloured designs and drawings of all kinds of animals.[50] Cassius Dio, describing the same campaign, remarked that 'There are two principal races of the Britons, the Caledonians and the Maeatians.... The Maeatians live near the cross wall which cuts the island in two, and the Caledonians are behind them.'[51] In both sources the term 'Britons' was rather confusingly used to mean only those outside the empire.

The Maeatians (Miathi in Brittonic) do not appear in Ptolemy's *Geography* and may represent a tribal regrouping in response to the campaigns of Agricola. The name Dumyat at the western end of the Ochil Hills, overlooking Stirling, is probably derived from Dun Miathi, 'hill fort of the Miathi'. It has the remains of a hill fort on its summit. Myothill, west of Falkirk, also seems to preserve the tribal name.[52]

Pagan Picts and Scots

In AD 305 Constantius Chlorus claimed a victory over the 'Caledones and other Picts'.[53] This is the first reference to *Picti*, a late Roman nickname for all the northern British tribes beyond their borders. It means 'painted' in Latin. Isidore of Seville tells us that it refers to the use of plant dye to create tattoos.[54] When the Romans first encountered the Insular Celts , they noted the British habit of dyeing their bodies with woad, which left a blue colour.[55]

Genetics: the Picts

Geneticist James Wilson noted in 2011 that a particular haplotype of Y-DNA R1b-L21 is not only strongly Scottish in distribution, but appears most densely in the area with Pictish symbols. Could this be a clue to Pictish ancestry?[56] Now the cluster has been more securely identified genetically by its own marker, L1065, so we can see how it fits on to the L21 tree. [see 102] Its parent is found in Wales. That is indeed what we would expect if L1065 reflects native Pictish ancestry, rather than the Irish who arrived in Scotland in the post-Roman period (see Chapter 9).

77 Meigle Museum in the Scottish Highlands houses 27 carved Pictish stones. Meigle 4, shown here, depicts a horseman at the top of the stone, with two interlaced serpents behind him. Under the horse's hooves is another entwined serpent, a Pictish Beast and another animal, with a second horseman to the right. The Pictish symbol of a crescent with V rod occupies the lower left of the stone.

As the Britons within the Roman empire gradually adopted Roman ways, those outside it would be easily distinguished by their tattoos. In a similar way and at around the same time the Romans coined the name *Scoti* for the people of Ireland.[57] When British Christian scholars began to write about the peoples of northern Britain and of Ireland they used the names they found in Latin histories. The Irish only really embraced the name Scot for those of their number who turned the land of the Picts into Scotland.

A barbarian conspiracy fell upon Britannia in AD 367. Picts, Saxons, Scots and Attacotti attacked simultaneously from several directions, laid waste to towns and drove off prisoners and cattle. [78, 79] (The Attacotti were Irish

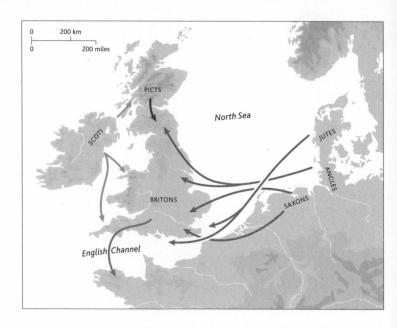

78 The Roman province of Britannia came under attack from three directions in the 4th century. These attacks by the Picts, Scots and Germani continued after Britannia became independent of the Roman empire in AD 410.

79 Roman dice-tower boasting of the downfall of the Picts. It was discovered near the villages of Vettweiss and Froitzheim, Germany, close to the Rhine. The front face of the tower bears the words: 'Pictos victos; hostis delta; lvdite secvri' ('the Picts are defeated; the enemy is destroyed; play in safety').

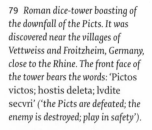

vassal peoples known as *aithechthuatha*.) One Roman general was killed and another captured. The emperor Valentinian I sent the energetic commander Theodosius to restore order. He succeeded with the aid of a strong army.[58] This presaged the upheavals that were to follow Britain's departure from the empire in AD 410.

Overview

- Over time, the Roman empire swallowed all the Celts except those of Ireland and northern Britain.

- The Cisalpine Gauls were defeated in the 2nd century BC. Their territory became a Roman province in 81 BC.

- The Roman conquest of Iberia began in urgent self-defence in 218 BC and ended in 19 BC as part of a policy of imperial expansion.

- Julius Caesar became governor of that part of Gaul already Roman in 58 BC and had conquered the rest of Gaul by 52 BC.

- Britain was conquered piecemeal AD 43–84, but the highlands and islands of the far north were largely excluded from the Roman province, a first step in the creation of what today is Scotland.

- *Picti* (Picts) was a late Roman nickname for all the northern British tribes beyond their borders. It means 'painted' in Latin. At around the same time the Romans coined the name *Scoti* (Scots) for the people of Ireland.

- Picts, Saxons, Scots and Attacotti attacked Britannia simultaneously in AD 367.

CHAPTER NINE

Christian Celts

> My name is Patrick. I am a sinner, a simple country person, and the
> least of all believers. I am looked down upon by many. My father
> was Calpornius. He was a deacon; his father was Potitus, a priest,
> who lived at Bannavem Taburniae [Bannaventa Burniae]. His home
> was near there, and that is where I was taken prisoner. I was about
> sixteen at the time. At that time, I did not know the true God. I was
> taken into captivity in Ireland, along with thousands of others. We
> deserved this, because we had gone away from God, and did not
> keep his commandments. We would not listen to our priests, who
> advised us about how we could be saved. The Lord brought his
> strong anger upon us, and scattered us among many nations even
> to the ends of the earth.[1]

When western Europe emerged from the centuries within the Roman
empire, Latin had been so firmly entrenched among the literate that
the earliest written sources from the British Isles are in that language. St
Patrick, a Briton by birth writing from Ireland, does so in Latin. The Briton
Gildas, wailing that the attacks of Saxons, Picts and Scots were God's pun-
ishment upon the sinful kings of the Britons, does so in Latin. It was the
language of Christianity. Latin had long unified the empire. Christianity
spread through the empire from Rome. Yet the names of the kings Gildas
reviles are Celtic.[2] Patrick tells us that Latin was not his first language.[3] Here
are clues that Britain would turn out to be different from the former Celtic-
speaking regions on the Continent. In Iberia and Gaul (except Armorica),
Celtic languages were irretrievably lost. Romance languages such as French
and Spanish, which evolved from Latin, are spoken there today.

Christianity had been a minority religion within the Roman empire
for centuries after the life of Jesus of Nazareth. Initially it was an annoy-
ance to Rome. The monotheism of Christianity was in direct conflict with
the expectation that loyal Romans would sacrifice to the deified emperor.
Christians were periodically persecuted. St Alban is the most famous of the

British martyrs. His shrine at Romano-British Verulamion gave the name St Alban's to the modern city there. From 260 there was a respite. Christianity became an approved cult until the Great Persecution of Diocletian from 303. By then Christianity was too entrenched to be uprooted, as the Edict of Toleration in 311 grudgingly recognized. In August 314 Constantine summoned the bishops of the western church to a council at Arles in Gaul. It was attended by the bishops of York, London and Lincoln, which were the capitals of three of the provinces into which Britannia was divided at that time.[4] This is evidence of an organized church in Britain in Late Roman times.

Sometime in the 4th century a Romano-Briton called Annianus tossed into the sacred spring at Aquae Sulis (Bath) evidence of his divided loyalties. Sulis Minerva was worshipped there. It was common for appeals to be made to the goddess on lead tablets. Annianus asked the Lady Goddess to retrieve six silver coins from whoever had stolen them, 'whether pagan or Christian'. Only a Christian would use such terminology. (Pagans did not refer to themselves as such.) Yet Annianus did not shrink from invoking the power of Sulis.[5] Judging by the coins still thrown into fountains and wishing wells today, there is a human urge at work here that neither Christianity nor modern science has managed to eradicate.

Soon after 350 a remarkable man was born in Britain. Pelagius was a Christian moralist, who preached the need for simple, virtuous living. He emigrated to Rome soon after Christianity was made the state religion of the Roman empire on 27 February 380. He left the city when it came under threat by Alaric the Goth in 409 and died not long after 418. His emphasis on salvation through good deeds appealed to many, but was seen by key figures in the Church of his day, St Augustine of Hippo and St Jerome, as diminishing the role of divine grace. This led to his excommunication as a heretic.[6] Pelagianism gained so much support in post-Roman Britain that Pope Celestine sent St Germanus of Auxerre to Britain in 429 to denounce it.[7]

By the time Britannia became independent of Rome in 410, Christianity was firmly established there. [80] In the quotation that begins this chapter Patrick suggests that religious apathy was so common as to bring down the wrath of God upon the Britons. Yet he was raised in a Christian environment. Though Gildas found much to complain about in his sinful countrymen, he never accused them of a return to paganism. Patrick tells us that he and thousands of other Britons were captured by Irish raiders and taken into

80 *This gold disc bears a monogram formed of the Greek letters chi (X) and rho (P), the first two letters of Christ's name, combined with alpha (A) and omega (W), the first and last letters of the Greek alphabet, and an appellation of Christ. It is part of a hoard of 4th-century Christian objects found at Water Newton, Cambridgeshire. It is the earliest group of Christian liturgical silver yet found within the former Roman empire.*

slavery in Ireland. This makes it possible that Christianity first arrived in Ireland unwillingly, though other Britons were migrating to Ireland of their own free will, as we shall see (pp. 169–70). As early as 431 there were enough Christians in Ireland for Pope Celestine to send Palladius to be the first bishop of the Irish (see below).[8]

Ogham

The oldest recorded form of the Gaelic languages is Primitive Irish, which is known only from ogham inscriptions. Given the centuries of contact between Ireland and the Roman world, the Latin alphabet was probably the first that the Irish encountered. Instead of adapting it to the writing of Gaelic, the Irish simply took the concept and created their own alphabet. The ogham symbols, formed of strokes along or across a line, are reminiscent of tally notches. [81] The letters they represent were chosen to fit the needs of Primitive Irish, which had no 'p' sound.[9]

Ogham inscriptions are found in Ireland and western Britain from the 4th to the 6th centuries. They are funerary memorial stones. The densest concentration is in southwest Ireland in counties Kerry, Cork and Waterford. Kerry alone has a third of the total number in Ireland. This is a region of Ireland with no ecclesiastical foundation known before AD 600. In the whole corpus of over 300 Irish ogham stones, hardly more than a dozen show any sign of Christian affiliation.[10] So for a body capable of overseeing such memorials, we may look to the druids.[11]

Druidic control of the language of ogham might well explain its antique character. It is strikingly similar to Latin. Near Slane in Co. Louth, there

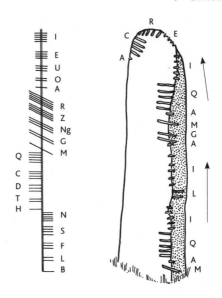

81 *The ogham alphabet was written on the edge of stones, the edge marking the division between strokes to the left and strokes to the right. This inscription from Ballyeightragh, Co. Kerry reads MAQI LIAG MAQI ERCA, the name of the person commemorated.*

is an ogham stone in memory of Mac Caírthinn Uí Enechglaiss (d. 446), to use the modern Irish version of his name. It reads *MAQI CAIRATINI AVI INEQUAGLAS*.[12] Primitive Irish is markedly more ancient than Old Irish (see below), which appears in manuscripts from the 6th century onwards. The latter represents a giant leap towards Modern Irish, including the presence of the letter 'p'. Such a language change over so short a period would be unusual. It has been argued therefore that Primitive Irish represents the last bastion of the sacred language of the pagan Celts, passed down from druid to druid, retaining features that had long disappeared from the vernacular speech of non-druids.[13]

Where ogham inscriptions are found in Britain we can be sure of Irish settlement. The strongest concentration is in Dyfed, southwest Wales. They are also found in Devon and Cornwall, northwest Wales and parts of Scotland. The Isle of Man has six ogham inscriptions.[14] Manx Gaelic, descended from Old Irish, replaced a Brittonic language there.

Irish in Dyfed

In Roman times the people of what is now southwest Wales were the Demetae.[15] Their territory of Demetia appears to have passed seamlessly to the medieval kingdom of Dyfed. Gildas, in his tirade against the 6th-century kings of British tribes, does not spare 'Vortipor, tyrant of the Demetae'.[16] A memorial stone to Voteporis has usually been identified with the Vortipor of Gildas.[17] [82] The fact that this stone is inscribed both in Latin and in Irish (using ogham) lends support to the claim in the 8th-century Irish epic *The Expulsion of the Déisi* that Eochaid son of Artchorp settled in Demed (Demetia) and founded a dynasty.[18]

Déisi simply means 'vassal peoples'. But by the 8th century *déisi* communities in the southeast of Ireland had formed the sub-kingdom of Déisi Muman (*déisi* of Munster). *The Expulsion of the Déisi* promulgated the notion of the Déisi as an ancient tribe expelled from Tara. The tale of Eochaid son of Artchorp is an intriguing digression from the main story. It preserves a pedigree for the kings of Dyfed which has similarities with the Dyfed royal line in Welsh genealogies, at least as far back as Triffyn. He appears in the

82 A memorial stone inscribed MEMORIA VOTEPORIGIS PROTICTORIS ('The monument of Voteporix the Protector'), found at Castell Dwyran, Carmarthenshire, Wales. Ogham letters just visible at the top and down the left side give the Gaelic version of the name: Votecorix.

Irish genealogy as Triphun, the great-grandson of Eochaid, but in the Welsh version as a descendant of Maxen Wledic. Both pedigrees include Vortipor (Gwrthefyr in Welsh) as the grandson of Triffyn.[19]

Maxen Wledic is the Welsh rendering of Magnus Maximus, a Galician-born Roman general who was assigned as commander to Britain in 380. In 383 Maximus was proclaimed Western emperor by his soldiers. He made his son Victor his colleague in power, but their imperial ambitions led to both their deaths in 388.[20] Maximus appears as the improbable progenitor of several Welsh royal lines. This could result from the deduction of pedigrees from king-lists, starting with Maximus as overlord.

The Irish of southwest Wales could have been bands of landless warriors (fianna), who had been recruited by the Roman authorities in the latter half of the 4th century to protect Demetia from Irish raids. In that case Triffyn would be the first Irish protector of Demetia , which title passed down to Vortipor.[21] Another Irish group which settled in south Wales and also in Cornwall was the Uí Liatháin (descendants of Liatháin) of east Cork.[22] The Historia Brittonum tells us that the 'sons of Liethan' occupied the country of the Demetae, as well as Gower and Kidwelly.[23]

Early Christian Ireland

The Confession written by Patrick in old age, carefully copied by his disciples and handed down through the ages, ensured him a fame denied to his fellow missionaries in Ireland. The self-portrait that leapt from his pen was of a passionate advocate of his faith, driven by dreams in which he sensed the divine will. Having escaped from servitude in Ireland, Patrick trained for the ministry in Britain. Then he returned to Ireland intent on spreading Christianity.[24] The stirring figure of Patrick has attracted a huge body of tradition. For centuries he has been known as the patron saint and apostle of Ireland. St Patrick's Day is celebrated not only in Ireland, but throughout the Irish diaspora, especially in the USA.

By comparison Palladius, the first bishop in Ireland, has been almost lost to sight. He came from Auxerre in Gaul and presumably belonged to the aristocratic Gallo-Roman family of the Paladii, which had controlled that region for generations. Since he was sent in 431 to minister to those in Ireland who were already Christian, he may not have sought conversions as Patrick so plainly did. Two apparently Continental clerics, bishops Auxilius

Genetics: Déisi Muman

Irish surnames such as Whalen, Phelan and O'Phelan are derived from the personal name Faeláin (wolf). Faeláin is recorded a number of times among the Irish royal houses, so we may guess that it would have been popular among lesser folk too. We would expect therefore a number of different Y-DNA haplogroups among men of these surnames. That is indeed the finding of the Family Tree DNA project for this group of surnames. The majority of men within it fall into the common Irish haplogroup R1b-L21, but that does not necessarily make them closely related.

One particular Faeláin is of interest for the story of an Irish dynasty in Dyfed, founded by Eochaid son of Artchorp (see p. 166), for this same Artchorp appears in an early pedigree as an ancestor of Faeláin, son of Cormac, king of the Déisi Muman.[25] *The Annals of Ulster* record the demise in 966 of this Faeláin. His descendants appear in the same annals as Ua Faeláin by 1085, a step towards surname development. So it is quite possible that some Whalens and Phelans descend from him.

A group of men of these surnames carry the R1b-L144 subclade of R1b-L21 and have ancestry from counties Laois or Waterford in Ireland, overlapping with the territory of the Déisi Muman (Munster). The genetic marker L144 has also been found in men of the Welsh surnames Prosser and Griffith.[26] The Welsh long retained the system of naming by genealogy (see p. 207), so when they eventually adopted hereditary surnames, these chiefly reflected paternal names. Griffith is derived from the Welsh personal name Gruffydd. There will be many unrelated men with that surname. The Welsh equivalent of 'son' is *map*, shortened to *ap* or *ab*, which in some cases was partly merged with the paternal name to form a surname. Dafydd ap Rosser would become David Prosser.[27] So here we have surnames both Irish and Welsh linked by Y-DNA. It can only be a guess that the link might have arisen from Irish settlement in southwest Wales. In the same haplogroup are men of two surnames derived from places in the north of England: Kendall and Bracewell.

and Secundinus, represented as disciples of Patrick in later sources, are more likely to belong to the mission of Palladius. They left a legacy in the place-names Killashee (*Cell Auxili* 'the cell of Auxilius') in Co. Kildare, and Dunshaughlin (*Dún Sechlainn* 'the fort of Secundinus') in Co. Meath. These two places lie in the centre of eastern Ireland.[28]

In Muirchú's *Life of Saint Patrick*, the saint's mission is connected to the northeast of Ireland, rather than the centre.[29] [83] This suggests that the home from which he was taken was somewhere in the north of what had been Roman Britain. In the surviving copies of Patrick's *Confession*, his birthplace appears as Bannavem Taburniae, which makes no sense as a Romano-British place-name. The Latin of his period often omitted breaks between words. If we place the break more logically, we get Bannaventa Burniae. There was a Bannaventa in what is now Northamptonshire. That can be ruled out as Patrick's birthplace, which was close to the Irish Sea, according to Muirchú. So the addition of Burniae or Berniae would distinguish this unknown Bannaventa from the one in Northamptonshire.[30] There has been a mass of contradictory speculation on its location, but no certainty. Even the dates for Patrick are uncertain. The *Annals of Ulster* give no fewer than four alternative dates for his death. A clue that tips the balance in favour of the last of these, 493, is that a British disciple of Patrick, Mochta, who founded a monastery at Louth in Ireland, died in 535.[31]

Patrick and Mochta were not the only Britons to enter northeast Ireland of their own volition. The Irish annals refer to warbands of British people rampaging around Ireland. The earliest reference tells us of the 'killing of Colman Mor, son of Diarmaid, in his chariot, by Dubhshlat Ua Treana, one of the Cruithni', in 552.[32] *Cruithni* or *Cruithin* is the Irish version of the Welsh *Prydyn* (Britons). From this we can reconstruct an earlier Brittonic version, *Pritani*, meaning literally 'figured folk', usually interpreted as 'tattooed

83 *Domhnall Ua Lochlainn, king of Ireland, commissioned this ornate bronze shrine in Armagh c. 1100 to encase a quadrangular bell reputed to have belonged to St Patrick. The front and sides of the shrine are decorated with silver and gold filigree wound into curvilinear patterns; those on the sides depict elongated beasts intertwined with ribbon-bodied snakes, characteristic of the final, Viking-influenced, style of Irish Celtic art.*

people'. It seems that ancient Greek travellers, hearing *Pritani*, wrote a Greek approximation which became *Britanni* in Latin.[33] From this ethnonym, Greeks and Romans created the island name Britannia, which they preferred to Albion. They also coined terms which translate as 'the British Isles' to include Ireland and the smaller islands of the group.[34] This was simply a geographical convenience, identifying the archipelago by the name of the largest island. It continues to this day.

The fact that these *Cruithin* arrivals from Britain had no specific tribal label (such as Brigantes) makes them part of a changing society. Tribal society in Ireland gradually dissolved in the centuries after 400. The earliest memorial stones found there frequently record the tribal affiliation of the deceased. By the time the first true annals for Ireland start in the middle of the 6th century, new dynastic kindreds were in evidence, which came to dominate the island politically.[35] *Cruithin* dynasties emerged in Ulster: the Dál nAraidi of southern Antrim and their offshoot the Uí Echach Cobha.

Both these dynastic names incorporate a personal name, that of the founder of the kindred. Uí Echach Cobha means 'descendants of Echu of Cobha'. Magh Cobha lay within what became the Barony of Iveagh (*Uíb Echach*) in Co. Down.[36]

A lineage can be pieced together for the Uí Echach Cobha, starting with the death of Eochu in 553. The annal entry helpfully tells us that he was the progenitor of the Uí Echach Ulad, another name for the Uí Echach Cobha. This information could only have been added retrospectively, so we cannot trust the genealogical detail that he was the son of Conlaed, king of Ulaid.[37] In the 8th century the Dál nAraidi were anxious to cast off their 'foreign' label. The term *Cruithin* disappeared from the annals after 773, and the Dál nAraidi claimed to be descended from the older-established Ulaid.[38]

The deaths of successive chiefs of Uí Echach Cobha and Iveagh are recorded in the annals. Surnames gradually developed within this kindred. One Aonghusa (Angus) had a son who was described as Mac (son of) Aonghusa in the usual Irish system of identification by genealogy. It so chanced that he lived at a time when hereditary surnames were developing, so MacAonghusa became the surname McGuinness. This lineage became lords of the Barony of Iveagh in the 12th century, taking over from another branch of the family.[39] It is interesting then that several men of this surname carry a Y-DNA haplogroup that seems to have arrived in Ireland from Britain.

Genetics: the Cruithin

A Y-DNA haplogroup that seems to have arisen in Britain has been found in some men who can trace descent from the Uí Echach Cobha, a *Cruithin* (British) dynasty in Ireland. When this link was first noticed, the phylogenetic tree of Y-DNA was a slender thing by comparison with its bushy growth today, so the name of the haplogroup in question has changed. Brian McEvoy and Dan Bradley of Trinity College Dublin identified it as simply a subclade of I1c.[40] I1c was the name in about 2005 of the present I2a2a (M223). The subclade they had in mind is currently known as I2a2a1a1 (M284). It has now itself been divided into subclades by newly discovered markers.

Haplogroup I2a2a1a1 (M284) is very rare outside the British Isles, except among those of British and Irish origin. Trace amounts are found in France and Germany, and a slightly higher percentage in Portugal, England's oldest ally. To judge by the estimated date that it burgeoned into sub-lineages, it was one of the I2 family that travelled with early farmers. So it could pre-date the Celts in Britain. The bearers of I2a2a1a1 (M284) have a mixed bag of surnames including English, Welsh, Scottish and Irish. Its descendant clade I2a2a1a1a1 (L126/S165) is more common in Scotland. Its offshoot I2a2a1a1a1a (S7753) includes men of several surnames of Irish Gaelic origin, such as McGuinness, Callahan, McConville and McManus, indicating that S7753 arrived in Ireland before the development of surnames. The estimated date of the haplogroup is around AD 500, which makes a neat fit to the earliest reference to the *Cruithin* in AD 552 (see p. 169).[41]

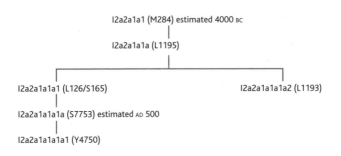

84 *Tree of Y-DNA haplogroup I2a2a1a1 (M284).*

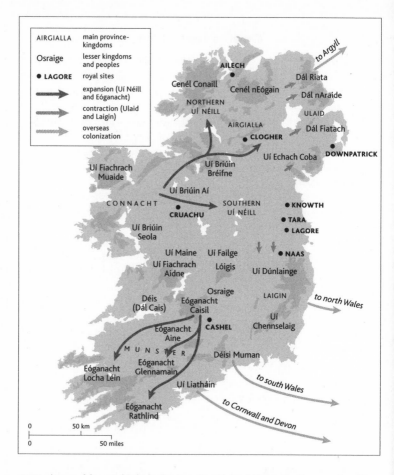

85 *Provinces and dynastic kindreds of early medieval Ireland, illustrating the expansion of the Uí Néill in the north and the Eóganacht of Munster, and Irish migrations to parts of Britain.*

If the ancestors of the *Cruithin* came to Ireland in the post-Roman period, then we cannot be surprised at their absence from Ptolemy's map of Ireland around AD 150. [see 67] Yet we should not interpret every population missing from this map as arrivals in Ireland after AD 150. The Romans had no reason to survey Ireland in detail. As for the dynasties that rose from obscurity into power in the 7th century, why should we expect a clue to their existence before they were formed?

Under the hegemony of these new dynasties, the Uí Néill in the north and the Eóganacht of Munster, there was a language shift in Ireland. [85] When Christianity replaced druids with priests in Ireland, it also replaced Primitive Irish with Latin as the sacred language. The Latin alphabet was also used to create a new written form of Irish. [86] This was Old Irish, taught in the monastic schools alongside Latin. It sprang from everyday spoken Irish – the vernacular.[42] The Old Irish period gave birth to a new word for the Irish. That ethnonym was *Féni*. A clue to its origins lies in the Old Irish view that in the past 'there were three principal peoples in Ireland, namely *Féni*, *Ulaid*, and *Gaileóin*, that is *Laigin*'. Thus the rulers of Connacht and the Uí Néill dynasties were *Féni*, as opposed to the men of Ulster and Leinster.[43]

86 *The Kilnasaggart Stone in Co. Armagh marks the site of an early Christian cemetery. It has an inscription in Irish, which records that Ternohc, son of little Ciaran, dedicated the place to the Apostle Peter. Above the inscription is a Latin cross, and beneath is a cross within a circle. There are other crosses on other faces of the pillar. Since Ternohc died in 716, the stone can be dated to c. 700, which makes it the earliest datable Christian monument in Ireland.*

Perhaps it is just a coincidence that the earliest Irish grammar primer declares that the battle of Moira, Co. Down, in 637 was crucial in its own creation. This battle marked the beginning of the end of Ulaid power and the triumphal rise of the Uí Néill and their allies in Ulster. The primer poetically declares that the battle dashed the 'brain of oblivion' out of the head of its first author, who settled down to amass knowledge of poetry and other writings. The man in question was Cenn Fáelad mac Ailill (d. 679) of an Ulster dynasty, the Cenél nÉogain. He wrote his Irish primer in Derryloran, Co. Derry. This and his other writings in Gaelic helped to establish the earliest vernacular literature in Europe.[44]

Anglo-Saxons and Britons

> Then all the councillors, together with that proud tyrant
> [Vortigern], were so blinded, that, as a protection to their
> country, they sealed its doom by inviting in among them like
> wolves into the sheep-fold, the fierce and impious Saxons, a
> race hateful both to God and men, to repel the invasions of the
> northern nations. Nothing was ever so pernicious to our country,
> nothing was ever so unlucky.[45]

So Gildas rants at the folly that brought Saxons down upon the Britons. The choice of Saxon mercenaries to guard Britain does seem perverse. The *Gallic Chronicle* tells us that the Saxons laid waste the British provinces in 408.[46] The result of hiring warriors from the enemy could have been predicted by those who knew the history of Gaul (see p. 149). The mercenaries grew restive, complained that their remuneration was inadequate, broke their treaty and began a campaign of plunder, calling support from fellow Saxons.[47] Or so Gildas says, and it is a reasonable explanation of how the Saxons first gained a toe-hold in Britain. Bede, writing in the monastery of Jarrow in the 7th century, gives us a more detailed picture. The incoming Germani were Angles, Saxons and Jutes.[48] He was himself of Anglian descent, and gave preference to the Angles in the title of his history, *The Ecclesiastical History of the English People*, which probably did much to ensure that the name England (Angle-land) was adopted. People might be speaking a Romance language in England today, had these newcomers not burst upon the scene, bringing the dialects that developed into English. The most

Romanized population of Britain was in the rich lowlands, dotted with bustling towns. Latin was probably widely spoken in southern Britain by late Roman times. This was the very area that turned English. The good agricultural land of the south attracted Anglo-Saxon settlement. Towns were abandoned.[49]

What happened to the Latin-speakers? Some may have perished on Saxon swords. Some may have adopted the language of the incomers. Yet it is intriguing that the Celtic which survived in the British highland zone developed a Latin accent at around this time, as though a rush of Romance refugees had arrived.[50] That would fit the picture that Gildas painted of the 'miserable remnant' of the Romano-British making for the mountains, fleeing overseas or surrendering themselves to be slaves to their foes, as the only alternative to famine.[51]

By 441 the Saxons ruled 'the British provinces', according to the *Gallic Chronicle*.[52] Britannia had been divided into several provinces by Late Roman times. So had all former Romano-British territory fallen to the Saxons? It might have seemed that way to an observer across the Channel, but other sources show how complex the political map of Britain actually was in these changing times. Wales, the southwest and the *Yr Hen Ogledd* were ruled by British kings. *Yr Hen Ogledd* (The Old North) was the Welsh term for the region that is now southern Scotland and northern England where a language akin to Welsh was spoken.

Genetics: Britons and Anglo-Saxons

There have been several attempts to work out from the DNA of the living the influence of the Anglo-Saxons on the gene pool of England. Most recently the large People of the British Isles study suggested a substantial contribution to the English population spreading in from the east, putatively the Anglo-Saxons.[53]

No certainty is possible without directly comparing the DNA of people in Britain before the Anglo-Saxon advent and after it. This was the aim of a study that has generated the first ancient genome sequences from Britain. The study sampled five individuals from Hinxton, Cambridgeshire, eastern England. Two men lived just before the Roman period and three women lived in the middle of the Anglo-Saxon period. All five samples are broadly similar to modern northern European peoples. Yet there are enough differences between the Britons and Anglo-Saxons to distinguish them.[54]

87 *The kingdoms and principal places of southern Britain c. 600. British kingdoms remained in the west, but a huge swathe of what is now England had been taken by Angles and Saxons.*

When the Saxons began to advance into the southwest and further north from around 550, there had been time for generations of inter-marriage between Briton and Saxon in the borderlands between the two. [87] The early kings of the Hwicce in the Severn Valley had Germanic names, yet they were Christian and probably of the British Church.[55] Cerdic, founder of the royal line of Wessex, has a name that seems like a Germanization of the British name Caraticos.[56] The laws of Ine of Wessex (ruled 688–726) recognize the existence within his domain of Welsh (as the Saxons called the British), though according them a lower status.[57] Saxon settlement in the far southwest was so slow that Cornwall retained a Brittonic language for centuries afterwards (see below pp. 180, 187.) So the impact of the Anglo-Saxons varied by region.

Kingdoms of Wales

Just as the Romans can be seen as creating Scotland, so in a way the Anglo-Saxons created Wales. Before their arrival, what is now Wales was part of Britannia, united to the rest of the Roman province by culture and language. Once the Angles and Saxons had overrun much of lowland Britain, Wales emerged as a separate country. The Welsh names for Wales (*Cymru*) and its people (*Cymry*) were unknown in Roman times. The term *Cymry* (people of the same home region) first appears in a poem addressed to the king of Gwynedd about 632/4.[58] It was the Anglo-Saxons who christened them 'Welsh', from the Old English word *walh* or *wealh*, meaning 'foreign'. The great earthwork known as Offa's Dyke was designed by King Offa of Mercia (d. 796) to keep the Welsh at bay.[59] It has roughly marked the border between England and Wales ever since.

Medieval Wales was a patchwork of often contending kingdoms. [87] The continuity between the Romano-British Demetia and medieval Dyfed in southwest Wales has already been mentioned (pp. 165–67). It is a similar picture in southeast Wales, where the territory of the Silures became the medieval kingdom of Gwent. This was the most Romanized region of Wales. Imported Mediterranean pottery shows that trade with Constantinople (Byzantium) continued following the collapse of the Roman empire. The name Gwent derives from Venta Silurum, the capital of the *civitas* of the Silures. By contrast, the large medieval kingdom of Powys in east Wales was not a direct successor to a post-Roman polity. The relentless pressure of the encroaching Angles created its eastern border, as the Britons were pushed into the upper valleys.[60]

In north Wales Gwynedd had natural advantages. The flatland of the Isle of Anglesey (Ynys Môn) was ideal for arable farming. The island was protected by the sea and the soaring bastion of Snowdonia. In Roman times north-west Wales seems to have been at least part of the territory of the Ordovices ('hammer-fighters').[61] A 5th-century inscription at Penbryn in southwest Wales commemorates a man of the tribe, who died far from home.[88] So how did the name Gwynedd arise? A memorial stone found at Ffestiniog, from around 500, records the new name. It is inscribed in Latin: *CANTIORIX HIC IACIT. VENEDOTIS CIVES FUIT CONSOBRINOS MAGLI MAGISTRATI* ('Cantiorix lies here. He was a citizen of *Venedota* [Gwynedd], a cousin of Maglos the magistrate').[62] The use of Late Latin and the terminology of citizenship and magistracy is powerful evidence that a Romano-British polity had survived for a century in this corner of Wales. Four former district names in Gwynedd are derived from Roman personal names.[63]

Yet several scholars have favoured the idea that the name *Venedota* is derived from the Old Irish *Féni* (see p. 173). One argument is that the Féni of Connacht had broken through the barrier of the Laigin of Leinster to reach the Irish Sea *c.* 500 and so theoretically could have crossed that sea to north Wales.[64] It is an ingenious idea, but strained. The root word *weni-* is found in Brittonic and Gaulish, with the probable sense of 'family, kindred', preserved in the Breton word *gwenn*, meaning 'race'.[65] This is the type of word, signifying 'us' as opposed to 'them', that often becomes the basis of ethnonyms, as we have seen with *Cymry*. The Breton name of the present-day town of Vannes is Gwened [see 92], a parallel to Gwynedd. Vannes takes its name from the Veneti tribe of Armorica, whose territory became an early Christian diocese centred at Vannes.[66]

In the case of Gwynedd, the distinction of 'us' versus 'them' probably began as a way to *exclude* the Irish. There is evidence of Irish settlement in Gwynedd, though by the Laigin rather than the Féni. The name of the Llŷn Peninsula here is derived from the Laigin, and the same root appears in Porthdinllaen, a coastal village on the peninsula. The power base of the first dynasty of Gwynedd was Anglesey, not Llŷn. Gildas calls Maelgwyn, an early 6th-century king of Gwynedd, the 'dragon of the island'.[67] Maelgwyn's descendant Cadfan (d. *c.* 625) has a memorial stone at Llangadwaladr on Anglesey to the 'most wise and renowned of all kings'. [see 6] It is built into the fabric of the church, and was probably moved there when his grandson had the church built. Llangadwaladr means 'church of Cadwaladr'. It lies close to Aberffraw, known to be a royal site at a later date.[68]

Later kings of Gwynedd, of a second dynasty, had a tradition that Maelgwyn's great-great-grandfather, Cunedda, came south from Manaw Gododdin, on the Firth of Forth, and expelled the Irish from Wales.[69]

88 A Latin inscription at Penbryn, Ceredigion: CORBALENGI IACIT ORDOVS. ('Here lies Corbalengos the Ordovix.') His tribe was no doubt mentioned because he was buried outside its territory in north Wales.

That would explain why a 5th-century elegy on the death of the northern Cunedda son of Edern was preserved in Wales.[70] Modern historians tend to be dismissive.[71] Genealogies can be tampered with. One argument is that the head of the second dynasty of Gwynedd, Merfyn Frych (d. 844), may have been from the Isle of Man, and could have aimed to legitimize his foreign origin by selecting an immigrant as the founder of the first dynasty.[72] This reasoning seems positively tortuous. We may doubt that Cunedda himself came south, but knowledge of him did. The most probable source of that knowledge would be his descendants.

Britons abroad

The Roman *civitas* of the Dumnonii, with its capital at Isca (Exeter), became the kingdom of Dumnonia after Britain separated from the Roman empire. It remained British long after the Anglo-Saxons had taken over southeastern Britain. In about 540 Gildas ranted at its king, Constantine, 'the tyrant whelp of the filthy lioness of Dumnonia'.[73] The learned Aldhelm, abbot of Malmesbury, addressed a letter around 675 to King Geraint of Dumnonia pressing him to adopt Catholic (Roman) church practice.[74] This Geraint (or perhaps a son of the same name) was attacked by Ine of Wessex around 710.[75] By about 813 the inroads of the kings of Wessex had reduced Dumnonia to *Cerniw* (in Welsh) or *Kernow* (in Cornish). The name is derived from the Celtic root *corn*, meaning 'horn', referring to the southwestern peninsula of Britain. The Anglo-Saxons added their word *walh* for 'Britons' to create the present county name Cornwall.

Dumnonia had absorbed immigrants from Ireland earlier. This may have been the initial impetus for British migration to the province of Armorica in Gaul, followed by another wave as the Saxons of Wessex penetrated Dumnonia. [89] There was so strong a flow from Britain to Armorica that the latter gained the name Brittany. For the French, Brittany is Bretagne, while Britain is Grand Bretagne (Great Britain). Most of the incomers appear to have come from the southwest of Britain, for the early medieval kingdoms of Dumnonea and Kernev appeared in Brittany.[76]

Tangible evidence of British settlement are the many Breton churches named after their local founders, following the same practice as in Cornwall and Wales. Some of these Brittonic saints were venerated in both Cornwall and Brittany, such as Samson and Petroc, but the great majority were honoured in just a single church dedication. In the Middle Ages St Petroc was the most revered Cornish saint. The place-name Padstow (holy place of St Petroc) records his ministry there. Petroc appears to have died and been buried at Padstow, but his relics were moved to Bodmin. His cult spread to Brittany, as is manifest in the place-names formed with his name (Perec in Breton).[77]

89 *The migration of Britons to Armorica and Galicia in the Post-Roman period.*

6th-century Briton settlements

HIBERNIA

BRITANNIA

ARMORICA

GALLAECIA

0   200 km

0   200 miles

The *Life of St Samson of Dol* is the earliest written narrative from Brittany. It tells us that the saint was born in south Wales and dedicated to God while still an infant. As an adult he travelled through Cornwall to Brittany. A Samson was present at the Council of Paris in 562, who could be the St Samson who founded the monastery at Dol-de-Bretagne.[78] Mobility within the Brittonic-speaking region is the thread running through these lives.

A separate Brittonic settlement in the former Roman province of *Gallaecia* in Spain was known as Britonia. *Gallaecia* was larger than the present region of Galicia, encompassing Asturias and Leon (Spain) and northern Portugal. A British diocese there is first mentioned in 572, with its see probably at the monastery of Santa Maria de Bretoña near Mondoñedo. The parish churches belonging to this diocese extended from Mondoñedo north to the sea, and east across the River Eo into what is now Asturias, suggesting a substantial migration of Brittonic speakers.[79]

Christian Picts and Scots

We know and from the chronicles and books of the ancients we find that among other famous nations our own, the Scots, has been graced with widespread renown.... The Britons they first drove out, the Picts they utterly destroyed.

Thus the Declaration of Arbroath in 1320 boosted a claim to Scottish independence. It suited the Scottish nobility of the time to claim the utter destruction of the native Celtic tribes north of the Antonine Wall by the incoming Irish (*Scoti*). Such a genocide is highly unlikely, but the Picts were no longer an independent people after 900.[80] How had this come about? Until recently the explanation seemed simple: Gaels from Ireland had invaded Argyll. There are certainly some ogham inscriptions in Argyll. Yet there is no sudden cultural shift. Archaeologist Ewan Campbell suggested that the people west of the mountain spine of Scotland, isolated by geography from the linguistic changes elsewhere in Britain, had simply retained the ancient Gaelic language of the British Isles.[81] That idea founders on the fact that Scottish Gaelic is a descendant of Old Irish. Geography does seem crucial though. Kintyre reaches out to the northeast tip of Ireland. [90] Around it are islands, so transport by boat would be commonplace. Trade, marriages and alliances could weave an invisible web across the water.

In the 8th century Bede had heard that the Irish 'came from Ireland under their leader Reuda and won lands from the Picts either by friendly treaty or by the sword.... They are still called Dalreudini after this leader.'[82] 'Dalreudini' is recognizable as the Gaelic kingdom of Dál Riata or Dalriada, which emerged around 700 from the union of several kindreds. Though mainly in Scotland, Dál Riata during part of its existence encompassed a small part of northeast Ireland. As for 'their leader Reuda', it seems that two of these kindreds, those of Kintyre and Cowel, promoted the idea of their joint descent from a Domangart Réte who died around 507. A separate kingroup that held sway in Islay seems an offshoot of the Dál Fiatach, ruling dynasty of the Ulaid. By contrast, the dominant kindred on Skye begins with

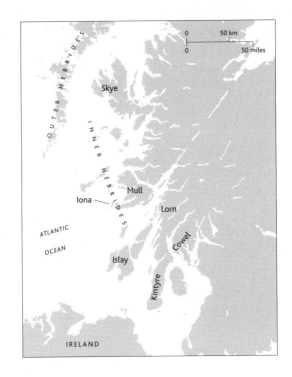

90 *The early medieval kingdom of Dál Riata was composed of territories on the west coast of Scotland and the Inner Hebrides that had earlier belonged to separate kindreds. Most of the territory of Dál Riata became the historic county of Argyll.*

Pictish names, yet spent three years in exile in Ireland in the 660s. Another three kindreds ruled Lorn. After all these regions were welded together as the Gaelic kingdom of Dál Riata, a genealogy was concocted descending all the kindreds from an Irish Eochaid.[83]

At the same time that Bede absorbed the approved history of Dál Riata, he was fed an origin story by the Picts that involved a cunning piece of propaganda. In this fiction, when the Picts settled in northern Britain they had no wives and asked the Irish for some. 'The latter consented to give them women only on condition that, in all cases of doubt, they should elect their kings from the female royal line.' Bede innocently reported that the custom had been observed among the Picts to his day.[84] The supposed matrilineal succession of the Picts was taken seriously until modern times, when historians realized that a contemporary of Bede was the Gaelo-Pictish Bridei, who had claimed a Pictish throne through his Pictish mother. The origin story conveniently legitimized this.[85]

Even more startling is the modern unpicking of the traditional view of Kenneth MacAlpin (d. 878), long heralded as the Scot who vanquished the Picts. Critical scrutiny of the sources reveals that he was in fact more probably Pictish himself, and was tagged on to the lineages of Dál Riata by later genealogists. He was the first to rule both Pictavia and Dál Riata. The crucial shift to a Gaelic-speaking court seems to have occurred in the time of his grandsons. They may have spent their youth sheltering with their aunt Máel Muire (d. 913), who married two high kings of Ireland in succession. It is in their time that the concept emerges of the kingdom of Alba, which encompassed both Picts and Scots.[86]

The closer one looks at this complex picture, the less it seems like one huge Irish army rushing up the beaches around 500, establishing a kingdom in Argyll that would eventually vanquish the native Picts. Gaelic could have been introduced to Scotland partly through a web of alliances, with threads of religion, politics and marriage. This would not rule out the actual movement of people from Ireland to Scotland. Far from it. It would just make the process more diffuse and drawn out. Among the Irish welcomed into the Gaelic enclave in western Britain was St Columba, who founded his famous abbey on the little Hebridean island of Iona in 563.[87] He is seen as the apostle of the Picts, completing the conversion to Christianity of all the peoples of the British Isles.

91 *The* Book of Kells *contains the four Gospels in Latin, written in a type of uncial script devised in Ireland. In addition to the ten full-page illuminations, the text is enlivened by many illuminated initials, such as this one from Matthew.*

Irish art came with Columba and the community he founded. The swirling La Tène style had continued to develop in Ireland after the Continental heartlands of La Tène and most of Britain were absorbed into the Roman sphere. As Ireland embraced Christianity, Irish art blossomed in such masterpieces as the famed *Book of Kells*, a gospel book created around 800 in a Columban monastery in Britain or Ireland. In addition to the well-known full-page illuminations, almost all the folios of the *Book of Kells* contain initial letters decorated with intertwining art with bird or animal features. [91]

Overview

- The Roman province of Britannia was Christian when it left the Roman empire in AD 410.

- Latin was the language of Christianity, yet it was not the first language of all the Romano-British. Celtic had survived there, as well as in those parts of the British Isles outside the Roman empire: Ireland and northern Britain.

- The Irish developed their own form of writing using ogham signs. Irish settlement in parts of Britain can be identified by ogham inscriptions.

- The Romano-British *civitas* of the Demetae became the medieval kingdom of Dyfed in southwest Wales. There is an ogham and Latin memorial there to Vortipor, identified by genealogies as one of an Irish royal dynasty of Dyfed.

- St Patrick was among thousands of Britons captured and enslaved by Irish raiders in the 5th century. St Patrick escaped and later returned to take Christianity to the pagan Irish.

- Genetic evidence supports the arrival of *Cruithin* (Britons) in northeastern Ireland in the post-Roman period.

- Tribal society in Ireland gradually dissolved in the centuries after AD 400. Dynastic kindreds emerged which dominated Ireland by the 7th century.

continued overpage

- Angles, Saxons and Jutes gained control of the southeast of Britain in the 5th century. Genetic evidence suggests that this involved mass movement. Celtic polities remained in the rest of Britain, but were reduced by later Anglo-Saxon expansions which penned Brittonic speakers into Wales and Cornwall.

- The concept of Wales as a separate country emerged from the process of Anglo-Saxon expansion. Poetry created in the Old North was preserved in Wales. That survival supports the tradition that the first royal dynasty of Gwynedd came south from Manaw Gododdin.

- The Roman *civitas* of the Dumnonii, with its capital at Isca (Exeter) became the kingdom of Dumnonia in southwest England. A stream of migration left Dumnonia for Armorica, which changed its name to Brittany. A second Brittonic settlement in northwestern Iberia was known as Britonia.

- The medieval claim that Scots from Ireland had utterly destroyed the native Picts is not supported by the evidence, including from genetics. Even the traditional concept of Irish invasion now appears simplistic. Irish movement to Scotland seems to have come about in complex ways.

- The Irish St Columba founded an abbey on the Hebridean island of Iona in 563. He is seen as the apostle of the Picts.

CHAPTER TEN

Loss and Revival

> Great nations, I mean such as have been famous, and made a
> considerable figure in the world, are almost like great rivers, that
> are never thoroughly known, unless you ascend to their very spring
> and original: it is with some measure of justice that the Celtae,
> a people better known by the name of Gauls, should be reputed
> great, either upon account of the number of their people, valiant
> actions, or the antiquity of descent.[1]

In Brittany, Ireland, Scotland and Wales live at least some people for whom a Celtic language is a mother-tongue, passed down a chain of ancestors from prehistory to the present. They grow fewer every day. English and French have almost swallowed up those Celtic languages that survived into the Middle Ages. In Continental Europe, Celtic languages were lost to Latin during the Roman empire. Romance languages derived from Latin had sprung up in Armorica and Galicia before the arrival of colonies of Britons there in the post-Roman period. Only in Armorica did the influx of Brittonic-speakers return the region to a Celtic language.

Cumbric, the Brittonic language of the Old North, vanished so long ago that few have even heard of it. It sank under the tide of English washing north and becoming tinted into Scots, the dialect of the Scottish Lowlands.[2] [see 94] In the 18th century Lowland Gaelic too gave way to Scots. Cornish died out in the 19th century.[3] The last native Manx speaker, Ned Maddrell, died on 27 December 1974, but the shift to English was already under way on Man when he was born in 1877.[4]

Of the living Celtic languages, Welsh is in the healthiest condition. Though UNESCO sees Welsh as vulnerable, Irish and Scottish Gaelic are classified as definitely endangered, and Breton as severely endangered. Almost two million people spoke Breton at the beginning of the 20th century. That number has now declined to around 250,000.[5] [92]

That Breton has survived into the 21st century at all is remarkable on several counts. Breton has never been an elite language. Latin was the language of the Church, and French that of the Breton nobility from as early as the 10th century. Breton was the speech of the illiterate majority. This left Breton almost without a written literature. Then in the white heat of revolutionary fervour, the Republic of France in 1794 sought to stamp out regional languages and dialects in favour of Standard French. Breton remains unrecognized today by national government as an official or regional language.[6]

By contrast Irish is the national language of the Republic of Ireland, yet the pattern of survival is similar. It is spoken as a community language only in a few rural areas mostly in the west of the country, collectively known as the Gaeltacht. [see 1] The measures taken for its support since Ireland's independence from Britain have not reversed its decline as a first language, though it is growing as a second language. Similarly in Scotland, Gaelic is found as a mother tongue furthest away from the main population centres. Its main stronghold is the Outer Hebrides, where over half the inhabitants speak it. [see 1]

92 *Percentage of Breton-speakers in each Breton county in 2004. Rennes and Nantes, the main towns of Brittany, lay outside the Breton sphere even in the 9th century, to judge from place-name evidence.*

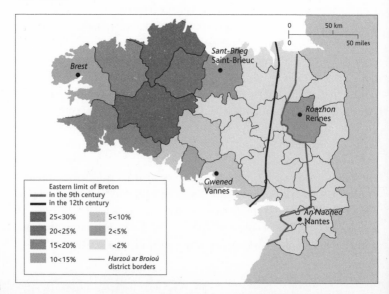

188

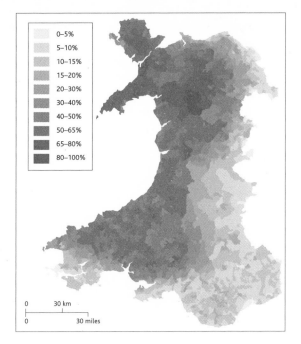

93 *The proportion of respondents in the 2011 census who said they could speak Welsh.*

0–5%
5–10%
10–15%
15–20%
20–30%
30–40%
40–50%
50–65%
65–80%
80–100%

0   30 km
0   30 miles

In Wales the decline in Welsh-speaking was inexorable over the course of the 20th century, from nearly one million speakers down to half that. [93] By 1991 there were none left speaking Welsh alone. Yet for the first time ever, the 2001 census showed that the percentage of people speaking Welsh had increased, thanks to the teaching of Welsh as a second language in schools. It is the decline in Welsh-speaking households that causes most concern.[7]

Immigrants and emigrants medieval to modern

Part of the reason for the decline of Celtic-speaking is that people do not always choose to live in the land of their parents. Populations have not remained static since the early medieval period. Indeed there has been far more moving to and from the remaining Celtic-speaking regions than can be encompassed by one short section of this book, but we must touch on some crucial trends.

Viking settlement left a legacy of Norse speech in Orkney and Shetland, which survived the transfer of these islands from the Danish crown to

Scotland in 1468. This language, known as Norn, had also been spoken in Caithness, the northeastern tip of mainland Scotland. Then Scots-speaking settlers took their language to Caithness and the Northern Isles [94]. In the islands it gradually overtook Norn. Pictish areas were first Gaelicized and then Anglicized by the creation of ethnically diverse burghs, with early Scots probably serving as a lingua franca and replacing other languages by about 1350.[8]

The Norman conquest of England added a great deal of French vocabulary to English, but left no other linguistic legacy. It was the language of the elite. However, the subsequent Anglo-Norman incursions into Wales and Ireland began a process of language shift to English. By the end of the Tudor period southern Pembrokeshire was known as 'Little England beyond Wales'. The linguistic frontier between English and Welsh in the county, known as the Landsker, has been remarkably stable ever since. It is also a cultural divide, revealed in place-names and church-types, which take us back to the period when Norman barons seized southern Pembrokeshire.[9]

It was from Pembrokeshire that an exiled Irish king set sail for home in 1167, triggering the Anglo-Norman invasion of Ireland. Gerald of Wales, a contemporary witness, blamed a fickle woman. It put him in mind of Helen of Troy. At the time Ireland was still divided into often embattled kingdoms. In 1152 Dermot MacMurrough, king of Leinster, abducted Derbforgaill, the wife of the king of Breifne. According to Gerald, she was nothing loath, having conceived a passion for Dermot. Modern historians see politics rather than romance in the episode. Either way, the king of Breifne held a grudge and in 1166 persuaded the high king of Ireland to banish Dermot MacMurrough. The deposed Dermot then made the classic error of seeking foreign aid to regain his throne. Henry II of England did no more than grant him permission to seek allies in Henry's domains, on condition of Dermot's oath of allegiance. It was Richard FitzGilbert, Earl of Pembroke, who actually pledged troops to Dermot, in return for Dermot's eldest daughter to wife and the succession to his kingdom. The result in the short term was victory for Dermot MacMurrough in 1170. He had little time to enjoy it; he died in May 1171. The consequences were profound. Henry II arrived in Ireland in October 1171, intent on ensuring that the gains of his vassals should come under his lordship.[10] It was the start of a long struggle over Ireland.

English settlers in Cornwall, Wales and Ireland inevitably reduced the percentage of people there speaking Celtic languages. Elizabeth I encouraged

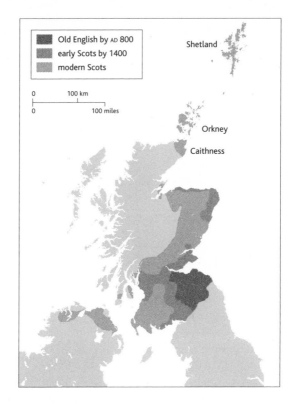

94 *History of Scots in Scotland and Ulster. Scots developed from the Old English spoken in Northumbria by Anglian settlers. It became so different from standard English that it has gained official status as a regional language.*

Old English by AD 800
early Scots by 1400
modern Scots

0   100 km
0   100 miles

Shetland

Orkney

Caithness

English settlement in Ireland. Her successor James I of England and VI of Scotland fostered the Plantation of Ulster by colonists from Britain. Most of these colonists came from the Scottish lowlands and brought with them their Scots language. [94] No less important was traffic out of Brittany, Ireland, Scotland and Wales, taking fluent Celtic-speakers away from their linguistic community. Over the centuries many Bretons moved into other parts of France, particularly the Paris area, in search of wider opportunities. Similarly there is a long history of immigration from Ireland, Scotland and Wales to England, with London attracting large numbers. The industrial cities of the Midlands were another draw after the Industrial Revolution. The European discovery of the Americas, Australia and New Zealand opened up vistas for the more adventurous. Only rarely did they form a Celtic-speaking colony, such as that of the Patagonian Welsh in South America and the enclaves of Scottish Gaelic in Canada. Both immigration and emigration resulted in many marriages across linguistic lines. Where one partner is English-speaking and the other bilingual, English is commonly the language of the home, and becomes the mother-tongue of any children reared in it.

The dominance of English

There is no doubt that over the centuries there have been deliberate attempts by government and other authorities to suppress the Celtic languages within the British Isles. The irony is that suppression was scarcely necessary, if the aim was an anglophone society. The seeds of its development were already in place.

The major factors in favour of language replacement are time and numbers. The longer two languages are in contact, the more time there is for the speakers of one or both groups to become bilingual. If one of the two groups is much larger than the other, the members of the smaller group are more likely to become bilingual, which is the most common route to the death of the minor language.[11]

English-speakers have long been in the overwhelming majority within Britain. The first census of Britain was taken in 1801. Even then, before the great industrial boom sucked workers from the Celtic fringe into expanding English cities, England was well ahead with over eight million people, while Scotland had one and a half million, and Wales only half a million. If the highlands of Britain had stunning mountain scenery, the lowlands had fields of wheat, which could feed more mouths. London dominated Britain's trade. It was also the seat of political power and hub of the judiciary. Knowledge of English was a prerequisite for participation in education, the professions and country-wide commerce. This is a typical pattern in which minority languages are lost.

This fundamental problem explains the limited success of modern revivals. Gaelic has been taught in the schools of the Republic of Ireland for decades. Yet few speak it at home. Ardent supporters of the revival of Cornish have made an effort to learn the language, but they have to communicate in English most of the time, since that is the majority language. [see 100] Indeed, English has become the lingua franca of international communications. Only determined efforts can prevent the loss of the living Celtic languages.

Rediscovering a forgotten family

One reaction to English dominance over the Celts of the British Isles was a defiant enthusiasm for all things Celtic. First there needed to be an understanding that Welsh, Gaelic and Cornish *are* Celtic languages. This began with the intellectual quickening of the Renaissance, with its revival of interest in Classical sources. Any scholar familiar with the works of Caesar and Tacitus could fit together the crucial facts: the names Celt and Gaul were synonymous, and the British spoke a similar language to Gaulish.[12] The finest scholars did more than simply absorb Classical knowledge though. They fell in love with logical deduction.

This blast of fresh air generated a healthy scepticism about the pseudo-histories hitherto accepted as genuine (see Chapter 1). The Scottish scholar George Buchanan (1506–1582) poured scorn on such fables. [95] If Caesar and Tacitus had failed to find out the origins of the British even after diligent enquiry, whence came this tale of Brutus as the founder of Britain?[13]

95 *The Scottish scholar George Buchanan at the age of 76, painted by Arnold Bronckorst in 1581.*

The English antiquary William Camden (1551–1623) gave an answer as good as any since. He set Brutus in the context of other stories of eponymous founders, such as Scota for the Scots and Danus for the Danes. These characters were invented to fill a gap in knowledge.[14]

Buchanan's history of the Scots was published in the year of his death, four years before the first edition of Camden's *Britannia*. So to Buchanan goes the credit for the first detailed work of scholarship to place the British Isles linguistically within the Celtic sphere. Using Classical sources which recorded the Late Iron Age expansions of the Gauls, he reasoned that they also spread into Britain. He not only recognized that place-names incorporating -*brig*- and -*dunum* were Celtic in origin, but argued for them being spread from Gaul.[15] It was the start of a still flourishing debate (see pp. 133–35). Buchanan's book was a glorious polemic. Camden described himself as 'a plain honest and diligent searcher after the truth'. He drew deep on Roman writers to demonstrate the similarities of culture, religion and language between Britannia and Gaul.[16]

Old ideas were not completely abandoned. Buchanan could not resist the strange tale of Pictish origin found in Bede (see p. 28). Camden drew on Genesis, just like medieval authors. So did the next scholar to come to our attention, which is scarcely surprising, given his vocation. Paul-Yves Pezron (1639–1706) was a Doctor in Divinity and Abbot of La Charmoy in France. Yet his scholarship was also marked by intensive use of Classical sources. His interest was in the origins of the Bretons.[17]

Archæologia Britannica,
GIVING SOME ACCOUNT
Additional to what has been hitherto Publish'd,
OF THE
LANGUAGES, HISTORIES and CUSTOMS
Of the Original Inhabitants
OF
GREAT BRITAIN:
From Collections and Observations in Travels through
Wales, Cornwal, Bas-Bretagne, Ireland and *Scotland.*

By EDWARD LHUYD M.A. of *Jesus College,*
Keeper of the ASHMOLEAN MUSEUM in OXFORD.

VOL. I.
GLOSSOGRAPHY.

O X F O R D,
Printed at the THEATER for the Author, MDCCVII.
And Sold by Mr. *Bateman* in *Pater-Noster-Row, London* : and *Jeremiah Pepyat* Bookseller at *Dublin.*

96 *The title-page of the first volume of Edward Lhuyd's* Archaeologia Britannica, *published in 1707.*

Welsh scholar Edward Lhuyd (1660–1709), at the time keeper of the Ashmolean Museum in Oxford, commissioned a translation into English of Pezron's book, which appeared in 1706.[18] Lhuyd was deeply interested in the relationship between the living languages of the Celtic group (not that he so labelled them). In the absence of published dictionaries for them all, he travelled through Cornwall, Scotland, Ireland and Brittany taking notes. In 1707 the first volume of his *Archaeologia Britannica* appeared. [96] It provided the first detailed account of the Insular Celtic languages, exploring their affinity with each other and with Gaulish. The concept of the Celtic language family was thus set on a solid footing.

A passion for Celtic

It was a concept with a considerable romantic appeal. Other countries might be richer in Greek and Roman antiquities, but these islands at the end of Europe had preserved linguistic treasures, remnants of a tongue elsewhere lost. British physician James Parsons (1705–1770) was born in Devon but educated in Dublin and Paris. His early years in Ireland had enabled him to learn Irish and he later learnt Welsh. His book *The Remains of Japhet* (1767) is based almost entirely on Genesis and pseudo-history. He deserves mention, though, for his fulminations against the English arrogance that could overlook the cultural achievements of their Celtic neighbours:

> It is too much the disposition of some among us to asperse,
> and set at nought, the natives of Ireland, Scotland and Wales....
> Both the Irish and the Welsh were ever well versed in the arts of
> music, poetry, government and war.... In music no nation was
> equal to Ireland.[19]

Others too were discovering what lay behind the language barrier. By 1757 the English poet Thomas Gray had penned an ode *The Bard*. He based it on 'a tradition current in Wales, that Edward the First, when he completed the conquest of that country, ordered all the bards, that fell into his hands, to be put to death'. It is a dramatic device to rage against the careless obliteration of so much lyrical eloquence by the encroaching English tongue. In the words of historian Eoin MacNeill, 'Its weird rhapsodical spirit contained the germ of the Celtic literary revival.'[20]

Travel to Wales and Scotland became popular among the English gentry from the latter half of the 18th century. Romantic scenery and ruined castles were eagerly sketched. Queen Victoria's love of her Highland hideaway at Balmoral, acquired in 1848, generated an even greater enthusiasm in England for all things Scottish.

In Victoria's reign there was also a revival of interest in Celtic art. It dovetailed with renewed appreciation of the exuberance of Gothic, despised in the previous century in favour of Neo-Classical purity. At the end of the 19th century, Art Nouveau rebelled altogether against the straitjacket of symmetry. There was a great attraction to undulating forms inspired by nature, harking back to Celtic art.[21] [97]

Happily, art knows no language barriers; so much in literature is lost in translation. Organizations sprang up to battle against the submergence of the Celtic languages. The Honourable Society of Cymmrodorion was officially founded in London in 1751 by Richard Morris and his brother Lewis, natives of Anglesey who had settled in London. It aimed to restore the literary heritage of the nation.[22] The Gwyneddigion Society was another London-based Welsh literary and cultural society, founded in 1770.

The Welsh tradition of *eisteddfodau*, festivals of poetry and music, in which bards and minstrels competed to win awards, was rescued almost from the

97 *Silver box designed by Archibald Knox in 1903/4 for Liberty & Co., in a series inspired by the Celtic crosses of his native Isle of Man.*

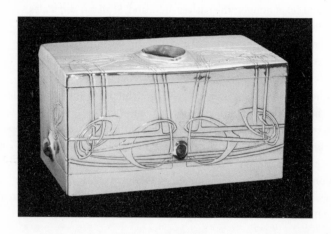

98 *The National Eisteddfod at Carnarvon Castle in 1862. An engraving from* The Illustrated London News.

brink of the grave. In medieval times, such grand events needed the patronage of princes. The bardic tradition petered out without the courts that had supported it. By the 18th century it had shrunk to a few devotees meeting in taverns. In 1789 one such devotee thought to petition the Gwyneddigion Society for patronage. A new era began. In September of that year an eisteddfod at Bala in Gwynedd paved the way for the modern institution. Even so, the first National Eisteddfod series in the 1860s [98] lost the will to promote the Welsh language, which was seen as having no utilitarian value. There could be no greater proof of the vulnerability of any language where money is minted in another tongue. However, Welsh became the official language of the National Eisteddfod in 1937.[23] The result was a more confidently Welsh institution. Today this annual festival embraces Welsh culture at its widest, including the visual and performing arts, and a science and technology pavilion. The message is clear. Welsh is a living language, not a fossil.

The Welsh National Eisteddfod became the inspiration for similar annual celebrations in Ireland, the Highlands of Scotland, Cornwall and the Isle of Man. A Pan-Celtic spirit is reflected in the Inter-Celtic Festival held

99 *Celtic dancers perform on 5 August 2007 in Lorient, Brittany, during the 37th Interceltic Music Festival of Lorient.*

at Lorient, Brittany, designed to foster contacts between the six modern 'Celtic nations' of Brittany, Cornwall, Ireland, the Isle of Man, Scotland and Wales. [99] 'Celtic nation' here means a people with a Celtic language that is either still spoken or was spoken into modern times.

In Ireland the *Feiseanna* and *Oireachtas*, respectively local and national festivals for the promotion of Gaelic language and culture, were consciously modelled on their Welsh predecessors.[24] They were licensed by the Gaelic League, founded in 1893 to preserve Irish language and culture. The new society was the brainchild of Eoin MacNeill (1867–1945), whom we have already met as an historian. He was also a revolutionary. His passion for the preservation of the Irish language and culture led him inexorably into Nationalist politics. He established the Irish Volunteers in 1913, a step towards the battle for independence. Though MacNeill personally opposed the idea of an armed rebellion, he was imprisoned for a year after the Easter Rising of 1916.[25] He went on to become a politician in the Irish Free State, created in 1922 as a dominion of the British Commonwealth. (Northern Ireland excluded itself.) This was followed by a fully independent Éire in 1937.

Political pressures

When Celtic pride pushed into politics, alarm bells began to sound. In the 20th century the power of nation states was threatened from above and below by pressures towards federalism and devolution. The determination on Irish independence from Britain was an example of the desire of a minority within a state to become a majority in its own state.

The counter urge towards federalism within Europe was driven partly by the desire to create a body large enough to compete economically with the massive power blocs of the US and USSR. More urgent though was the need to end the cycle of bloodshed that had taken Europe through two world wars. Closer co-operation between the countries of Europe held out hope of peace. On 18 April 1951 representatives of six nations signed the Treaty of Paris to create the European Coal and Steel Community. The founder nations were Belgium, France, Italy, Luxembourg, the Netherlands and West Germany. In 1957 the Treaty of Rome created the European Economic Community (EEC) for the same 'inner six' nations. Other European nations could see economic advantages in a common market. The 'outer seven' nations (Austria, Denmark, Norway, Portugal, Sweden, Switzerland and the United Kingdom) formed their own European Free Trade Association in 1960, but most were interested in links to the EEC. Denmark, Ireland and the United Kingdom joined the EEC on 1 January 1973. Fear of loss of sovereignty to Brussels has been a constant theme in British politics ever since.

At the same time the pressure for devolution was growing in Wales and Scotland. Plaid Cymru returned its first MP in 1966 and the Scottish National Party won its first seat at Westminster in 1967. Far more alarming, however, was the violence in Northern Ireland. The Provisional Irish Republican Army conducted an armed paramilitary campaign from 1969 until 1997, aimed at the forced birth of a united Ireland. Protestant paramilitary organizations fervently against a united Ireland contributed to the terror and lawlessness that blighted Ulster.

Against this background the *I Celti* exhibition held in the Palazzo Grassi in Venice in 1991 put a match to a powder keg of English anxiety. It was created by French and Italian learned societies, not a political body. Yet it was consciously designed to support the EEC with a vision of a pan-European culture in the deep past. The Berlin Wall fell as work began on the exhibition. So it was with hope of a reunited Europe that the exhibition opened.[26] Notably, the pan-European culture that the Palazzo Grassi proudly displayed was not the Roman empire, which imposed European unity by armed might. Federalism was not to be equated with empire. On view instead were the tribal Celts. Here was a society in which power was local, but trade was widespread.

In Spain under General Franco (dictator 1939–75) there was a strong urge to be seen as fully European, rather than a detached part of North Africa. (Spain's links to North Africa began with the Phoenicians, but were strongest in the centuries of Moorish control.) Celtic heritage was stressed, with its links to other parts of Europe. Ideologically this was bound up with an ultraconservative viewpoint.[27] The authoritarian Franco wanted to establish national homogeneity. He promoted the use of Castilian Spanish and suppressed other languages such as Catalan, Galician and Basque. He was emphatically a supporter of the nation state against devolution. The concept of the Celts, it seems, could serve a variety of political purposes, some of which could leave archaeologists distinctly uneasy.[28]

To state what will be obvious to the reader by now, the ancient Celts were never united in a federal system or any other. Their political organization when they emerged into history was tribal. Those who prepared the magnificent *I Celti* exhibition never pretended otherwise. The optimistic idea was to show that modern political boundaries may not be deeply rooted in the past. The real problem with using the Celts to carry that message was that they were just one of a number of peoples in Iron Age Europe. Millions of people in modern Europe do not identify themselves as descendants of Celts.

Celtoscepticism

The backlash can be seen in a rash of works in the 1990s, which not only (rightly) denied that the Celts had ever united Europe. They also argued that the word 'Celt' should not be used at all for any peoples of the British Isles.[29] A common theme was that only those peoples who had been firmly labelled as Celts by ancient authors should be so described. From the scholarly perspective, this was simplistic, betraying uncritical use of documentary sources and unfamiliarity with the fluidity of ethnonyms.

Identification labels are used to distinguish between 'them' and 'us', as we have seen. Different labels may be used as the focus shifts to a more inclusive 'us'. Today a person from the north of England could see himself as a Geordie, English, British or European, depending on the context. The concept 'European' requires an understanding that there are other continents on the planet. So Europeans in antiquity seldom identified themselves as European. Nonetheless in our modern eyes they were.

A familiar modern ethnonym for an ancient people may not have been used in antiquity at all (see the 'Italics' below), or may have arisen in the Roman period as a collective name for a group of tribes. The Germani had no collective name for themselves when they were first encountered by the Romans. They were a tribal people, for whom the important identification was the tribal name. When Tacitus enquired of Germani the origin of their name, he was informed that it just happened to be the name of the tribe who first crossed the Rhine and pushed into Gaul. While the tribe had since renamed themselves the Tungri, the name Germani had stuck in the minds of their enemies, and been recently adopted by the Germani themselves as the collective name for all their tribes.[30] By that time a collective name would have been useful to distinguish themselves from the non-Germanic-speaking peoples that they were encountering in their expansion.

The Celts of Britain and Ireland were likewise tribal. In day-to-day affairs, a person was identified by parentage and tribe, as we find on their memorials. Until Caesar paid his visit, the Celtic-speakers of Britain can very seldom have encountered anyone who did *not* speak a Celtic language. So there was no need for a collective name except in distinguishing themselves from those outside their particular island. The collective names were geographical (*Iwerni, Albiones, Pritani/Cruithin* etc). By contrast the Gauls had come in contact with Greeks long before, who labelled them *Keltoi* ('the tall ones').[31] Since Britain had waves of arrivals from Gaul before the Roman conquest, some notion of belonging to a Celtic-speaking 'us' versus 'non-Celts' may have penetrated Britain from Gaul, perhaps of interest to a few exceptionally well-travelled or learned individuals, but not in common use.

Greek and Roman writers were not reliable in their grasp of the origins even of peoples they knew well. 'Italic' was an obvious modern label for a language group spoken in Italy, but it was not used in antiquity. The Romans called themselves Roman and their language Latin. They were familiar with neighbouring peoples such as the Oscans and Umbrians, but without understanding their relationship to the Latins. Indeed one minor author, himself of Gaulish origin, claimed that the Umbrians were descended from the ancient Gauls.[32] It took modern scholarship to decipher inscriptions in the Umbrian language and classify it as related to Latin and Oscan.[33] Too much time had elapsed before the adoption of writing for any recollection of a common origin to be preserved by Roman authors.

So the modern discovery of the relationship between Celtic-speakers in the British Isles and on the Continent was part of a pattern. Linguistics was being used to shed light on prehistory and early history. In a similar way, archaeology in the modern era has enabled scholars to delve deeper than the written word. It has become an established principle that archaeologists should not be led or limited by documentary sources. We are no longer restricted to the works of ancient Greeks and Romans for our understanding of the European past.

No doubt many archaeologists accepted Celtoscepticism as appropriate scholarly caution, fitting the framework of an anti-migrationist mood that had dominated Anglophone archaeology for decades. In the post-Colonial era there was an understandable distaste for invasionist models in archaeology. It seemed preferable to think that ideas, styles, even languages, could move with minimal human agency. The questioning of invasionist assumptions served a useful purpose. Invasion is certainly not the only way that people have moved around. In recent years a fresh look at human mobility has begun to reveal its complexity. We have entered a new phase in the debate now that genetics can be used to test theories about population movement or the relationship between peoples.[34]

Back to the future

The most enlightening results have come from ancient DNA. What is emerging is a story that goes beyond Celtic roots to the origins of the entire Indo-European language family. Joining the dots of evidence, we can draw a line from a Siberian mammoth-hunting family (box p. 70) to many a modern-day speaker of Celtic (box pp. 26–27). It seems that the European gene pool was stirred vigorously in the Copper Age by migrants from the European steppe, long regarded as the most likely homeland of the Indo-European languages. Yet the answers generate more questions. That the Insular Celts were related to their Continental cousins seems clear enough, but scarcely satisfies the thirst for knowledge. Deductions about the details have been made in this book that require testing by ancient DNA. There is much more work to be done.

100 *In 2008 new signs welcoming people to Cornwall in both English and Cornish were erected on all ten entry roads and the Tamar Bridge (shown here). Cornish died out in the 19th century, but there is interest in its revival.*

Neither can the preservation of living Celtic languages be taken for granted, though there has been progress in this cause. Travel through Wales and you will see bilingual public signage everywhere. In Scotland that policy was first implemented in the Gaelic-speaking areas, but is gradually spreading. In Ireland road signs are bilingual, except in the Gaeltacht, where Irish alone is used. To stay alive languages need to be spoken and heard. Radio and television programmes in Welsh and Gaelic from the BBC and in Irish from RTÉ and TG4 have a crucial role therefore. Even more important has been the steady increase in the number of primary schools in Brittany, Wales and Ireland (including Northern Ireland), and the opening of one on the Isle of Man, offering education through the medium of a Celtic language. This immersion in the language produces confident and fluent speakers. Democracy in the 1990s delivered devolution within the UK in the form of the Welsh Assembly, Scottish Parliament and Northern Ireland Assembly, all of which have measures in place to support the Celtic languages. So we end on a note of hope that the story of the Celts is far from over. [100, 101]

It will be clear from this book that today's Celtic-speakers are not stuck in a time warp. The Celtic languages have such deep roots in the past that constant linguistic evolution and adaptation is as much a part of their story as their common origin. Material cultures too are always changing. Whether they generate new phases by colliding with another culture, or by sending shoots out into a new environment, or by inventing a better mousetrap, cultures do not stand still. They mutate almost like living things. Two identical cultural 'capsules' placed in two different locations will immediately start to accumulate different experiences. The modern Bretons, Cornish, Irish, Manx, Scots and Welsh cherish their own particular identities. Though they may acknowledge some commonality, each has its own history, partly reflected in their genes. For example a characteristic genetic cluster can be detected in the Cornish today which is distinct from those found in the modern Welsh.[35] In short the human past is a mixture of continuity and change. Today's Celt has a life very different

101 *A druidic ceremony at Névez, Finistère, Brittany, marking the springtime Beltaine festival, symbol of renewal and fecundity, celebrated each year on 1 May.*

from that of his or her ancestors 4,000 years ago. A singer then could be heard only as far as the voice can carry. Today a song can wing its way across the world.

Overview

- The percentage of fluent Celtic-speakers has declined in modern times. Causes include the weak position of a minority language where the majority language is required for educational, social and economic functions, immigration and emigration, and mixed-language households.

- Renaissance scholarship rediscovered the relationship between the Insular and Continental Celtic languages.

- In the 18th and 19th centuries there was a resurgence of interest in the Celtic languages, literature, art and music within the British Isles.

- Organizations were formed to support the Insular Celtic languages and culture. Some campaigners saw a need for political change.

- In the 20th century the power of nation states was threatened from above and below by pressures towards federalism and devolution.

- Celtoscepticism was one reaction. Anglophone archaeologists argued that the word Celtic should not be used about Insular Celts.

- Genetics has entered the debate. DNA from human remains can track the movement of people. It is beginning to answer some of the burning questions about the Celts, but more work is needed to fill in the details.

- Measures are in place to support the surviving Celtic languages.

Surnames and DNA

Y-DNA is handed down from father to son, as have surnames generally been, so can links be found between the two? This has proved a fruitful area of research. It is not always practicable though. Certain British and Irish surnames, such as Brown, Davies, Evans, Jones, Kelly, Murphy, Roberts, Smith, Taylor, Thomas, Walker, Williams and Wilson, are so common that there will be hundreds if not thousands of unrelated lineages with the same name.

This is not surprising when we consider the origins of surnames. Names such as Smith and Taylor are occupational, and there were many men with the same occupation who were not closely related. Jones (son of John) is the most common name in Wales and found so widely in England too that just over 1 per cent of British people are so named.[1] Murphy (descendant of Murchadha) is the commonest surname in Ireland and has been carried into England and Scotland by Irish immigration. Another common Irish name is Kelly (descendant of Ceallaigh).[2] Murphy and Kelly are found in 1.2 per cent of the Irish population each, and genetically men of these surnames have numerous patrilineal lineages, none of which overwhelmingly predominates. That is what we would expect, since the surnames derive from personal names which were common in the past.[3] Rarer surnames might still have more than one origin, but strong clusters can emerge from DNA testing that help to distinguish between the possible origins (see box p. 208).

Origins of surnames

At the time of the Norman conquest of England in 1066, surnames in the modern sense were unknown. A person was simply identified by a personal name, bestowed at the font. Now and then it might be necessary to distinguish one person from others of the same name. This was done by a descriptive addition, known as a by-name, referring to some striking personal quality (Robert le Gros), or occupation (Alfred the Steward), or father's name (Roger FitzRalph), or place of origin (John the Dane), or place of residence (Alstan of Boscombe). There was no consistency in this and for centuries afterwards the same person might appear in different records with a different appellation. Only very gradually did hereditary surnames develop from such descriptors. The knightly class began to adopt dynastic names in the 12th century. Surnames had filtered down to most English families by 1400, though their form was still evolving.[4]

In Wales most people only began to adopt hereditary surnames under the Tudors and even in the 19th century some men were still taking their father's Christian name as their surname. In the Scottish Highlands that custom was abandoned in the 18th century, but the clan system resulted in large numbers of people with the same surname. Chiefs of clans increased the number of their followers by attaching men of other descents, who took the clan name.[5] In both cases we can expect many unrelated lineages with the same surnames.

Some Irish surnames can be traced back further than any others in the British Isles, with a few appearing in the early 10th century AD, though most were created during the 11th and 12th centuries. Previously, standard Gaelic naming was predominantly genealogical. A man would be identified as *mac* (son of), or *ua* (grandson or descendant of), which became simplified to Ó. For example O'Brien meant grandson/descendant of Brian. Surnames in the form O'Brien could easily be passed down to the next generation, becoming inherited surnames. In time the Mac forms were also handed down, both in Ireland and Scotland.

Descendants of Brian Boru

The most famous Brian in Irish history was Brian Boru, High King of Ireland. As I write, the millennial celebration is under way of his victory at the Battle of Clontarf on 23 April 1014, often inaccurately portrayed as the decisive defeat of the Vikings by the Gaels. In reality the battle was a dynastic struggle in which Irish and Vikings were allied. Brian Boru was supported by the Limerick Vikings against the Norse of Dublin and the men of Leinster. Brian Boru came of a minor *déisi* lineage in Munster who lived around the head of the Shannon estuary. They were in the line of devastation as Viking longships snaked up the Shannon in 836. At the time, Brian's ancestors were known as the Déis Tuaiscirt. Later they took the name Dál Cais.[6] [see 85] This lineage rocketed to power in two generations. Brian's father Cennétig

Genetics: Irvine surname

A surname dictionary may give several possible origins for surnames such as Erwin, Irwin or Irvine. In fact one well-researched dictionary warns against confusion between Erwin (which can also appear as Everwin, Irwin, Irwine, Irwing and Urwin) and Irvin (with its variants Irvine, Irving, Ervin, Erving and Urvine). The first is derived from an Old English personal name Eoforwine ('boar-friend') as shown by its appearance in England in 1185 in the form 'William son of Irwine'. The second group of names derives from the place-name Irvine in Ayrshire. It is first recorded in Scotland in 1226 in the form 'Robert of Hirewyn'.[7]

The Clan Irwin Surname DNA Study has succeeded in identifying 30 separate genetic families for men of these two clusters of surnames. The largest by far is a group with origins in the Scottish Borders, who carry the rare Y-DNA haplogroup R1b1a2a1a2c1j1 (L555/S393).[8] [102]

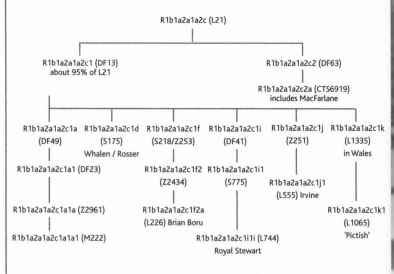

102 *A selective phylotree of Y-DNA haplogroup L21, showing those haplogroups mentioned in the text.*

mac Lorcán (Kennedy son of Lorcan) was described on his death in 951 as the king of Tuadmumu (north Munster),[9] later anglicized as Thomond. Two of his sons managed to unseat an Eóghanacht king to become king of Munster. Brian was the second of these, and went on to take the throne

Genetics: descendants of Brian Boru

The current Baron Inchiquin is Sir Conor Myles John O'Brien, whose Y-DNA has been tested. His haplogroup was revealed to be R1b1a2a1a2c1f2a (L226/S168) [see 102], which confirmed previous deduction that this rare marker was linked to Dál Cais kindred.[10]

of Tara from the Uí Neill. Sadly his triumph at Clontarf was a disaster for his family. Brian and many of his relatives were killed.[11] Descendants of Brian Boru continued to hold the kingdom of Thomond, with some interruptions, until in 1543 Murchadh Ó Briain (Murrough O'Brien) was created Baron Inchiquin and Earl of Thomond by Henry VIII of England, in return for abandoning his native title.[12]

Royal Stewart line

The movements between different parts of the British Isles over the centuries have been so complex that the lines of descent of any one family could zigzag across the Isles like a cat's-cradle. Brittany must be included in that weave. The army that William the Conqueror brought to Britain included Bretons. Most probably some were returning to the land of their ancestors. One particular Breton line was to rise to the Crowns of both Scotland and England. David I of Scotland was exiled in England for some years before taking the throne of Scotland in 1124. He spent time at the court of Henry I (1100–1135). There he was influenced by Norman culture and gained Norman and Breton allies.[13] Walter Fitzalan (d. 1177) entered David's service and rose to become Steward of Scotland, which became an hereditary office. Walter was the third son of a Breton knight, Alan fitz Flaad, lord of Oswestry, descended from the hereditary stewards of Dol in Brittany. Walter was granted the district which later became Renfrewshire and extensive other lands in Scotland, where he and his descendants settled knights and other men recruited from the Welsh border country. Walter's descendants eventually acquired the surname Stewart from their office. Walter, 6th High Steward of Scotland, married Marjorie Bruce, daughter of Robert I of Scotland. On the death without heirs in 1371 of Marjorie's brother, David II, his nephew Robert Stewart took the throne of Scotland.[14]

The House of Stewart ended with Mary, Queen of Scots, but since she married her cousin Henry Stewart or Stuart, Lord Darnley (descendant of Alexander, 4th High Steward of Scotland), their son continued the line, and brought it to England, as James VI of Scotland and I of England. One of his descendants in the male line is the present Duke of Buccleuch. The title was created on 20 April 1663 for James, Duke of Monmouth, the illegitimate son of Charles II, on his marriage to Anne Scott, sister and heiress of the 2nd Earl of Buccleuch.[15]

Other descendants of Alexander, 4th High Steward of Scotland, survive, which has made it possible to cross-check the royal Stewart DNA (see box below). They include members of the Appin Stewart branch, descended from a grandson of Alexander.

James II of England and VII of Scotland was deposed in 1688 after a son was born to his Catholic queen. Parliament feared the return of Catholicism. In this they reflected the views of the majority in England, Wales and the strongly Presbyterian Scotland. James had two Protestant daughters, Mary and Anne, who reigned in turn after him, followed by the Protestant descendants of James I of England and VI of Scotland. The deposed king found some of his strongest support in the Scottish highlands among his own kin. The Stewarts of Appin loyally supported his cause. They were involved in the Jacobite risings claiming the throne for the former king's son James Francis ('The Old Pretender') and grandson Charles Edward ('The Young Pretender' or 'Bonny Prince Charlie'). Charles Stewart of Ardsheal, head of a cadet branch of Appin, led the Appin Regiment at the Battle of Culloden in 1746. It ended in a rout for the Young Pretender which effectively finished the Jacobite cause. The Appin Regiment suffered massive losses and Charles Stewart of Ardsheal had to flee the country to escape execution. A descendant of his is now clan chief of the Appin Stewarts.

Genetics: Royal Stewart

In 2012 the DNA of the 10th Duke of Buccleuch was tested. His Y-DNA haplogroup was found to be an exact match to that of a descendant of Charles Stewart of Ardsheal. The haplogroup is R1b1a2a1a2c1i1a (L744/S388).[16] It fits on the end of a chain downwards from the widespread British and Breton marker R-L21. [see 102]

Genetics: MacFarlane

The great majority of men who carry R1b-L21 fall into the subclade defined by the marker DF13. The brother marker DF63 is found much more rarely. Within the latter branch is a subclade defined by CTS6919. [102] A number of MacFarlane and MacFarland men carry this haplogroup, some of whom have a documented lineage from the Arrochar line.[17]

Clan MacFarlane

The region around lovely Loch Lomond is now Dunbartonshire. It was once the district of Lennox. The old Scottish title Mormaer of Lennox was held by a family with origins before the era of surname development. Their personal names were Gaelic, apart from that of the 1st and 2nd Earls of Lennox, both named Alwyn. This obviously Germanic name has caused confusion. Scholars battled over whether Alwyn I was a Celt or an Anglo-Saxon. It seems he was both. Paternally Alwyn I was a son of Murdac, Mormaer of Lennox. Maternally he was a grandson of an Alwyn, most likely Alwyn MacArkyl, who was prominent at the court of King David I (1124–1153). A poem probably written to celebrate his coming of age describes him as Alwyn the younger, which could cause further confusion, since he became Alwyn the elder after his son Alwyn was born. In the poem he is being distinguished from his maternal grandfather.[18]

In the 13th century Gilchrist, a younger son of Alwyn II, was granted the feudal barony of Arrochar between Loch Long and Loch Lomond by his eldest brother, the 3rd Earl of Lennox. Gilchrist became the ancestor of Clan MacFarlane. The surname derives from Gilchrist's great-grandson Phàrlan, 4th Baron of Arrochar. His son was Malcolm Mac Phàrlan. MacPhàrlan, later spelled MacFarlane, then became an hereditary surname. Since Phàrlan was an uncommon personal name, there is less likelihood of unrelated MacFarlanes than is the case with names such as Donald and Gregor.

In the 16th century, the MacFarlanes were caught up in the drama of the royal succession. Protestants and Catholics battled over the choice of marriage partner for the infant Mary, Queen of Scots. Duncan MacFarlane of Arrochar supported the Earl of Lennox against the Catholic party in the Battle of Glasgow Muir in 1544. He was a staunch supporter of the

Reformation. However, when the Protestant Henry VIII sought to gain by force the marriage of Mary to his infant son in 1547, Duncan fought and died for Scotland at the Battle of Pinkie Cleugh.

His descendant William MacFarlane sold Arrochar in 1784. Other MacFarlanes had earlier settled in Ulster, and moved from there to the US, while another branch chose to make their home in Co. Dublin.[19] This scattered clan provides a test case for the usefulness of DNA testing (see box on p. 211.)

Notes

Prologue

1. Tacitus, *Germania*, 4.
2. Tacitus, *Agricola*, 11.
3. MacNeill 1920, 1–3.

Chapter 1: The Voices of the Celts

1. *Fled Bricrend* 27–29.
2. Koch and Carey 2003, 324.
3. Ptolemy, II.2; Rivet and Smith 1979, 508–09; Koch 2006, 824.
4. Driscoll and Yeoman 1997, 220–26.
5. Koch and Carey 2003, 326.
6. Rendered in Welsh as Golistan.
7. Koch and Carey 2003, 323.
8. Lapidge, Blair, Keynes and Scragg 1999, 163, 503.
9. Fraser 2009, 131.
10. Koch and Carey 2003, 322, stanza B2.26.
11. Koch and Carey 2003, 53.
12. Koch 2006, 997–98.
13. Meyer 1911, 99, from St Gall MS 904.
14. Skene 1868, I, 523
15. Caesar, VI.13–14.
16. *The Light Fantastic* (1986).
17. Geoffrey of Monmouth, VIII. 10–12.
18. Koch and Carey 2003, 59.
19. Koch and Carey 2003, 59–63, 108, 110–13.
20. Koch 2006, 352–53.
21. Bieler 1979, Muirchú, Life of Saint Patrick.
22. Carney 2005, 451, 454.
23. Adamnan.
24. Clancy and Márkus 1995, 104–15.
25. *Lives of Saints Declan and Mochuda*, 93.
26. Adamnan, chapter 35.
27. *Táin Bó Cúailnge*.
28. *Annals of Tigernach*, 404, 407.
29. Mac Carron and Kenna 2012.
30. Walsh 1993.
31. Lynn 1989.
32. Hurl, McSparren and Moore 2002.
33. Koch 2006, 261–64.
34. Ó hUiginn 2006.
35. Jackson 1964.
36. Mallory 1992.
37. Koch and Carey 2003, 158.
38. Ó Corráin 2006.
39. Baillie 1995, 65–67.
40. Warner 1990.
41. Mallory 1993.
42. Gildas, II.4.
43. *Historia Brittonum*.
44. Ó Cróinín 2005, 182.
45. Crick 2004.
46. Geoffrey of Monmouth, dedication.
47. *Historia Regum Britanniae*, ed. Wright, xvi.
48. William of Newburgh, 29–37; Gerald of Wales, *The Journey Through Wales*, 1.5.
49. *Historia Regum Britanniae*, ed. Wright, xviii.
50. Thorpe 1966, 50. The manuscript is BL Harleian MS 3859, ff. 174v–198r.
51. Rivet and Smith 1979, 396–98, 443–44.
52. Isidore, IX.ii.102.
53. Summerfield 2011.
54. Genesis 6–10.
55. Ross 1981.
56. Flavius Josephus, I.6.
57. Reynolds 1983.
58. Ross 1981, 23.
59. *Lebor Gabála Érenn*, I.10–11.
60. Ross 1981.
61. Isidore, IX.ii.26.
62. Koch 2006, 775.
63. Flavius Josephus, I.6.
64. Novembre 2008; Tian 2008; Tian 2009; O'Dushlaine 2010.
65. Schiffels 2014; Felix Jeyareuben Chandrakumar for the Y-DNA haplogroup allocation from raw data accompanying Schiffels.
66. Bede, chapter 1.
67. *Historia Brittonum* III, 13, 15; Carey 1994.
68. Ó Cróinín 2005, 185–86; Carey 1994; Koch 2006, 739
69. *Lebor Gabála Érenn*, vol. 2 (Irish Texts Society 35), 252.

Chapter 2: The Gauls and Celtic

1. Koch and Carey 2003, 12–13: translation by Philip Freeman of Diodorus Siculus, *Library of History*, 5.28–30.
2. Koch and Carey 2003, 8–9, translation of Polybius, *History*, 2.28.3–10.
3. Caesar, I.1; and see Pausanias, 1.4.1.
4. Sims-Williams 2006, 180–82.
5. Stephani Byzantini, 539, 581. For a translation see Koch and Carey 2003, no. 3.
6. Herodotus, II.33, IV, 49.
7. Aristotle, *Meteorology*, I.13.350.
8. Smith 1854, I, 106.
9. Herodotus, IV, 49.
10. Cunliffe 1997, 28–31.
11. Koch (ed.) 2006, 887.
12. Hummler 2007; Cunliffe 1997, 31.
13. Livy, V.34–35.
14. Cunliffe 1997, 32; Frey 1995, 520.
15. Koch 2006, 832–33.
16. Ritchie 1995.
17. Koch 2007, §83.
18. Moore and Chiriotti 2010.
19. Ó hUiginn 2006.
20. Caesar, V.15–19.
21. Tacitus, *Annals*, 14.35, trans. J. T. Koch and J. Carey in Koch and Carey 2003, 43.
22. Koch and Carey 2003, 322, stanza B2.37.
23. Adamnan, VII.
24. Greene 1972; Mallory 1998.
25. Nutt 1900.
26. Koch and Carey 2003, 90, 139–43. MacKillop 2004, under Liath Macha.
27. Homer, *Iliad*, XVI.
28. Walters Art Museum, Maryland.
29. Isidore, XVIII.xxxvi.
30. de Leeuw 2008.
31. Greene 1972; Mallory 1998; Karl 2003; Karl 2006.
32. Berggren and Jones 2000.
33. Talbert 2000, 118, 155; Rivet and Smith 1979, 437–38.
34. Lejars 2003.
35. Koch and Carey 2003, 13–14: translation by Philip Freeman of Diodorus Siculus, *Library of History*, 5.31.
36. Morley 2008.
37. Jay 2013.
38. Jay 2012.
39. Jay 2012.
40. Boyle 2008.
41. Carter and Hunter 2003; Carter 2010.
42. Polybius II, 29.

43. Caesar, VII.81.
44. Information from National Museums Scotland, where both the original and the replica are displayed.
45. Gilbert, Brasseur, Dalmont and Maniquet 2012.
46. Ptolemy, II.6.
47. Gilbert, Brasseur, Dalmont and Maniquet 2012.
48. Caesar, VI.17.
49. Gilbert, Brasseur, Dalmont and Maniquet 2012.
50. Caesar, V.12.
51. Koch 2007, 19; Mallory 2013, 163.
52. Herodotus, I.163; IV.152; Roller 2006, 34–36.
53. Aubet 2001, 33–34, 162, 259–62; Mata 2001; Aubet 2008; Deamos 2009.
54. Freeman 2010, 312.
55. Herodotus, I.163. I use the Greek version of his name here.
56. Mallory and Adams 2006, 242.
57. Prósper 2010/2011, 58 and fn. 5.
58. Herodotus, I.163–65 and note.
59. Manco 2015, 26–27: table 1.
60. Scozzari 2012. The mutation V20 defined C7 at that point, which was renamed C6 and then C1a2 in 2014.
61. Koch 2010 and 2011.
62. Valério 2014.
63. Roller 2006, 9–11, 74–77; Koch 2006, 1270.
64. Avienus, trans. Murphy, lines 90–100 and p. 86. Strabo, I. 4.5 and IV, 4.1 records the names used by Pytheas.
65. Freeman 2001, Kindle locations 706–11.
66. Koch 2006, 38–39, 709; Rivet and Smith 1979, 40.
67. Rivet and Smith 1979, 247–48; Koch 2006, 38–39.
68. Hubert 1934, 186; Dillon and Chadwick 1967, 4; Corcoran 1970, 24; Anthony 2007, 367; Cunliffe 2010, 34.

Chapter 3: Bell Beakers and Language

1. Childe 1930, 4–5.
2. Hubert 1934, 186; Dillon and Chadwick 1967, 4; Corcoran 1970, 24; Anthony 2007, 367; Cunliffe 2010, 34.
3. Manco 2015, chapter 10.
4. Sherratt 1987.
5. Childe 1958, 223.
6. Dietrich 2012.
7. Dineley 2004.
8. Rojo-Guerra 2006.
9. Guerra-Doce 2006.
10. Czebreszuk and Szmyt 2003.
11. Shepherd 2012.
12. Sarauw 2007 and 2008.
13. Østmo 2012; Prescott 2012.
14. Identification by Roger Taylor, Royal Albert Memorial Museum & Art Gallery, Exeter.
15. Parker Pearson 1995.
16. Querré and Convertini 1998.
17. Salanova 2011.
18. Vander Linden 2007.
19. O'Brien 2004.
20. Northover, O'Brien and Stos 2001.
21. Warner, Moles and Chapman 2010.
22. Pare 2000.
23. Senna-Martinez 2011.
24. Sofia Martinez, O Primeiro Alquimista: A Idade do Bronze em Portugal (2012).
25. Carlin and Brück 2012.
26. Jeunesse 2014.
27. Turek 2006; Fitzpatrick 2013; Peška 2013; Vergnaud 2013.
28. Peška 2013; Prieto-Martínez 2012.
29. Fitzpatrick 2009; Fitzpatrick 2013, 50–53; Darvill 2006, 151.
30. Maryon 1936; Taylor 1980, 22; Independent 5 August 2014.
31. Nocete 2014.
32. Chapman 2006; Warner, Moles and Chapman 2010.
33. Taylor 1994.
34. Armbruster 2013.
35. Heath 2012, 10–12, 39.
36. Fitzpatrick 2013, 53.
37. Jay, Parker Pearson 2012.
38. Price, Knipper, Grupe and Smrcka, 2004.
39. Menk 1979; Cox and Mays 2000, 281–83; Nicolis 2001, 2, 403; Budziszewski, Haduch and Włodarczak 2003.
40. Lee 2012.
41. 1000 Genomes Project Consortium 2010; Myres 2011; Wei 2013; Sikora, Colonna, Xue and Tyler-Smith 2013.
42. Sims-Williams 2006, 17.
43. Talbert 2000, 18.
44. Ptolemy, II.2; Koch 2007, maps 15.2 and 21.2.
45. Rivet and Smith 1979, 129.
46. Fraser 2009, 20.
47. Sims-Williams 2006, 179.
48. Koch and Carey 2003, 8.
49. Fortson 2010, 276–77.
50. Watkins 1966.
51. Kortlandt 1981.
52. Cowgill 1970; Ringe, Warnow and Taylor 2002; Nakhleh, Ringe and Warnow 2005; Schrijver 2006; Hamp and Adams 2013.
53. Manco 2015, 166–67, revised.
54. De Alarcão 2001.
55. Krahe 1963.
56. Mees 2003.
57. Villar 2000, 2004.
58. Kitson 1996.

Chapter 4: The Indo-European Family

1. Jones, Works, III, 34. Spellings modernized by the present author.
2. ODNB; Canon and Franklin 2004.
3. Muller 1986; Canon and Franklin 2004; Mallory and Adams 2006, 4–6.
4. Mallory 1989, 143.
5. Renfrew 1987.
6. Diamond and Bellwood 2003.
7. Mallory and Adams 2006, 101–03, 166, 241, 260–62.
8. Gray and Atkinson 2003; Bouckaert 2012.
9. Anthony 2013; Anthony and Ringe 2015; Pereltsvaig and Lewis 2015.
10. Chang, Cathcart, Hall and Garrett 2015.
11. Bryce 2005, 11–12, 21–39.
12. Watkins 2001; Goedegebuure 2008; Josephson 2012.
13. Mallory 1989; Anthony 2007; Anthony and Ringe 2015.
14. Anthony 2007, 72–75; Anthony and Ringe 2015.
15. Carpelan, Parpola and Koskikalio 2001.
16. Huehnergard 2011; Militarev 2005.
17. Nichols 1997, 125–28; Mallory and Adams 2006, 82–83.
18. Anthony 2007, 287–97.
19. Anthony 2007, 94–95; Häkkinen 2012.
20. Vasil'ev 1999.
21. Inizan 2012.
22. Clark 1982.
23. Inizan 2012.

24. Hartz, Terberger and Zhilin 2010.
25. Stupak 2006; Smyntyna 2007.
26. Altinbilek, Astruc, Binder and Pelegrin 2012.
27. Raghavan 2014.
28. Gatsov and Nedelcheva 2011.
29. Manco 2015, 96–98; Anthony 2007, 171 fig. 9.3.
30. Anthony 2007, 148–49.
31. Anthony 2007, chapters 8–9.
32. Nikitin 2012.
33. Mallory and Adams 2006.
34. Anthony 2007, chapter 13.
35. Anthony and Chi 2009.
36. Haas 1998; O'Brien 1995.
37. Manco 2015, 113.
38. Lazaridis 2014.
39. Haak 2015.
40. Nikitin 2012; Wilde 2014.
41. Haak 2015.
42. Lazarovici 2010; Anthony 2007, 164–74.
43. Sherratt 1981; Bogucki 1993; Greenfield 2010; Marciniak 2011.
44. Manzura 2005a, 327.
45. Parpola 2008.
46. Kohl 2007, 45–46; Korvin-Piotrovskiy 2012.
47. Kirtcho 2009.
48. Outram 2009; Anthony 2007, chapter 10.
49. Anthony 2007, 287–93; Chernykh 2008.
50. Morgunova and Khokhlova 2013.
51. Anthony 2007, chapter 13.
52. Anthony 2007, 328–39.
53. Harrison and Heyd 2007, chapter 9; Kristiansen 2005.
54. Homer, Iliad, 17.51–52.
55. Harrison and Heyd 2007, chapter 9; Kristiansen 2005.
56. Anthony 2007, 43–48, 75, 249–59, 260–62, fig. 13.11; Anthony 2013.
57. Thissen 1993; Bauer 2006.
58. Kremenetski, Chichagova and Shishlina 1999; Kremenetski 2003.
59. Anthony 2007, 64–65, 307–11; Anthony 2013.
60. Mallory and Mair 2000.
61. Anthony 2007, chapter 14; Anthony 2008; Wlodarczak 2009; Manco 2015, 131–32.
62. Haak 2015.
63. Kroonen 2012.
64. Anthony 2007, 361–67; Heyd 2011.

65. Martirosyan 2013; Mallory and Adams 1997, 26–30.
66. Sherratt 1986.
67. Manzura 2005b; Sherratt 1986; Andreu 2010, 646; Koukouli-Chrysanthaki and Papadopoulos 2009.
68. Anthony 2007, 343–48.
69. Anthony 2007, 371–82, 389–411, 452–57.
70. Kuzmina 2007, 379–413.
71. Keyser 2009.

Chapter 5: Stelae to Bell Beaker
1. Tertullian, 57, citing Nicander of Colophon, a Greek author of the 2nd century BC.
2. Labaune 2013, 181, fig. 3.
3. Robb 2009.
4. Harrison and Heyd 2007.
5. Mallory 1989, 203–05; Telegin and Mallory 1994; Mallory and Adams 1997, 544–46; Anthony 2007, 268–71, 291, 320–21, 338–39, fig 13.11.
6. Mallory 1989, 203–05; Telegin and Mallory 1994, 23.
7. Schloen and Fink 2009; Pardee 2009; Struble and Herrmann 2009.
8. Telegin and Mallory 1994.
9. Zavaroni 2009.
10. Heyd 2011, 541.
11. Gogâltan 2013.
12. Höppner 2005.
13. Mazzieri and Dal Santo 2007.
14. Maggi and Pearce 2005.
15. Mallory and Adams 1997, 217–18, 317–18, 482–83, 485–86.
16. Manco 2015, 113.
17. Dolfini 2010.
18. Dolfini 2013.
19. De Marinis 1998.
20. De Saulieu 2013.
21. Velušček 2004; Čufar, Kromer, Tolar and Velušček 2009.
22. Carozza and Mille 2007; Roberts 2009.
23. Bernard, Carles, Picavet and Morin 2005.
24. Nocete 2006; Nocete 2011, 3278–95; Hanning, Gauß and Goldenberg 2010; Roberts 2008.
25. Lira 2010.
26. Bendrey 2012.
27. Kunst 2007.
28. Cardoso 2000.
29. Müller 2007.
30. Diaz-Guardamino Uribe 2010.

31. Gallay 1978 and 1995.
32. Harrison and Heyd 2007.
33. Harrison and Heyd 2007, 134–35, 142, 146, 151, 161–64.
34. Harrison and Heyd 2007, 147, 149, 160.
35. Telegin and Mallory 1994, 40–41.
36. Harrison and Heyd 2007, 158–59, 170–71.
37. Harrison and Heyd 2007, 154–55, 171–72.
38. Vander Linden 2013; Beckerman 2012.
39. Müller and van Willigen 2001; Wlodarczak 2009; Cardoso 2014.
40. Heyd, Husty and Kreiner 2004; Lechterbeck 2014.
41. Salanova 2008.
42. Bettencourt and Luz 2013.
43. Kunst 2001; Carvalho-Amaro 2013.
44. Kunst 2001; Ferreira 2003; Carvalho-Amaro 2013.
45. Turek 2012.
46. Among Cucuteni and Svobodnoe types: Anthony 2007, figs. 11.4, 12.6, 12.9.
47. Odriozola and Hurtado Pérez 2007; Curtis, Popovic, Wilson and Wright 2010; Všianský, Kolář and Petřík 2014.
48. Parkinson 2010; Roberts, Sofaer and Kiss 2008.
49. Cardoso 2014.
50. Cunliffe and Koch 2010; Koch and Cunliffe 2013.
51. Hyllested 2010.
52. Manco 2015, 183.
53. Hickey 2002; Shisha-Halevy 2003.
54. Matasović 2008 and 2012.
55. Lemercier 2012; Salanova 2004.
56. Gibson 2013, 76.
57. Endrődi and Horváth 2006.
58. Endrődi 2013.
59. Price, Knipper, Grupe and Smrcka 2004.
60. Desideri and Besse 2010.
61. Anthony 2007, 183, 250; fig. 11.10, 256, 298; Ruzickova 2009.
62. Piguet and Besse 2009; Kulcsár and Szeverényi 2013.
63. Sheridan 2008.
64. Heyd 2007.
65. Harrison and Heyd 2007, 185–87, 192.
66. Chiaradia, Gallay and Todt 2003; Menk 1979.

67. Lemercier 2012.
68. Garrido Pena 1997; Rios 2013; Kulcsár and Szeverényi 2013.
69. Koch 2006, 364–65, 374.
70. Gibson 2014.
71. Fitzpatrick 2013, 56–58 and fig. 2.8; Gibson 2013, 78.
72. Fokkens, Achterkamp and Kuijpers 2008; Woodward and Hunter 2011.
73. De Bernardo Stempel 2007; Nicolaisen 1982.
74. Mallory 2013, chapter 9, particularly p. 261.
75. Stevens and Fuller 2012; Whitehouse 2014.
76. Rocca 2012.
77. Burgess and O'Connor 2008.
78. Kristiansen 1998, 144; Henderson 2007, chapter 3; Cunliffe 2008, 254–58.
79. Tinsley 1981; Turner 1981.
80. Lorrio and Zapatero 2005, 221–27; De Alarcão 2001; Burgess and O'Connor 2008.
81. Manco 2015, 166–67.
82. De Alarcão 2001.
83. Prósper 2014; García Quintela 2005.

Chapter 6: The Iron Sword

1. Aristotle, Nicomachean Ethics, 3.7.
2. Manti and Watkinson 2008.
3. Mödlinger 2013.
4. Bouzek 2001; Makhortyk 2008.
5. Makhortyk 2008.
6. Kristiansen 1998, 137.
7. Isaac 2010.
8. Kristiansen 1998, 161, 233.
9. Pare 1991.
10. Kristiansen 1998, 211–16; Manning 1995.
11. Kristiansen 1998, 254–63.
12. Fernández-Götz and Krausse 2013.
13. Fernández-Götz and Krausse 2013.
14. Olivier 1999; Verger 2006.
15. Piggott 1995.
16. Green 1996, 73.
17. Eluère 1991.
18. Diodorus Siculus, V.22.
19. Rolley 2003.
20. Aratus, lines 206ff.
21. Olivier 1999; Verger 2006.
22. Tacitus, Agricola, 16; Tacitus, Annals, 14.31.
23. Chaume and Reinhard 2011.
24. Chaume and Reinhard 2011.

25. Minerva 7 (5), 6.
26. Moscati 1991, 34, 136, 499–500.
27. Knipper 2014.
28. Knipper 2014.
29. De Marinis 1991; Uhlich 2007.
30. Caesar, IV.10.
31. Pliny, III.20.
32. Pliny, III.1.
33. De Marinis 1991.
34. De Marinis 1991.
35. Uhlich 2007.
36. Koch 2006, 463–64.
37. Koch 2006, 708–08.
38. Ptolemy, II.2, 7–8.
39. Ellis Evans 1995.
40. Koch 1992; Sims-Williams 2007; Matasović 2007.
41. Frey 1991, 129.
42. Fernández-Götz and Krausse 2013.
43. Cunliffe 1997, 63–64.
44. Koch 2007, §17.3, §17.4, §18.
45. Furger-Gunti 1991.
46. Karl 2003.
47. Megaw and Megaw 1995; Harding 2007, 63.
48. Megaw and Megaw 1995.
49. Karl 2006.
50. Maier 1991; Collis 1995, 161–62, 172.

Chapter 7: On the Move

1. Justin, XXIV.4.
2. Ammianus Marcellinus, 15.9.4.
3. Caesar, I.1; II.4.
4. Koch 2006, 195–99.
5. Koch 2007, maps § 17.3 and § 84.
6. Caesar, VI.44.
7. Halkon 2011.
8. Justin, XX.5.
9. Livy, V.34
10. Tinner 2003.
11. Livy, V.33.
12. Dionysius of Halicarnassus, XIII.11
13. Pliny the Elder, 12.2.
14. Diodorus Siculus, V. 26.
15. Caesar, II.15.
16. Diodorus Siculus, XV.70.
17. Polybius, II.17.
18. Dionysius of Halicarnassus, XIII.12; Livy V.34–35.
19. Frey 1995.
20. Polybius, II.17.
21. Livy V.34–35; Sims-Williams 2006, 91, 199.
22. Grassi 2011.
23. Vitali 1991; Frey 1995.
24. Uhlich 2007.

25. Karl 2006; Čižmář 1991; Bujnar and Szabó 1991.
26. Božič 1991; Guštin 2011; Jovanović 1991.
27. Polyaenus, XII.42; Theopompus, F40 – see Shrimpton 1991, appendix, 221.
28. Strabo, 7.3; Arrian, I.4.
29. Božič 1991; Guštin 2011.
30. Arrian, VII.15.
31. Pausanias, I.4.1; Diodorus Siculus, XX.19.1; Justin, XV.2.
32. Justin, XXIV.4–5.
33. Diodorus Siculus, XXII.9.1-3; Justin, XXIV.6-8; Pausanias, X.19.8–23.13.
34. Athenaeus, VI.234a–c.
35. Polybius, IV.46; Pausanias, X.19.7; Livy, XXXVIII.16.
36. Livy, XXXVIII.16.
37. Ammianus Marcellinus, XV.9.
38. Livy, XXXVIII.16.
39. Rankin 1987, chapter 9; Koch 2007, §19.2.
40. Strabo, IV.1.13.
41. Strabo, XII.5.1.
42. Koch 2006, 1350–51.
43. Acts 16:6.
44. NPNF2:6, 497.
45. Kelly 1975, 25–26, 37.
46. Eska 2006.
47. Lorrio and Zapatero 2005.
48. García Alonso 2006.
49. Lorrio and Zapatero 2005.
50. Villar 2004, 248.
51. Pliny, III.3.
52. Strabo, 3.1.6, 3.3.5; Talbert 2000, map 26.
53. Luján Martínez 2006.
54. Villar 2004, 256, 267–68; Talbert 2000; http://pleiades. stoa.org.
55. Turner 1981.
56. Cruciani, Trombetta and Antonelli 2011.
57. Chiaroni, Underhill and Cavelli-Sforza 2009.
58. Bertoncini 2012; Capocasa 2014.
59. Armit, Swindles and Becker 2013.
60. Chapman 2006.
61. Armit, Swindles and Becker 2013.
62. Mallory 2013, 185.
63. Caulfield 1977.
64. De Bernardo Stempel 2007.
65. MacNeill 1920, chap. 4.
66. Toner 2000; Darcy and Flynn 2008.
67. Busby 2012.

68. Moore 2006.
69. Lacey 2006.
70. Busby 2012.
71. Personal communication David Powell.
72. Caesar, V.12.
73. Koch 2007, 21, 109–10 and maps 50, 76, 252–67.
74. Ptolemy, II.2; II.8; Koch 2006, 357–58; Koch 2007, map 15.6; Cunliffe 2005.

Chapter 8: Celts vs Romans

1. Polybius, I.1.
2. Polybius, II.19–35.
3. Markoe 2000, 181–82.
4. Polybius, III, 9–11.
5. Polybius, III.34, 44, 82–118.
6. Arslan 1991.
7. Manco 2015, 182–83.
8. Polybius, III.15, 17, 20; Livy, XXI, 1–15.
9. Polybius, III.97–99.
10. Polybius, X.2, 6.
11. Polybius, X.6–15, 18, 34–38.
12. Livy, XXVIII, 1–2; Polybius, XI. 20–24a, 33.
13. Livy, XXVI. 50.
14. Polybius, X.17.
15. Silva 2013.
16. Livy, XLIII.2.
17. Diodorus Siculus, XXXIII.1; Cassius Dio, XXII.73; Justin, XLIV.2.
18. Plutarch, Caesar, 12.
19. Caesar, I.2–4, VII.4.
20. Lintott 1999, 109–13.
21. Plutarch, Caesar, 3–6, 14.
22. Caesar, I.2–8.
23. Karl 2001.
24. Caesar, I.9–29.
25. Caesar, I.30–32; VI.11–12; Strabo IV.3.2.
26. Caesar, I.34–54.
27. Caesar, II.1.
28. Caesar, II.3.
29. Caesar, II.3–4
30. Caesar, II.8–35.
31. Caesar, VII.4.
32. Caesar, VII.
33. Caesar, VII.89.
34. Plutarch, Caesar, 27.
35. Caesar, IV.20–38; V.1–23.
36. Tacitus, Agricola, 13.
37. Res Gestae Divi Augusti, 32; Manley and Rudkin 2005.
38. Koch 2006, 520.
39. Cassius Dio, 60.19–20 refers to Berikos, generally taken to be Vericos.

40. Tacitus, Agricola, 12.
41. Tacitus, Annals, XII, 36-8.
42. Tacitus, Histories, III.45.
43. Tacitus, Histories, III.45; Tacitus, Agricola 17; Tacitus, Annals XII.40.
44. Raftery 2005, 174–76.
45. Ó Floinn 2000.
46. Koch 2006, 750.
47. Tacitus, Agricola, 22–38.
48. Tacitus, Agricola, 14, and note 48; Ptolemy, II.2; Koch 2007, map 15.6; Koch 2006, 1362.
49. Ptolemy, II.2; Koch 2007, maps §15.2 and §21.2; Fraser 2009, 20.
50. Herodian, III.14.
51. Cassius Dio, LXXVII.12.
52. Fraser 2009, 15–17.
53. Panegyrici Latini VI: Panegyric of Constantine 226–27 and note 27.
54. Isidore, XIX.xxiii.7.
55. Caesar, V.14; Pomponius Mela, III, 51.
56. Moffat and Wilson 2011, 159.
57. Freeman 2001.
58. Ammianus Marcellinus, XXVI.4.5; XXVII.8; Rance 2001.

Chapter 9: Christian Celts

1. Patrick, Confession, 1.
2. Gildas, 27–33.
3. Patrick, Confession, 9.
4. Thomas 1981, 46–48, 197.
5. Tomlin 1992, 16–17.
6. Rees 1998.
7. Murray 2003, IV.16: Chronicle of Prosper of Aquitaine.
8. Murray 2003, IV.16: Chronicle of Prosper of Aquitaine.
9. McManus 1996.
10. Ó Cróinín 1995, 33–34, 305.
11. Mallory 2013, 263.
12. Ó Cróinín 1995, 53.
13. Koch 1995.
14. Koch 2007, 18, §20, §391; Edwards 2007.
15. Ptolemy, II.2.
16. Gildas, III.31.
17. Edwards 2007; Koch 2007, §391, no. 145; Charles-Edwards 2013, 174–75.
18. Expulsion of the Dessi 112-13.
19. Archaeologia Cambrensis, 5th series, 9 (1892), 64–65.
20. Murray 2003, IV.16: Chronicle of Prosper of Aquitaine.
21. Rance 2001. See Thornton 2003, chapter 5 for a more critical review of the evidence.

22. Ó Cróinín 1995, 19.
23. Historia Brittonum, III.14.
24. Patrick, Confession.
25. O' Brien 1962, 253.
26. Family Tree DNA: R1b L21 and Subclades Project.
27. Hey 2000, 93.
28. Ó Cróinín 1995, 20–23.
29. Bieler 1979 includes Muirchú's Life of Saint Patrick.
30. Rivet and Smith 1979, 511–12.
31. Ó Cróinín 1995, 23-27.
32. Annals of the Four Masters.
33. Rivet and Smith 1979, 280–82.
34. Pliny, IV, 30; Ptolemy, II, 1–2.
35. Ó Cróinín 1995, chapter 2.
36. Muhr 1996, 1–7, 151–53.
37. Annals of Ulster.
38. Ó Cróinín 1995, 48.
39. O'Laverty 1878, lvii, 35.
40. McEvoy and Bradley 2010, 117.
41. Family Tree DNA I-M223 Y-Haplogroup Project; Moffat and Wilson 2011, 24–25; estimated dates supplied by Kenneth Nordtvedt.
42. Koch 1995.
43. Koch 2006, 738–39.
44. Annals of Ulster; Auraicept Na N-Éces, lines 63-78; Lacey 2006, 229–32.
45. Gildas, 23.
46. Murray 2003, IV.17: Gallic Chronicle.
47. Gildas, 23.
48. Bede, 15.
49. Lane 2014.
50. Schrijver 2007.
51. Gildas, 25.
52. Murray 2003, IV.17: Gallic Chronicle.
53. Winney 2012; Leslie 2015.
54. Schiffels 2014.
55. Bede, 193; Manco 1998, 31.
56. Lapidge, Blair, Keynes and Scragg 1999, 93.
57. Laws of the Earliest English Kings 36–61.
58. Koch 2006, 532.
59. Asser, 14.
60. Charles-Edwards 2013, 14–17.
61. Charles-Edwards 2013, 20–21; Rivet and Smith 1979, 434.
62. Edwards 2013.
63. Koch 2006, 518–19.
64. Charles-Edwards 2013, 176–79.
65. Rivet and Smith, 491.
66. Koch 2007, §24.
67. Gildas, 33.

68. Koch 2007, §391, no. 90; Edwards 2013; Charles-Edwards 2013, 476.
69. *Historia Brittonum*, section 62; Koch 2006, 518–20.
70. Koch 2006, 1261–62.
71. Fraser 2009, 153; Charles-Edwards 2013, 190.
72. Thornton 2003, chapter 4.
73. Gildas, III.28.
74. *Aldhelm: the Prose Works*, Letter IV.
75. *Anglo-Saxon Chronicle*.
76. Koch 2006, 275–78, 750.
77. Orme 2000, 1, 214–19.
78. Koch 2006, 1558.
79. Koch 2006, 291.
80. Woolf 2007, chapter 8.
81. Campbell 2001.
82. Bede, 11.
83. Fraser 2009, 145–46, 156–60, 203–06.
84. Bede, 11.
85. Fraser 2009, 54, 239.
86. Woolf 2007, 93–98, 110–25, 220, 320–21.
87. Fraser 2009, chapter 4.

Chapter 10: Loss and Revival

1. Pezron trans. Jones 1706, 1–2.
2. Jones 1997.
3. Jenner 1904, 19–22.
4. Broderick 1999, 5, 75.
5. Moseley 2010.
6. Ternes 1992, 372–77.
7. Jones 2012.
8. Johnston 1997.
9. John 1972.
10. Gerald of Wales, *Conquest of Ireland*; Ó Cróinín 1995, 285–88.
11. Thomason 2001, 66 and chapter 9.
12. Caesar, I.1; Tacitus, *Agricola*, 11.
13. Buchanan 1582, II, 1–2, 6–8.
14. Camden 1607, I.
15. Buchanan 1582, II.
16. Camden 1607, I.
17. Pezron trans. Jones 1706, i.
18. Pezron trans. Jones 1706.
19. Parsons 1767, ix–x.
20. MacNeill 1920, 7.
21. Moscati 1991, 29–30.
22. Koch 2006, 527–29.
23. Edwards 2006.
24. Koch 2006, 737–38.
25. Ó Croidheáin 2006, 138, 151–53.
26. Moscati 1991, foreword.
27. Burillo Mozota 2005.
28. Dietler 1994.
29. Chapman 1992; Dietler 1994; Collis 1997 and 2003; James 1999.
30. Tacitus, *Germania*, chapter 2.
31. De Bernardo Stempel 2008.
32. Solinus, 2.11, citing Marcus Antonius [Gnipho], a grammarian of Gaulish origin who taught in Rome in the 1st century bc; repeated by Isidore, IX.ii.87.
33. Buck 1904.
34. Manco 2015.
35. Leslie 2015.

Appendix: Surnames and DNA

1. McKie 2006, 174.
2. Reaney and Wilson 1997.
3. McEvoy and Bradley 2006.
4. Hey, 2000, 31, 51–53.
5. Reaney and Wilson 1997, Introduction; Redmonds, King and Hey 2011, 2–3.
6. Ó Cróinín 2005, 237, 266–67; Duffy 2013.
7. Reaney and Wilson 1997, 157, 249.
8. http://dnastudy.clanirwin.org
9. *Annals of Ulster*.
10. Wright 2009; Family Tree DNA: R-L226 Project; Dennis Wright personal communication.
11. Ó Cróinín 2005, 276; Duffy 2013.
12. *Complete Peerage*, XII (1), 702–03.
13. Chibnall 2000, 69.
14. Barrow 2004.
15. *Complete Peerage*, II, 366.
16. Family Tree DNA: Stewart Stuart DNA Project.
17. Family Tree DNA projects MacFarlane and DF63 and subclades.
18. *Complete Peerage*, VII, 585–93.
19. Burke and Burke 1847, II, 800–01; MacFarlane 1922.

Bibliography

Abbreviation: *PNAS = Proceedings of the National Academy of Sciences of the United States of America*

1000 Genomes Project Consortium. 2010. A map of human genome variation from population-scale sequencing, *Nature*, 467, 1061–73.

Adamnan. *Life of Saint Columba by Adomnán of Iona*, ed. and trans. R. Sharpe. 1995. London: Penguin.

Aldhelm: *the Prose Works*, ed. and trans. M. Lapidge and M. Herren. 1979. Ipswich: D.S. Brewer.

Allen, M. J., Gardiner J. and Sheridan, A. (eds). 2012. *Is There a British Chalcolithic? People, Place and Polity in the Later 3rd Millennium*. Oxford and Oakville, CT: The Prehistoric Society/Oxbow Books.

Altinbilek-Algül, C., Astruc, L., Binder, D., Pelegrin, J. 2012. Pressure blade production with a lever in the Early and Late Neolithic of the Near East, chapter 5 in Desrosiers (ed.) 2012, 157–79.

Ammianus Marcellinus. *Roman History*, trans. C. D. Yonge. 1862. London: Bohn.

Andreu, S. 2010. The Northern Aegean, in E. H. Cline (ed.), *The Oxford Handbook of the Bronze Age Aegean*, 643–59. New York: Oxford University Press.

Anglo-Saxon Chronicle, ed. and trans. M. Swanton. 1996. London: J. M. Dent.

Annals of the Four Masters, ed. and trans. John O'Donovan, *Annala Rioghachta Eireann: Annals of the kingdom of Ireland by the Four Masters, from the earliest period to the year 1616. Edited from MSS in the Library of the Royal Irish Academy and of Trinity College Dublin with a translation and copious notes*, 7 vols. 1848–51. Dublin: Hodges and Smith.

Annals of Tigernach, trans. W. Stokes, *Revue Celtique*, ed. H. D'Arbois de Jubainville, 16–18 (1895–97). Digital edition: CELT: Corpus of Electronic Texts.

Annals of Ulster. The Annals of Ulster (to A.D. 1131), ed. and trans. S. Mac Airt and G. Mac Niocaill. 1983. Dublin: Dublin Institute for Advanced Studies.

Anthony, D. W. 2007. *The Horse, the Wheel and Language: How Bronze Age Riders from the Eurasian Steppes Shaped the Modern World*. Princeton and Oxford: Princeton University Press.

Anthony, D. W. 2008. A new approach to language and archaeology: the Usatovo Culture and the separation of Pre-Germanic, *Journal of Indo-European Studies*, 36 (1–2), 1–51.

Anthony, D. W. 2013. Two IE phylogenies, three PIE migrations, and four kinds of steppe pastoralism, *Journal of Language Relationship*, 9, 1–22.

Anthony, D. W. and Chi, J. Y. (eds). 2009. *The Lost World of Old Europe: The Danube Valley, 5000–3500 BC*. New York and Princeton: Institute for the Study of the Ancient World/Princeton University Press.

Anthony, D. W. and Ringe, D. 2015. The Indo-European homeland from linguistic and archaeological perspectives, *Annual Review of Linguistics*, 1, 199–219.

Aratus. *Phaenomena*. Included in A. W. Mair and G. R. Mair (trans.), *Callimachus, Hymns and Epigrams. Lycophron.*

Aratus. 1921 (Loeb Classical Library). London: William Heinemann.

Aristotle. *Meteorology*, in *Works of Aristotle*, trans. E. W. Webster, vol. 3. 1931. Oxford: Clarendon Press.

Aristotle. *Nicomachean Ethics*, vol. 19 of *Aristotle in 23 Volumes*, trans. H. Rackham. 1934. Cambridge, MA: Harvard University Press; London: William Heinemann Ltd.

Armbruster, B. 2013. Gold and gold-working of the Bronze Age, chapter 25 in *The Oxford Handbook of the European Bronze Age*, A. Harding and H. Fokkens (eds), 454–68. Oxford: Oxford University Press.

Armit, I., Swindles, G. T. and Becker, K. 2013. From dates to demography in later prehistoric Ireland? Experimental approaches to the meta-analysis of large 14C data-sets, *Journal of Archaeological Science*, 40 (1), 433–38.

Arrian. *The Anabasis of Alexander*, trans. E. J. Chinnock. 1884. London: Hodder and Stoughton.

Arslan, E. 1991. The Transpadane Celts, in Moscati et al. (eds) 1991, 461–70.

Asser. *Alfred the Great: Asser's Life of King Alfred and Other Contemporary Sources*. S. Keynes and M. Lapidge (trans.). 1983. Harmondworth: Penguin Books.

Athenaeus. *Deipnosophistae*, trans. Charles Burton Gulick. 1927–41. 7 vols (Loeb Classical Library). Cambridge, MA: Harvard University Press.

Aubet, M. E. 2001. *The Phoenicians and the West: Politics, Colonies and Trade* (2nd ed.). Cambridge: Cambridge University Press.

Aubet, M. E. 2008. Political and economic implications of the new Phoenician chronologies, in *Beyond the Homeland: Markers in Phoenician Chronology* (Ancient Near Eastern Studies, Supplement 28), C. Sagona (ed.), 247–59. Leuven and Dudley, MA: Peeters.

Auraicept Na N-Éces, ed. and trans. G. Calder. 1917. Edinburgh: John Grant.

Avienus, Rufus Festus. *Ora Maritima: A Description of the Seacoast from Brittany to Marseilles [Massilia]*, trans. J. P. Murphy. 1977. Chicago: Ares Publishing.

Baillie, M. G. L. 1995. *A Slice Through Time: Dendrochronology and Precision Dating*. London: Batsford.

Barrow, G. W. S. 2004. Stewart family (per. c. 1110–c. 1350), *Oxford Dictionary of National Biography*.

Bauer, A. A. 2006. Between the steppe and the sown: prehistoric Sinop and inter-regional interaction along the Black Sea coast, chapter 12 in *Beyond the Steppe and the Sown*, D. L. Peterson, L. M. Popova and A.T. Smith (eds), 225–46. Leiden and Boston: Brill.

Beckerman, S. 2012. Dutch beaker chronology re-examined, *Palaeohistoria* 53/54, 25–64.

Bede. *The Ecclesiastical History of the English People, The Greater Chronicle, Bede's Letter to Egbert*, ed. and trans. J. McClure and R. Collins. 1994. Oxford and New York: Oxford University Press.

Bendrey, R. 2012. From wild horses to domestic horses: a European perspective, *World Archaeology*, 44 (1), 135–57.

Berggren, J. L. and Jones, A. 2000. *Ptolemy's Geography: An Annotated Translation of the Theoretical Chapters*. Princeton and Woodstock: Princeton University Press.

Bernard, C., Carles, J., Picavet, R. and Morin, A. 2005. Etude préliminaire sur des poignards gravés de type Remedello découverts dans les Préalpes du Sud (Chastel-Arnaud, Drôme, France) et réflexions sur leur insertion dans le Néolithique final régional, *Bulletin de la Société préhistorique française*, 102 (2), 345–59.

Bertoncini, S. et al. 2012. A Y variant which traces the genetic heritage of Ligures tribes, *Journal of Biological Research*, 84 (1), 143–46.

Bettencourt, A. M. S. and Luz, S. 2013. A corded-mixed Bell Beaker vase at the monumental enclosure of Forca, Maia, North of Portugal, chapter 1 in Prieto-Martínez and Salanova (eds) 2013, 15–20.

Bieler, L. (ed. and trans.). 1979. *The Patrician Texts in the Book of Armagh*. Scriptores Latini Hiberniae, 10. Dublin: Dublin Institute for Advanced Studies.

Bogucki, P. 1993. Animal traction and household economies in Neolithic Europe, *Antiquity*, 67 (256), 492–503.

Bouckaert, R. et al. 2012. Mapping the origins and expansion of the Indo-European language family, *Science*, 337, 957–60.

Bouzek, J. 2001. Cimmerians and early Scythians: the transition from geometric to early orientalising style in the North Pontic area, in *North Pontic Archaeology: Recent Discoveries and Studies* (Colloquia Pontica 6), G. R. Tsetskhladze (ed.), 33–44. Leiden, Boston and Köln: Brill.

Boyle, A. et al. 2008. Site D (Ferry Fryston) in the Iron Age and Romano-British periods, in *The Archaeology of the A1(M) Darrington to Dishforth DBFO Road Scheme*, F. Brown et al., 121–59. Oxford: Lancaster Imprints, Oxford Archaeology North.

Božič, D. 1991. The Taurisci, in Moscati et al. (eds) 1991, 471–77.

Broderick, G. 1999. *Language Death in the Isle of Man: An Investigation into the Decline and Extinction of Manx Gaelic as a Community Language in the Isle of Man*. Tubingen: Niemeyer.

Bryce, T. 2005. *The Kingdom of the Hittites*. Oxford and New York: Oxford University Press.

Buchanan, G. 1582. *Rerum Scoticarum Historia*. Translated as *The History of Scotland*, 1690.

Buck, C. D. 1904. *A Grammar of Oscan and Umbrian*. Boston: Ginn.

Budziszewski, J., Haduch, E. and Włodarczak, P. 2003. Bell Beaker Culture in South-Eastern Poland, in *The Northeast Frontier of Bell Beakers: Proceedings of the symposium held at the Adam Mickiewicz University, Poznań (Poland), May 26–29 2002*, J. Czebreszuk and M. Szmyt (eds). BAR International Series 1155, 155–81. Oxford: Archaeopress.

Bujnar, J. and Szabó, M. 1991. The Carpathian Basin, in Moscati et al. (eds) 1991, 277–85.

Burgess, C. and O'Connor, B. 2008. Iberia, the Atlantic Bronze Age and the Mediterranean, in *Contacto cultural entre el Mediterráneo y el Atlántico (siglos XII-VIII ANE). La precolonización a debate* (Serie Arqueológica 11),

S. Celestino, N. Rafel, and X.-L. Armada (eds), 41–58. Escuela Española de Historia y Arqueología en Roma-CSIC. Madrid.

Burillo Mozota, F. 2005. Celtiberians: Problems and Debates, *e-Keltoi: the Journal of Interdisciplinary Celtic Studies*, 6: The Celts in the Iberian Peninsula, 411–80.

Burke, J. and Burke, J. B. 1847. *Genealogical and Heraldic Dictionary of the Landed Gentry of Great Britain and Ireland*. London: Henry Colburn.

Busby, G. B. J. et al. 2012. The peopling of Europe and the cautionary tale of Y chromosome lineage R-M269, *Proceedings of the Royal Society B: Biological Sciences*, 279 (1730), 884–92.

Caesar. *The Conquest of Gaul*, trans. S. A. Handford, rev. J. F. Gardner. 1982. London and New York: Penguin Books.

Camden, W. 1607. *Britannia*, trans. P. Holland. London.

Campbell, E. 2001. Were the Scots Irish?, *Antiquity*, 75, 285–92.

Campbell, J., John, E. and Wormwald, P. 1982. *The Anglo-Saxons*. London and New York: Penguin Books.

Canon, G. and Franklin, M. J. 2004. A Cymmrodor claims kin in Calcutta: an assessment of Sir William Jones as philologer, polymath, and pluralist, *Transactions of the Honourable Society of Cymmrodorion*, New Series, 11, 50–69.

Capocasa, M. et al. 2014. Linguistic, geographic and genetic isolation: a collaborative study of Italian populations, *Journal of Anthropological Sciences*, 92, 201–31.

Cardoso, J. L. 2000. The fortified site of Leceia (Oeiras) in the context of the Chalcolithic in Portuguese Estramadura, *Oxford Journal of Archaeology*, 19 (1), 37–55.

Cardoso, J. L. 2014. Absolute chronology of the Beaker phenomenon north of the Tagus estuary: demographic and social implications, *Trabajos De Prehistoria*, 71 (1), 56–75.

Carey, J. 1994. *The Irish National Origin-Legend: Synthetic Pseudohistory*. Cambridge: University of Cambridge.

Carlin, N. and Brück, J. 2012. Searching for the Chalcolithic: continuity and change in the Irish Final Neolithic/Early Bronze Age, in Allen, Gardiner and Sheridan (eds) 2012, 193–210.

Carney, J. 2005. Language and literature to 1169, chapter 13 in Ó Cróinín (ed.) 2005, 451–510.

Carozza, L. and Mille, B. 2007. Chalcolithique et complexification sociale: quelle place pour le métal dans la définition du processus de mutation des sociétés de la fin du Néolithique en France? in *Le Chalcolithique et la construction des inégalités, 1, le continent européen*, J. Guilaine (ed.), 195–232. Paris: Editions Errance.

Carpelan, C., Parpola, A. and Koskikalio, P. (eds). 2001. *Early Contacts between Uralic and Indo-European: Linguistic and Archaeological Considerations: Papers Presented at an International Symposium Held at the Tvärminne Research Station of the University of Helsinki, 8–10 January 1999* (Mémoires de la Société Finno-Ougrienne 242). Helsinki: Finno-Ugrian Society.

Carter, S. and Hunter, F. 2003. An Iron Age chariot burial from Scotland, *Antiquity*, 77 (297), 531–35.

Carter, S. et al. 2010. A 5th century BC Iron Age chariot burial from Newbridge, Edinburgh, *Proceedings of the Prehistoric Society*, 76, 31–74.

Carvalho-Amaro, G. 2013. Pre-Bell Beaker ware from Estremadura, Portugal, and its likely influence on the appearance of Maritime Bell Beaker ware, chapter 18 in Prieto Martínez and Salanova, L. (eds) 2013, 197–208.

Cassius Dio. *Roman History*, trans. E. Cary. 1914–27. 9 vols (Loeb Classical Library) Cambridge, MA: Harvard University Press.

Caulfield, S. 1977. The Beehive Quern in Ireland, *The Journal of the Royal Society of Antiquaries of Ireland*, 107, 104–38.

Celtic Inscribed Stones: Online database created by University College London, 1999.

Chang, W., Cathcart, C., Hall, D. and Garrett, A. 2015. Ancestry-constrained phylogenetic analysis supports the Indo-European steppe hypothesis, *Language*, 91 (1)

Chapman, M. 1992. *The Celts. The Construction of a Myth*. London and New York: St Martin's Press.

Chapman, R. J. et al. 2006. Microchemical characterisation of natural gold and artefact gold as a tool for provenancing prehistoric gold artefacts: a case study in Ireland, *Applied Geochemistry*, 21 (6), 904–18.

Charles-Edwards, T. M. 2013. *Wales and the Britons 350–1064*. Oxford: Oxford University Press.

Chaume, B. and Reinhard, W. 2011. Les statues du sanctuaire de Vix-Les Herbues dans le contexte de la statuaire anthropomorphe hallstattienne, in Gruat and Garcia (eds) 2011, 293–310.

Chernykh, E. 2008. The 'steppe belt' of stock-breeding cultures in Eurasia during the Early Metal Age, *Trabajos de Prehistoria*, 65 (2), 73–93.

Chiaradia, M., Gallay, A. and Todt, W. 2003. Different contamination styles of prehistoric human teeth at a Swiss necropolis (Sion, Valais) inferred from lead and strontium isotopes, *Applied Geochemistry*, 18, 353–70.

Chiaroni, J., Underhill, P. and Cavalli-Sforza, L. L. 2009. Y chromosome diversity, human expansion, drift and cultural evolution, *PNAS*, 106 (48), 20174–79.

Chibnall, M. 2000. *The Normans*. Malden, MA: Wiley-Blackwell.

Childe, V. G. 1930. *The Bronze Age*. London and New York: Cambridge University Press.

Childe, V. G. 1958. *The Dawn of European Civilization* (6th ed.). New York: Alfred A. Knopf.

Čižmář, M. 1991. The Celtic population of Moravia in the fourth century B.C., in Moscati et al. (eds) 1991, 273–76.

Clancy, T. O. and Márkus, G. 1995. *Iona: The Earliest Poetry of a Celtic Monastery*. Edinburgh: Edinburgh University Press.

Clark, J. E. 1982. Manufacture of Mesoamerican prismatic blades: an alternative technique, *American Antiquity*, 47 (2), 355–76.

Collis, J. 1995. The first towns, chapter 10 in Green 1995, 159–75.

Collis, J. 1997. Celtic myths, *Antiquity*, 71 (271), 195–201.

Collis, J. 2003. *The Celts: Origins, Myths & Inventions*. Stroud: Tempus Publishing.

Complete Peerage = The Complete Peerage of England, Scotland, Ireland, Great Britain and the United Kingdom by G. E. C [okayne], ed. V. Gibbs et al. (2nd ed.) 12 vols. 1910–1959. London: The St Catherine Press.

Corcoran, J. X. W. P. 1970. The origins of the Celts: the archaeological evidence, chapter 1 in N. Chadwick, *The Celts*. Harmondsworth and New York: Penguin.

Cowgill, W. 1970. Italic and Celtic superlatives and the dialects of Indo-European, in G. Cardona et al. (eds), *Indo-European and the Indo-Europeans*, 113–53. Philadelphia: University of Pennsylvania Press. Reprinted in J. Klein (ed.), 2006. *The Collected Writings of Warren Cowgill*. New York: Beech Stave Press.

Cox, M. and Mays, S. 2000. *Human Osteology in Archaeology and Forensic Science*. London: Greenwich Medical Media.

Crick, J. C. 2004. Monmouth, Geoffrey of (d. 1154/5), *Oxford Dictionary of National Biography*. Oxford: Oxford University Press.

Cruciani, F., Trombetta, B., Antonelli, C. et al. 2011. Strong intra- and inter-continental differentiation revealed by Y chromosome SNPs M269, U106 and U152, *Forensic Science International: Genetics*, 5 (3), e49–52.

Čufar, K., Kromer, B., Tolar, T. and Velušček, A. 2010. Dating of 4th millennium BC pile-dwellings on Ljubljansko barje, Slovenia, *Journal of Archaeological Science*, 37, 2031–39.

Cunliffe, B. 1997. *The Ancient Celts*. Oxford and New York: Oxford University Press.

Cunliffe, B. 2005. *Iron Age Communities in Britain: An Account of England, Scotland and Wales from the Seventh Century BC until the Roman Conquest* (4th ed.). Abingdon: Routledge.

Cunliffe, B. 2008. *Europe Between the Oceans: Themes and Variations: 9000 BC–AD 1000*. New Haven and London: Yale University Press.

Cunliffe, B. 2010. Celticization from the West, chapter 1 in Cunliffe and Koch (eds) 2010, 13–38.

Cunliffe, B. and Koch, J. T. (eds). 2010. *Celtic from the West: Alternative Perspectives from Archaeology, Genetics, Languages and Literature* (Celtic Studies Publications 15). Oxford: Oxbow Books.

Curtis, N., Popovic, L., Wilson, N. and Wright, M. 2010. The moon, the bonfire and the beaker? Analysing white inlay from Beaker pottery in Aberdeenshire, *Past: The Newsletter of the Prehistoric Society*, 65, 1–3.

Czebreszuk, J. (ed.) 2004. *Similar but Different: Bell Beakers in Europe*. Poznan: Adam Mickiewicz University. Reprinted in 2014. Leiden: Sidestone Press.

Czebreszuk, J. and Szmyt, M. (eds) 2003. *The Northeast Frontier of Bell Beakers: Proceedings of the symposium held at the Adam Mickiewicz University, Poznań (Poland), May 26–29 2002* (BAR International Series 1155). Oxford: Archaeopress.

Darcy, R. and Flynn, W. 2008. Ptolemy's map of Ireland: a modern decoding, *Irish Geography*, 41 (1), 49–69.

Darvill, T. 2006. *Stonehenge: The Biography of a Landscape*. Stroud: Tempus.

De Alarcão, J. 2001. Novas perspectivas sobre os Lusitanos (e outros mundos), *Revista Portuguesa De Arqueologia*, 4, 2.

Deamos, M. B. 2009. Phoenicians in Tartessos, chapter 8 in Dietler and López-Ruiz (eds) 2009, 193–228.

De Bernardo Stempel, P. 2007. Pre-Celtic, Old Celtic layers, Brittonic and Goidelic in ancient Ireland, in *Language Contact in the Place-names of Britain and Ireland*, P. Cavill and G. Broderick (eds), 137–63. Nottingham: English Place-Name Society.

De Bernado Stempel, P. 2008. Linguistically Celtic ethnonyms: towards a classification, in *Celtic and Other Languages in Ancient Europe*, J. L. García Alonso (ed.), 101–18. Ediciones Universidad Salamanca.

de Leeuw, H. 2008. Chariots on High Crosses: Celtic or Christian?, *The Journal of the Royal Society of Antiquaries of Ireland*, 138, 5–25.

De Marinis, R. 1991. Golasecca Culture and its links with Celts beyond the Alps, in Moscati et al. (eds) 1991, 93–102.

De Marinis R. C. 1998. The eneolithic cemetery of Remedello Sotto (BS) and the relative and absolute chronology of the Copper Age in Northern Italy, *Notizie Archeologiche Bergomensi*, 5, 33–51.

De Saulieu, G. 2013. Rock carvings and Alpine statue-menhirs, from the Chalcolithic to the Middle Bronze Age, chapter 16 in *The Oxford Handbook of the European Bronze Age*, A. Harding and H. Fokkens (eds), 291–310. Oxford: Oxford University Press.

Desideri, J. and Besse, M. 2010. Swiss Bell Beaker population dynamics: eastern or southern influences?, *Archaeological and Anthropological Sciences*, 2 (3), 157–73.

Desrosiers, P. M. (ed.). 2012. *The Emergence of Pressure Blade Making: From Origin to Modern Experimentation*. New York and London: Springer.

Diamond, J. and Bellwood, P. 2003. Farmers and their languages: the first expansions, *Science*, 300 (5619), 597–603.

Díaz-Guardamino Uribe, M. 2010. *Las Estelas Decoradas en la Prehistoria de la Península Ibérica*, PhD Thesis, Madrid.

Dietler, M. 1994. 'Our Ancestors the Gauls': archaeology, ethnic nationalism, and the manipulation of Celtic identity in modern Europe, *American Anthropologist*, 96 (3), 584–605.

Dietler, M. and López-Ruiz, C. (eds). 2009. *Colonial Encounters in Ancient Iberia: Phoenician, Greek and Indigenous Relations*. Chicago and London: University of Chicago Press.

Dietrich, O. et al. 2012. The role of cult and feasting in the emergence of Neolithic communities. New evidence from Göbekli Tepe, south-eastern Turkey, *Antiquity*, 86, 674–95.

Dillon, M. and Chadwick, N. 1967. *The Celtic Realms*. London: Weidenfeld & Nicolson.

Dineley, M. 2004. *Barley, Malt and Ale in the Neolithic* (BAR S1213). Oxford: Archaeopress.

Diodorus Siculus. *The Library of History*, trans. C. H. Oldfather. 1933–67. 12 vols (Loeb Classical Library). Cambridge, MA: Harvard University Press.

Dionysius of Halicarnassus. *Roman Antiquities*, trans. E. Cary. 7 vols. 1937–50. (Loeb Classical Library) Cambridge, MA: Harvard University Press.

Dolfini, A. 2010. The origins of metallurgy in central Italy: new radiometric evidence, *Antiquity*, 84 (325), 707–23.

Dolfini, A. 2013. Early Metallurgy in the Central Mediterranean, chapter 15 in *Archaeometallurgy in Global Perspective*, B. W Roberts and C. P. Thornton (eds), 473–506. New York: Springer.

Driscoll, S. T. and Yeoman, P. 1997. *Excavations within*

Edinburgh Castle in 1988–91 (Monograph Series no. 12). Edinburgh: Society of Antiquaries of Scotland.

Duffy, S. 2013. *Brian Boru and the Battle of Clontarf*. Dublin: Gill & Macmillan.

Edwards, H. T. 2006. Eisteddfod and Eisteddfod Genedlaethol Cymru, in Koch (ed.) 2006, 664–68.

Edwards, N. 2007. *A Corpus of Early Medieval Inscribed Stones and Stone Sculpture in Wales, 2: South-West Wales*. Cardiff: University of Wales Press.

Edwards, N. 2013. *A Corpus of Early Medieval Inscribed Stones and Stone Sculpture in Wales, 3: North Wales*. Cardiff: University of Wales Press.

Ellis Evans, D. 1995. The early Celts: the evidence of language, chapter 2 in Green (ed.) 1995, 8–20.

Eluère, C. 1991. The Celts and their gold: origins, production and social role, in Moscati et al. (eds) 1991, 349–55.

Endrődi, A. 2013. Recent data on the settlement history and contact system of the Bell Beaker–Csepel Group, in *Moments in Time: Papers Presented to Pál Raczky on his 60th Birthday*, A. Anders and G. Kulcsár (eds), 693–705. Ősrégészeti Tanulmányok / Prehistoric Studies, I.

Endrődi, A. and Horváth, A. 2006. Kora Bronzkori arany korong Csepel–Szigetről, *Budapest Régiségei*, 40, 21–30.

Eska, J. 2006. The Galatian language, in Koch (ed.) 2006, 788.

Expulsion of the Dessi, The, ed. K. Meyer, *Y Cymmrodor*, 14 (1901), 101–35.

Fernández-Götz, M. and Krausse, D. 2013. Rethinking Early Iron Age urbanisation in Central Europe: the Heuneburg site and its archaeological environment, *Antiquity* 87, 473–87.

Ferreira, S. D. 2003. Os Copos no Povoado Calcolítico de Vila Nova de São Pedro, *Revista Portuguesa de Arqueologia*, 6 (2), 181–228.

Fitzpatrick, A. 2009. In his hands and in his head, The Amesbury Archer as a metalworker, in *Bronze Age Connections: Cultural contact in prehistoric Europe*, P. Clark (ed.), 176–88. Oxford: Oxbow Books.

Fitzpatrick, A. P. 2013. The arrival of the Bell Beaker set in Britain and Ireland, chapter 2 in Koch and Cunliffe (eds) 2013, 41–70.

Flavius Josephus. *Antiquities of the Jews*, trans. William Whiston. 1895. London.

Fled Bricrend [The Feast of Bricriu], trans. G. Henderson. 1899. London: David Nutt for The Irish Texts Society.

Fokkens, H., Achterkamp, Y. and Kuijpers, M. 2008. Bracers or bracelets? About the functionality and meaning of Bell Beaker wrist-guards, *Proceedings of the Prehistoric Society*, 74, 109–40.

Fortson, B. W. 2010. *Indo-European Language and Culture: An Introduction* (2nd ed.). Chichester: John Wiley & Sons.

Fourdringier, E. 1878. *Double sépulture gauloise de la Gorge Meillet, territoire de Somme-Tourbe (Marne)*. Paris and Châlons sur Marne: privately published.

Fraser, J. E. 2009. *From Caledonia to Pictland: Scotland to 795*. (The New Edinburgh History of Scotland 1) Edinburgh: Edinburgh University Press.

Freeman, P. 2001. *Ireland and the Classical World*. Austin, TX: University of Texas Press. Kindle edition.

Freeman, P. 2010. Ancient references to Tartessos, chapter 10 in Cunliffe and Koch (eds) 2010.

Frey, O.-H. 1991. The formation of the La Tène culture in the fifth century BC, in Moscati et al. (eds) 1991, 127–45.

Frey, O.-H. 1995. The Celts in Italy, chapter 27 in Green (ed.) 1995.

Furger-Gunti, A. 1991. The Celtic war chariot: The experimental reconstruction in the Schweizerisches Landesmuseum, in Moscati et al. (eds) 1991, 356–59.

Gallay, A. 1978. Stèles néolithiques et problématique archéologique, Archives Suisses d'Anthropologie Générale 42 (2), 75–103.

Gallay, A. 1995. Les stèles anthropomorpes du site mégalithique du Petit-Chasseur à Sion (Valais, Suisse), in Statue-stele e massi incisi nell'Europa dell'Età del Rame, S. Casini, R. C. De Marinis and A. Pedrotti (eds), 167–94, Notizie Archeologiche Bergomensi 3.

García Alonso, J. L. 2006. -Briga Toponyms in the Iberian Peninsula, e-Keltoi: the Journal of Interdisciplinary Celtic Studies, 6: The Celts in the Iberian Peninsula, 689–714.

García Quintela, M. V. 2005. Celtic Elements in Northwestern Spain in Pre-Roman times, e-Keltoi: the Journal of Interdisciplinary Celtic Studies, 6: The Celts in the Iberian Peninsula, 497–569.

Garrido Pena, R. 1997. Bell Beakers in the southern Meseta of the Iberian Peninsula: socioeconomic context and new data, Oxford Journal of Archaeology, 16, 187–209.

Gatsov, I. and Nedelcheva, P. 2011. Neolithic chipped stone assemblages in North Western Anatolia, Turkey, Eurasian Prehistory, 8 (1–2), 89–95.

Geoffrey of Monmouth. History of the Kings of Britain, trans. A. Thompson, revised J. A. Giles. 1999. Cambridge, Ontario: In Parentheses Publications.

Gerald of Wales. The Journey Through Wales and the Description of Wales, trans. L. Thorpe. 1978. London and New York: Penguin.

Gerald of Wales. The Conquest of Ireland, in The Historical Works of Giraldus Cambriensis, trans. F. Forester, ed. T. Wright. 1863. London: Henry G. Bohn.

Gibson, C. 2013. Beakers into Bronze: tracing connections between western Iberia and the British Isles 2800–800 BC, chapter 3 in Koch and Cunliffe (eds) 2013.

Gibson, C. 2014. Closed for business or cultural change? Tracing the re-use and final blocking of megalithic tombs during the Beaker period throughout Atlantic Europe. Paper presented at the conference Atlantic Europe in the Metal Ages, Cardiff, 12 April 2014.

Gilbert, J., Brasseur, E., Dalmont J.-P. and Maniquet, C. 2012. Acoustical evaluation of the Carnyx of Tintignac, Proceedings of the Acoustics 2012 Nantes Conference, 3955–59.

Gildas. The Ruin of Britain, and other works, trans. M. Winterbottom. 1978. London: Phillimore.

Goedegebuure, P. M. 2008. Central Anatolian languages and language communities in the colony period: a Luwian-Hattian symbiosis and the independent Hittites, in Anatolia and the Jazira during the Old Assyrian period, J. G. Dercksen (ed.) (Old Assyrian Archives, Studies, 3. PIHANS 111), 137–80. Leiden: The Netherlands Institute for the Near East.

Gogâltan, F. 2013. Transilvania şi spaţiul Nord-Pontic. relaţii interculturale între sfârşitul Epocii Cuprului şi începutul Epocii Bronzului (CCA. 3500–2500 A. Chr.) Terra Sebus. Acta Musei Sabesiensis, 5, 31–76.

Grassi, E. 2011. Attività metallurgiche a Mediolanum tra archeologia e archeometria: Metallurgy in Mediolanum between archaeology and archaeometry, Archeologia Uomo Territorio, 30.

Gray, R. and Atkinson, Q. 2003. Language-tree divergence times support the Anatolian theory of Indo-European origin, Nature, 426, 435–39.

Green, M. (ed.). 1995. The Celtic World. Abingdon: Routledge.

Green, M. A. 1996. Celtic Art: Reading the Messages. London: Weidenfeld & Nicolson.

Greene, D. 1972. The chariot as described in Irish literature, in Iron Age in the Irish Sea Province, C. Thomas (ed.), CBA Research Report 9, 59–73. London: Council for British Archaeology.

Greenfield, H. J. 2010. The Secondary Products Revolution: the past, the present and the future, World Archaeology, 42 (1), 29–54.

Gruat, P. and Garcia, D. (eds). 2011. Stèles et statues du début de l'âge du Fer dans le Midi de la France (VIIIe-IVe s. av. J.-C.): chronologies, fonctions et comparaisons. Documents d'Archéologie Méridionale, 34.

Guerra-Doce, E. 2006. Exploring the significance of Beaker pottery through residue analyses, Oxford Journal of Archaeology, 25 (3), 247–59.

Guštin, M. 2011. On the Celtic tribe of Taurisci: local identity and regional contacts in the ancient world, in The Eastern Celts: The Communities Between the Alps and the Black Sea (Annales Mediterranei), M. Guštin and M. Jevtić (eds), 119–28. Koper: Univerza na Primoerskem.

Haak, W. et al. 2008. Ancient DNA, Strontium isotopes, and osteological analyses shed light on social and kinship organization of the Later Stone Age, PNAS, 105 (47), 18226–31.

Haak, W. et al. 2010. Ancient DNA from European early Neolithic farmers reveals their Near Eastern affinities, PloS Biology, 8 (11), e1000536.

Haak, W. et al. 2015. Massive migration from the steppe is a source of Indo-European languages, Nature, published online 2 March 2015.

Haas, J. et al. 1998. Synchronous Holocene climatic oscillations recorded on the Swiss Plateau and at timberline in the Alps, The Holocene, 8 (3), 301–09.

Häkkinen, J. 2012. Early contacts between Uralic and Yukaghir, in Per Urales ad Orientem Iter polyphonicum multilingue Festkrift tillägnad Juha Janhunen på hans sextioårsdag den 12 februari 2012 (Mémoires de la Société Finno-Ourgrienne 264), T. Hyytiäinen, L. Jalava, J. Saarikivi and E. Sandman (eds), 91–101. Helsinki: Finno-Ugrian Society.

Halkon, P. 2011. Iron, landscape and power in Iron Age East Yorkshire, The Archaeological Journal, 168, 133–65.

Hamp, E. P. and Adams, D. Q. 2013. The Expansion of the Indo-European Languages: An Indo-Europeanist's Evolving View. Sino-Platonic Papers 239.

Hanning, E., Gauß, R. and Goldenberg, G. 2010. Metal for Zambujal: experimentally reconstructing a 5000-year-old technology; Metal para Zambujal: reconstrucción experimental de una tecnología de 5.000 años, *Trabajos de Prehistoria*, 67 (2), 287–304.

Harding, D. W. 2007. *The Archaeology of Celtic Art*. Abingdon and New York: Routledge.

Harrison, R. and Heyd, V. 2007. The Transformation of Europe in the Third Millennium BC: the example of 'Le Petit-Chasseur I + III' (Sion, Valais, Switzerland), *Praehistorische Zeitschrift*, 82 (2), 129–214.

Hartz, S., Terberger, T. and Zhilin, M. 2010. New AMS-dates for the Upper Volga Mesolithic and the origin of microblade technology in Europe, *Quartär* 57, 155–69.

Heath, J. 2012. *Life in Copper Age Britain*. Stroud: Amberley Press.

Henderson, J. 2007. *The Atlantic Iron Age: Settlement and Identity in the First Millennium BC*. Abingdon and New York: Routledge.

Herodian of Antioch's History of the Roman Empire from the Death of Marcus Aurelius to the Accession of Gordian III, trans. E. C. Echols. 1961. Berkeley and Los Angeles: University of California Press.

Herodotus. *The Histories*, trans. R. Waterfield. 1998. Oxford and New York: Oxford University Press.

Hey, D. 2000. *Family Names and Family History*. London and New York: Hambledon and London.

Heyd, V. 2007. When the West meets the East: The eastern periphery of the Bell Beaker phenomenon and its relation with the Aegean Early Bronze Age, in *Between the Aegean and the Baltic Seas: Prehistory Across Borders: Proceedings of the International Conference, Bronze and Early Iron Age Interconnections and Contemporary Developments Between the Aegean and the Regions of the Balkan Peninsula, Central and Northern Europe University of Zagreb, 11–14 April 2005* (Aegaeum: Annales d'archéologie égéenne de l'Université de Liège et UT-PASP 27), I. Galanaki, H. Tomas, Y. Galanakis and R. Laffineur (eds), 91–104. Université de Liege and University of Texas at Austin.

Heyd, V. 2011. Yamnaya groups and tumuli west of the Black Sea, in *Ancestral Landscapes: Burial Mounds in the Copper and Bronze Ages*, E. Borgna and S. Müller Celka (eds), 536–55. Travaux de la Maison de l'Orient et de la Méditerranée 61. Lyon.

Heyd, V., Husty, L. and Kreiner, L. 2004. *Siedlungen der Glockenbecherkultur in Süddeutschland und Mitteleuropa*. Arbeiten zur Archäologie Süddeutschlands. Bd 17. Büchenbach: Verlag Dr. Faustus.

Hickey, R. 2002. Internal and external forces again: changes in word order in Old English and Old Irish, *Language Sciences*, 24 (3–4), 261–83.

Historia Brittonum, translated in *Six Old English Chronicles*, ed. J. A. Giles. 1848. London: Henry G. Bohn.

Historia Regum Britanniae of Geoffrey of Monmouth, I: Bern, Burgerbibliothek, MS 568, ed. N. Wright. 1985. Cambridge: D. S. Brewer.

Homer. *The Iliad*, trans. A. T. Murray (Loeb Classical Library). Cambridge, MA: Harvard University Press; London: William Heinemann Ltd. 1924; or trans. E. V. Rieu, revised P. Jones. 2003. London: Penguin Books.

Höppner, B. et al. 2005. Prehistoric copper production in the Inn Valley (Austria), and the earliest copper in Central Europe, *Archaeometry*, 47 (2), 293–315.

Hubert, H. 1934. *The Rise of the Celts*. London: Kegan Paul & Co.

Huehnergard, J. 2011. Proto-Semitic language and culture, in *The American Heritage Dictionary of the English Language* (5th ed.), 2066–69. Boston and New York: Houghton, Mifflin and Harcourt.

Hummler, M. 2007. Bridging the gap at La Tène, *Antiquity*, 81, 1067–70.

Hurl, D., McSparren, C. and Moore, P. 2002. Excavations at the Dorsey, Co. Armargh. Centre for Archaeological Fieldwork, Queen's University, Belfast. Data Structure Report no. 4.

Hyllested, A. 2010. The precursors of Celtic and Germanic, in *Proceedings of the 21st UCLA Indo-European Conference*, S. W. Jamison, H. C. Melchert and B. Vine (eds), 107–28. Bremen: Hempen.

Inizan, M. L. 2012. Pressure débitage in the Old world: forerunners, researchers, geopolitics, handing on the baton, chapter 2 in Desrosiers (ed.) 2012, 11–42.

Isaac, G. R. 2010. The origins of the Celtic languages: language spread from east to west, chapter 7 in Cunliffe and Koch 2010, 162–65.

Isidore. *The Etymologies of Isidore of Seville*, ed. and trans. S. A. Barney, W. J. Lewis, J. A. Beach and O. Bergho. 2006. Cambridge: Cambridge University Press.

Jackson, K. H. 1964. *The Oldest Irish Tradition: A Window on the Iron Age*. Cambridge and New York: Cambridge University Press.

James, S. 1999. *The Atlantic Celts: Ancient People or Modern Invention?* London: British Museum Press.

Jay, M. et al. 2012. Chariots and Context: new radiocarbon dates from Wetwang and the chronology of Iron Age burials and brooches in East Yorkshire, *Oxford Journal of Archaeology*, 31 (2), 161–89.

Jay, M. et al. 2013. British Iron Age chariot burials of the Arras culture: a multi-isotope approach to investigating mobility levels and subsistence practices, *World Archaeology*, 45 (3), 473–91.

Jay, M., Parker Pearson, M. et al. 2012. The Beaker People Project: an interim report on the progress of the isotope analysis of the organic skeletal material, in Allen, Gardiner and Sheridan (eds) 2012, 226–36.

Jenner, H. 1904. *A Handbook of the Cornish Language, chiefly in its latest stages with some account of its history and literature*. London: David Nutt.

Jeunesse, C. 2014. Pratiques funéraires campaniformes en Europe - Faut-il remettre en cause la dichotomie Nord-Sud? La question de la réutilisation des sépultures monumentales dans l'Europe du 3e millénaire, in *Données récentes sur les pratiques funéraires néolithiques de la Plaine du Rhin supérieur*, P. Lefranc, A. Denaire and C. Jeunesse (eds), BAR International Series 2633, 211. Oxford: Archaeopress.

John, B. S. 1972. The linguistic significance of the Pembrokeshire landsker, *The Pembrokeshire Historian: Journal of the Pembrokeshire Local History Society*, 4, 7–29.

Johnston, P. 1997. Older Scots phonology and its regional variation, chapter 3 in Jones (ed.) 1997, 47–111.

Jones, C. (ed.) 1997. *The Edinburgh History of the Scots Language*. Edinburgh: Edinburgh University Press.

Jones, H. M. 2012. *A Statistical Overview of the Welsh Language*. Cardiff: Welsh Language Board.

Jones, *Works = The Works of Sir William Jones*, ed. A. M. Jones, 13 vols (2nd ed.). 1807. London: J. Stockdale.

Josephson, F. 2012. Transfer of morphemes and grammatical structure in ancient Anatolia, in *Copies Versus Cognates in Bound Morphology*, L. Johanson and M. Robbeets (eds), 337–54. Leiden: Brill.

Jovanović, B. 1991. The Scordisci, in Moscati et al. (eds) 1991, 337–47.

Justin. Marcus Junianus Justinus. *Epitome of the Philippic History of Pompeius Trogus*, trans. with notes by the Rev. J. S. Watson. 1853. London: Henry G. Bohn.

Karl, R. 2001. ... on a road to nowhere ..: Chariotry and the road systems in the Celtic world, IRQUAS Online Project. New Perspectives in Irish Studies.

Karl, R. 2003. Iron Age chariots and medieval texts: a step too far in 'breaking down boundaries'?, *e-Keltoi: the Journal of Interdisciplinary Celtic Studies*, 5: *Warfare*, 1–30.

Karl, R. 2006. Boii and the Celts in Bohemia, in Koch (ed.) 2006, 222–26.

Kelly, J. N. D. 1975. *Jerome: His Life, Writings and Controversies*. London: Duckworth; New York: Harper & Row.

Keyser, C. et al. 2009. Ancient DNA provides new insights into the history of south Siberian Kurgan people, *Human Genetics*, 126 (3), 395–410.

Kirtcho, L. 2009. The earliest wheeled transport in Southwestern Central Asia: new finds from Altyn-Depe, *Archaeology, Ethnology and Anthropology of Eurasia*, 37 (1), 25–33.

Kitson, P. R. 1996. Reconstruction, typology and the 'original homeland' of the Indo-Europeans, in *Linguistic Reconstruction and Typology*, J. Fisiak (ed.). (Trends in Linguistics: Studies and Monographs 96), 183–239. Berlin: Mouton de Gruyter.

Knipper, C. et al. 2014. Social differentiation and land use at an Early Iron Age 'princely seat': bioarchaeological investigations at the Glauberg (Germany), *Journal of Archaeological Science*, 41, 818–35.

Koch, J. T. 1992. Gallo-Brittonic vs. Insular Celtic: The inter-relationships of the Celtic languages reconsidered, in *Bretagne et pays celtiques – langues, histoire, civilisation: Mélanges offerts à la mémoire de Léon Fleuriot*, Gw. Le Menn, J.-Y. Le Moing (eds), 471–95. Saint-Brieuc and Rennes.

Koch, J. T. 1995. The Conversion and the transition from Primitive to Old Irish *c.* 367–*c.* 637, *Emania* 13, 39–50.

Koch, J. T. (ed.) 2006. *Celtic Culture: A Historical Encyclopedia*, 5 vols. Santa Barbara, CA: ABC-CLIO.

Koch, J. T. 2007. *An Atlas for Celtic Studies: Archaeology and Names in Ancient Europe and Early Medieval Ireland, Britain and Brittany* (Celtic Studies Publications 12). Oxford: Oxbow Books and Celtic Studies Publications.

Koch, J. T. 2010. Paradigm shift? Interpreting Tartessian as Celtic, chapter 9 in Cunliffe and Koch (eds) 2010, 185–301.

Koch, J. T. 2011. *Tartessian 2: The Inscription of Mesas do Castelinho, *ro* and the Verbal Complex, Preliminaries to Historical Phonology*. Aberystwyth: University of Wales Centre for Advanced Welsh and Celtic Studies.

Koch, J. T. and Carey, J. (eds) 2003. *The Celtic Heroic Age: Literary Sources for Ancient Celtic Europe & Early Ireland & Wales* (4th ed.). Aberystwyth: Celtic Studies Publications.

Koch, J. T. and Cunliffe, B. (eds). 2013. *Celtic from the West 2: Rethinking the Bronze Age and the Arrival of Indo-European in Atlantic Europe*. Oxford and Oakville: Oxbow Books.

Kohl, P. L. 2007. *The Making of Bronze Age Eurasia* (Cambridge World Archaeology). Cambridge, New York and Melbourne: Cambridge University Press.

Kortlandt, F. 1981. More evidence for Italo-Celtic, *Ériu*, 32, 1–22. Reprinted in *Italo-Celtic Origins and Prehistoric Development of the Irish Language*, 25–50. 2007. Amsterdam and New York: Editions Rodopi B.V.

Korvin-Piotrovskiy, A. G. 2012. Tripolye Culture in Ukraine, in *The Tripolye Culture: Giant-settlements in Ukraine: Formation, Development and Decline*, F. Menotti and A. G. Korvin-Piotrovskiy (eds), 6–18. Oxford and Oakville: Oxbow Books.

Koukouli-Chrysanthaki, Ch. and Papadopoulos, S. 2009. The Island of Thassos and the Aegean in the prehistory, *Asmosia VII: Proceedings of the 7th International Conference of Association for the Study of Marble and Other Stones in Antiquity, Thassos, September 15–20, 2003*, Bulletin de Correspondance Hellénique Supplément 51.

Krahe, H. 1963. *Die Struktur der alteuropäischen Hydronomie*. Wiesbaden: Akademie der Wissenschaften und der Literatur.

Kremenetski, C. V. 2003. Steppe and forest-steppe belt of Eurasia: Holocene environmental history, chapter 2 in *Prehistoric Steppe Adaptation and the Horse* (McDonald Institute Monographs), M. Levine, C. Renfrew and K. Boyle (eds), 11–27. Cambridge: University of Cambridge.

Kremenetski, C. V., Chichagova, O. A. and Shishlina, N. I. 1999. Palaeoecological evidence for Holocene vegetation, climate and land-use change in the low Don basin and Kalmuk area, southern Russia, *Vegetation History and Archaeobotany*, 8 (4), 233–46.

Kristiansen, K. 1998. *Europe Before History* (New Studies in Archaeology). Cambridge and New York: Cambridge University Press.

Kristiansen, K. 2005. What language did Neolithic pots speak? Colin Renfrew's European farming-language-dispersal model challenged, *Antiquity*, 79 (305), 694–95.

Kroonen, G. 2012. Non-Indo-European root nouns in Germanic: Evidence in support of the Agricultural Substrate Hypothesis, in *A Linguistic Map of Prehistoric Northern Europe*, R. Grünthal and P. Kallio (eds), 239–60. Mémoires de la Société Finno-Ougrienne 266. Helsinki: Société Finno-Ougrienne.

Kulcsár, G. and Szeverényi, V. 2013. Transition to the Bronze Age: issues of continuity and discontinuity in the first half of the third millennium BC in the Carpathian Basin, in *Transitions to the Bronze Age. Interregional Interaction and Socio-Cultural Change in the Third Millennium BC Carpathian Basin and Neighbouring Regions*, V. Heyd, G. Kulcsár and V. Szeverényi (eds), 67–92. Budapest: Archaeolingua.

Kunst, M. 2001. Invasions? Fashion? Social Ranks? Consideration concerning the Bell Beaker phenomenon in Copper Age fortifications of the Iberian peninsula, in Nicolis (ed.) 2001, 81–90.

Kunst, M. 2007. Zambujal (Torres Vedras, Lisboa): relatório das escavações de 2001, *Revista Portuguesa de Arqueologia*, 10 (1), 95–118.

Kuzmina, E. E. 2007. *The Origin of the Indo-Iranians*, ed. J. P. Mallory. Leiden and Boston: Brill.

Labaune, M. 2013. Bell Beaker metal and metallurgy in Western Europe, chapter 16 in Prieto Martinéz and Salanova (eds) 2013, 177–88.

Lacan, M. 2011. Ancient DNA suggests the leading role played by men in the Neolithic dissemination, *PNAS*, 108 (45), 18255–59.

Lacey, B. 2006. *Cenél Conaill and the Donegal Kingdoms, AD 500–800*. Dublin: Four Courts Press.

Lane, A. 2014. Wroxeter and the end of Roman Britain, *Antiquity*, 88, 501–15.

Lapidge, M., Blair, J., Keynes, S. and Scragg, D. (eds). 1999. *Blackwell Encyclopaedia of Anglo-Saxon England*. Oxford: Blackwell.

Laws of the Earliest English Kings, ed. and trans. F. L. Attenborough. 1922. Cambridge: Cambridge University Press.

Lazaridis, I. et al. 2014. Ancient human genomes suggest three ancestral populations for present-day Europeans, *Nature*, 513, 409–13.

Lazarovici, C.-M. 2010. New data regarding the chronology of the Precucuteni, Cucuteni and Horodiştea-Erbiceni cultures, *PANTA RHEI: Studies on the Chronology and Cultural Development of South-Eastern and Central Europe in Earlier Prehistory Presented to Juraj Pavúk on the Occasion of his 75th Birthday. Studia Archaeologica et Mediaevalia*, 11, 71–94. Bratislava: Comenius University.

Lebor Gabála Érenn, 'The Book of the Taking of Ireland', Irish Texts Society, vols 34 (1938), 35 (1939), 39 (1940), 41 (1941) and 44 (1956).

Lechterbeck, J. et al. 2014. How was Bell Beaker economy related to Corded Ware and Early Bronze Age lifestyles? Archaeological, botanical and palynological evidence from the Hegau, Western Lake Constance region, *Environmental Archaeology*, 19 (2), 95–113.

Lee, E. J. et al. 2012. Emerging genetic patterns of the European neolithic: Perspectives from a late neolithic bell beaker burial site in Germany, *American Journal of Physical Anthropology*, 148 (4), 571–79.

Lejars, T. 2003. La nécropole celtique de Roissy, *Pour La Science*, 306.

Lemercier, O. 2012. Interpreting the Beaker phenomenon in Mediterranean France: an Iron Age analogy, *Antiquity*, 86 (331), 131–43.

Leslie, S. et al. 2015. The fine-scale genetic structure of the British population, *Nature*, 519, 309–14.

Lhuyd, E. 1707. *Archaeologia Britannica: giving some account additional to what has been hitherto publish'd, of the languages, histories and customs of the original inhabitants of Great Britain: from collections and observations in travels through Wales, Cornwall, Bas-Bretagne, Ireland and Scotland*, vol. 1: *Glossography*. Oxford: Printed for the author.

Lintott, A. 1999. *The Constitution of the Roman Republic*. Oxford and New York: Oxford University Press.

Lira, J. et al 2010. Ancient DNA reveals traces of Iberian Neolithic and Bronze Age lineages in modern Iberian horses, *Molecular Ecology*, 19 (1), 64–78.

Lives of Saints Declan and Mochuda, ed. and trans. P. Power. 1914. Irish Texts Society 16.

Livy. *History of Rome*, trans. Rev. Canon Roberts. 1905. London: J. M. Dent & Sons, Ltd. *History of Rome: Books Nine to Twenty-Six*, trans D. Spillan and C. Edmonds. 1868. London: Henry G. Bohn.

Lorrio, A. J. and Zapatero, G. R. 2005. The Celts in Iberia: an overview, *e-Keltoi: the Journal of Interdisciplinary Celtic Studies*, 6: *The Celts in the Iberian Peninsula*, 167–254.

Luján Martínez, E. R. 2006. The language(s) of the Callaeci, *e-Keltoi: the Journal of Interdisciplinary Celtic Studies*, 6: *The Celts in the Iberian Peninsula*, 715–48.

Lynn, C. J. 1989. An interpretation of 'The Dorsey', *Emania* 6, 5–10.

Mac Carron, P. and Kenna, R. 2012. Universal properties of mythological networks, *Epl (Europhysics Letters)*, 99, 28002.

McEvoy. B. and Bradley, D. G. 2006. Y-chromosomes and the extent of patrilineal ancestry in Irish surnames, *Human Genetics*, 119, 212–19.

McEvoy, B. P. and Bradley, D. G. 2010. Irish Genetics and Celts, chapter 5 in Cunliffe and Koch 2010, 107–20.

MacFarlane, J. 1922. *The History of Clan MacFarlane*. Glasgow: David J. Clark.

McKie, R. 2006. *The Face of Britain: How Our Genes Reveal the History of Britain*. London: Simon & Schuster.

MacKillop, J. 2004. *A Dictionary of Celtic Mythology*. Oxford: Oxford University Press.

McManus, D. 1996. Ogham, section 26 in *The World's Writing Systems*, P. T. Daniels and W. Bright (eds), 340–45. Oxford and New York: Oxford University Press.

MacNeill, E. 1920. *Phases of Irish History*. Dublin: M. H. Gill and Son.

Maggi, R. and Pearce, M. 2005. Mid fourth-millennium copper mining in Liguria, north-west Italy: the earliest known copper mines in Western Europe, *Antiquity*, 79 (303), 66–77.

Maier, F. 1991. The oppidum of Manching, in Moscati et al. (eds), 1991, 530–31.

Makhortyk, S. V. 2008. On the question of Cimmerian imports and imitations in Central Europe, in *Import and Imitation in Archaeology*, P. F. Biehl and Y. Ya. Rassamakin (eds), 167–86. Langenweißbach: Beier & Beran.

Mallory, J. P. 1989. *In Search of the Indo-Europeans: Language, Archaeology and Myth*. London: Thames & Hudson.

Mallory, J. P. 1992. The world of Cú Chulainn: the archaeology of the Táin Bó Cúailnge, in *Aspects of the Táin*, J. P. Mallory (ed.), 103–59. Belfast: December Publications.

Mallory, J. P. 1993. The Archaeology of the Irish Dreamtime, in *Proceedings of the Harvard Celtic Colloquium*, 13, B. Hillers, P. Hopkins and J. Hunter (eds), 1–24. Department of Celtic Languages and Literature: Harvard University.

Mallory, J. P. 1998. The Old Irish Chariot, in *Mír Curad: Studies in Honour of Calvert Watkins*, J. Jasanoff, H. C. Melchert and L. Olivier (eds), 451–64. Innsbruck: Sonderbruck.

Mallory, J. P. 2013. *The Origins of the Irish*. London and New York: Thames & Hudson.

Mallory, J. P. and Adams, D. Q. (eds). 1997. *Encyclopedia of Indo-European Culture*. London: Fitzroy Dearborn Publishers.

Mallory, J. P. and Adams, D. Q. 2006. *Oxford Introduction to Proto-Indo-European and the Proto-Indo-European World*. Oxford: Oxford University Press.

Mallory, J. P. and Mair, V. H. 2000. *The Tarim Mummies: The Mystery of the First Europeans in China*. London and New York: Thames & Hudson.

Manco, J. 1998. Saxon Bath: The Legacy of Rome and the Saxon Rebirth, *Bath History*, 7, 27–54.

Manco, J. 2015. *Ancestral Journeys: The Peopling of Europe from the First Venturers to the Vikings*. Revised and updated edition. London and New York: Thames & Hudson.

Manley J. and Rudkin, D. 2005. A pre-AD 43 ditch at Fishbourne Roman palace, Chichester, *Britannia*, 36, 55–99.

Manning, W. H. 1995. Ironworking in the Celtic world, chapter 17 in Green (ed.) 1995, 310–20.

Manti, P. and Watkinson, D. 2008. From Homer to hoplite: scientific investigations of Greek copper alloy helmets, *History of Mechanism and Machine Science*, 6, 167–79.

Manzura, I. 2005a. Steps to the steppe: or, how the North Pontic region was colonised, *Oxford Journal of Archaeology*, 24 (4), 313–38.

Manzura, I. 2005b. The proto-Bronze Age cemetery at Durankulak: a look from the East, in *Prehistoric Archaeology and Theoretical Anthropology and Education* (Reports of Prehistoric Research Projects 6–7), L. Nikolova, J. Fritz and J. Higgins (eds), 51–55. Salt Lake City and Karlovo.

Marciniak, A. 2011. The Secondary Products Revolution: empirical evidence and its current zooarchaeological critique, *Journal of World Prehistory*, 24, 117–30.

Markoe, G. E. 2000. *The Phoenicians* (Peoples of the Past). London: British Museum Press.

Martirosyan, H. 2013. The place of Armenian in the Indo-European language family: the relationship with Greek and Indo-Iranian, *Journal of Language Relationship*, 10, 85–137.

Maryon, H. 1936. Excavation of two Bronze age barrows at Kirkhaugh, Northumberland, *Archaeologia Aeliana* (4th series), 13, 207–17.

Mata, D. R. 2002. The ancient Phoenicians of the 8th and 7th centuries BC in the Bay of Cadiz: state of the research, in *The Phoenicians in Spain: An Archaeological Review of the Eighth–Sixth Centuries B.C.E. A Collection of Articles Translated from Spanish*, M. R. Bierling (ed. and trans.), 155–98. Winona Lake, IN: Eisenbrauns.

Matasović, R. 2007. Insular Celtic as a language area, in *The Celtic Languages in Contact: Papers from the Workshop within the Framework of the XIII International Congress of Celtic Studies, Bonn, 26–27 July 2007*, H. L. C. Tristram (ed.), 93–112. Potsdam: Universitätsverlag Potsdam.

Matasović, R. 2012. The substratum in Insular Celtic, *Journal of Language Relationship*, 8, 153–68.

Mazzieri, P. and Dal Santo, N. 2007. Il sito del Neolitico recente di Botteghino (Parma), *Rivista di Scienze Preistoriche*, LVII, 113–38.

Mees, B. 2003. Stratum and shadow: a genealogy of stratigraphy theories from the Indo-European West, in *Language Contacts in Prehistory: Studies in Stratigraphy: Papers from the Workshop on Linguistic Stratigraphy and Prehistory at the Fifteenth International Conference on Historical Linguistics, Melbourne, 17 August 2001*. (Amsterdam Studies in the Theory and History of Linguistic Science, Series IV: Current Issues in Linguistic Theory, 239), H. Anderson (ed.), 11–44. Amsterdam and Philadelphia: John Benjamins Publishing Company.

Megaw, R. and Megaw, V. 1995. The nature and function of Celtic art, chapter 20 in Green (ed.) 1995, 345–75.

Menk, R. 1979. Le phenomène campaniforme: structure biologiques et intégration historique, *Archives Suisses d'anthropologie générale*, 43, 259–84.

Meyer, K. (ed. and trans.). 1911. *Selections from Ancient Irish Poetry*. London: Constable & Company.

Militarev, A. Y. 2005. Once more about glottochronology and the comparative method: the Omotic-Afrasian case, *Aspects of Comparative Linguistics*, 1, 339–40.

Mödlinger, M. et al. 2013. Archaeometallurgical characterization of the earliest European metal helmets, *Materials Characterization*, 79, 22–36.

Moffat, A. and Wilson, J. 2011. *The Scots: A Genetic Journey*. Edinburgh: Birlinn.

Moore, C. and Chiriotti, C. 2010. Reinventing the wheel: new evidence from Edercloon, Co. Longford, chapter 5 in *Creative Minds: Production, Manufacturing and Invention in Ancient Ireland, Proceedings of a Public Seminar on Archaeological Discoveries on National Road Schemes, August 2009*, M. Stanley, E. Danaher and J. Eogan (eds). (Archaeology and the National Roads Authority, Monograph Series No. 7.) Dublin: National Roads Authority.

Moore, L. T. et al. 2006. A Y-chromosome signature of hegemony in Gaelic Ireland, *American Journal of Human Genetics*, 78 (2), 334–38.

Morgunova, N. L. and Khokhlova, O. S. 2013. Chronology and periodization of the Pit-Grave Culture in the region between the Volga and Ural Rivers based on radiocarbon dating and paleopedological research, in Proceedings of the 21st International Radiocarbon Conference, A. J. T. Jull and C. Hatté (eds), *Radiocarbon*, 55 (2–3), 1286–96.

Morley, C. 2008. Chariots and migrants in East Yorkshire: dismantling the argument, in *Movement, Mobility and Migration*, Archaeological Review from Cambridge, 23.2, E. Lightfoot (ed.), 69–91.

Moscati, S. et al. (eds) 1991. *The Celts*. Milan: Bompiani; London: Thames & Hudson.

Moseley, C. (ed.). 2010. *Atlas of the World's Languages in Danger* (3rd ed.). Paris: UNESCO Publishing. Online version.

Muhr, K. 1996. *Place-Names of Northern Ireland, 6: North-west County Down / Iveagh*. Belfast: Cló Ollscoil na Banríona.

Muller, J.-C. 1986. Early stages of language comparison from Sassetti to Sir William Jones (1786), *Kratylos*, 31, 1–31.

Müller, J. and van Willigen, S. 2001. New radiocarbon evidence for European Bell Beakers and the consequences for the diffusion of the Bell Beaker Phenomenon, in Nicolis (ed.) 2001, 59–75.

Müller, R. et al. 2007. Zambujal and the beginnings of metallurgy in southern Portugal, in *Metals and Mines: Studies in Archaeometallurgy: Selected papers from the Conference Metallurgy: A Touchstone for Cross-cultural Interaction held at the British Museum 28–30 April 2005 to celebrate the career of Paul Craddock during his 40 years at the British Museum*, S. La Niece, D. Hook and P. Craddock (eds), 15–26. London: Archetype Publications in association with the British Museum.

Murray, A. C. 2003. (ed. and trans.) *From Roman to Merovingian Gaul: A Reader*. Toronto, Ontario: Higher Education University of Toronto Press.

Myres, N. et al. 2011. A major Y-chromosome haplogroup R1b Holocene era founder effect in Central and Western Europe, *European Journal of Human Genetics*, 19 (1), 95–101.

Nakhleh, L., Ringe D. and Warnow, T. 2005. Perfect phylogenetic networks: a new methodology for reconstructing the evolutionary history of natural languages, *Language, Journal of the Linguistic Society of America*, 81 (2), 382–420.

Nichols, J. 1997. The epicenter of the Indo-European linguistic spread, in *Archaeology and Language I: Theoretical and Methodological Orientations*, R. Blench and M. Spriggs (eds), 122–48. London: Routledge.

Nicolaisen, W. F. H. 1982. Old European names in Britain, *Nomina* 6, 37–42.

Nicolis, F. (ed.) 2001. *Bell Beakers Today: Pottery, People, Culture, Symbols in Prehistoric Europe. Proceedings of the International Colloquium, Riva del Garda (Trento, Italy), 11–16 May 1998*. 2 vols. Trento: Provincia Autonoma di Trento.

Nikitin, A. et al. 2012. Mitochondrial haplogroup C in ancient mitochondrial DNA from Ukraine extends the presence of East Eurasian genetic lineages in Neolithic Central and Eastern Europe, *Journal of Human Genetics*, 57, 610–12.

Nocete, F. 2006. The first specialised copper industry in the Iberian peninsula: Cabezo Juré, *Antiquity*, 80 (309), 646–57.

Nocete, F. et al. 2011. Direct chronometry (14C AMS) of the earliest copper metallurgy in the Guadalquivir Basin (Spain) during the third millennium BC: first regional database, *Journal of Archaeological Science*, 38 (12), 3278–95.

Nocete, F. et al. 2014. Gold in the southwest of the Iberian peninsula during the 3rd Millennium BC, *Journal of Archaeological Science*, 41, 691–704.

Northover, J. P. N., O'Brien, W. and Stos, S. 2001. Lead isotopes and metal circulation in Beaker/Early Bronze Age Ireland, *Journal of Irish Archaeology*, 10, 25–47.

Novembre, J. et al. 2008. Genes mirror geography within Europe, *Nature*, 456, 98–101.

NPNF2:6 = *The Nicene and Post-Nicene Fathers*, second series, vol. 6: *Jerome: Letters and Select Works*, trans. W. H. Fremantle. 1893.

Nutt, A. T. 1900. *Cuchulainn, the Irish Achilles*. London: D. Nutt.

O'Brien, M. A. 1962. *Corpus Genealogiarum Hiberniae*, vol. 1. Dublin: The Dublin Institute for Advanced Studies.

O'Brien, S. R. et al. 1995. Complexity of Holocene climate reconstructed from a Greenland ice core, *Science*, 270 (5244), 1962–64.

O'Brien, W. 2004. *Ross Island: Mining, Metal and Society in Early Ireland* (Bronze Age Studies 6). Galway: National University of Ireland, Department of Archaeology.

Ó Corráin, D. 2006. Annals, Irish, in Koch (ed.) 2006, 69–75.

Ó Croidheáin, C. 2006. *Language from Below: The Irish Language, Ideology and Power in 20th-Century Ireland*. Oxford, Bern, Berlin, Bruxelles, Frankfurt am Main, New York, Wien: Peter Lang.

Ó Cróinín, D. 1995. *Early Medieval Ireland 400–1200* (Longman History of Ireland). Abingdon and New York: Routledge.

Ó Cróinín, D. 2005. Ireland, 400–800, chapter 7 in Ó Cróinín (ed.) 2005, 182–234.

Ó Cróinín, D. (ed.) 2005. *A New History of Ireland, vol. 1: Prehistoric and early Ireland*. Oxford and New York: Oxford University Press.

ODNB = Oxford Dictionary of National Biography. Oxford University Press 2004–14.

Odriozola C. P. and Hurtado Pérez, V. M. 2007. The manufacturing process of 3rd millennium BC bone based incrusted pottery decoration from the Middle Guadiana river basin (Badajoz, Spain), *Journal of Archaeological Science*, 34, 1794–803.

O'Dushlaine, C. T. et al. 2010. Population structure and genome-wide patterns of variation in Ireland and Britain, *European Journal of Human Genetics*, 18, 1248–54.

Ó Floinn, R. 2000. Freestone Hill, Co. Kilkenny: a reassessment, in *Seanchas. Studies in Early and Medieval Irish Archaeology, History and Literature in Honour of Francis J. Byrne*, A. P. Smyth (ed.), 12–29. Dublin: Four Courts Press.

Ó hUiginn, R. 2006. Táin Bó Cuailnge ('The Cattle Raid of Cooley'), in Koch (ed.) 2006, 1646–47.

Olalde, I. et al. 2014. Derived immune and ancestral pigmentation alleles in a 7,000-year-old Mesolithic European, *Nature*, 507, 225–28.

O'Laverty, J. 1878. *An Historical Account of the Diocese of Down and Conor, Ancient and Modern*, vol. 1. Dublin: James Duffy and Sons.

Olivier, L. 1999. The Hochdorf 'princely' grave and the question of the nature of archaeological funerary assemblages, chapter 8 in *Time and Archaeology*, T. Murray (ed.), 109–38. London and New York: Routledge.

Orme, N. 2000. *The Saints of Cornwall*. Oxford and New York: Oxford University Press.

Østmo, E. 2012. Late Neolithic expansion to Norway. The beginning of a 4000 year-old shipbuilding tradition, chapter 6 in Prescott and Glørstad 2012, 63–69.

Outram, A.K. et al. 2009. The earliest horse harnessing and milking, *Science*, 323 (5919), 1332–35.

Panegyrici Latini. In Praise of Later Roman Emperors: the Panegyrici Latini, ed. and trans. C. E. V. Nixon and B. Saylor Rodgers. 1995. Oakland, CA: University of California Press.

Pardee, D. 2009. A new Aramaic inscription from Zincirli, *Bulletin of the American Schools of Oriental Research*, 356, 51–71.

Pare, C. 1991. Fürstensitze, Celts and the Mediterranean World: Developments in the West Hallstatt Culture in the 6th and 5th centuries BC, *Proceedings of the Prehistoric Society*, 57 (2), 183–202.

Pare, C. F. E. 2000. Bronze and the Bronze Age, in *Metals Make the World Go Round: The Supply and Circulation of Metals in Bronze Age Europe. Proceedings of a Conference Held at the University of Birmingham in June 1997*, C. F. E. Pare (ed.), 1–32. Oxford: Oxbow Books.

Parker Pearson, M. 1995. Southwestern Bronze Age pottery, in *'Unbaked Urns of Rudely Shape': Essays on British and Irish Pottery for Ian Longworth*, I. Kinnes and G. Varndell, (eds), 89–100. Oxford: Oxbow.

Parkinson, W. A. et al. 2010. Elemental analysis of ceramic incrustation indicates long-term cultural continuity in the prehistoric Carpathian Basin, *Archaeology, Ethnology and Anthropology of Eurasia*, 38 (2), 64–70.

Parpola, A. 2008. Proto-Indo-European speakers of the Late Tripolye culture as the inventors of wheeled vehicles: Linguistic and archaeological considerations, in *Proceedings of the 19th Annual UCLA Indo-European Conference* (The Journal of Indo-European Studies Monograph Series 54), K. Jones-Bley, M. E. Huld, A. Della Volpe and M. Robbins Dexter (eds), 1–59. Washington, DC: Institute for the Study of Man.

Parsons, J. 1767. *The Remains of Japhet, being historical enquiries into the affinity and origins of the European languages*. London: Printed for the author.

Patrick. *Confessio*, trans. P. McCarthy. 2003. Dublin: Royal Irish Academy.

Pausanias. *Description of Greece*, trans. W. H. S. Jones and H. A. Ormerod. 1918. 5 vols (Loeb Classical Library). Cambridge, MA, Harvard University Press; London, William Heinemann Ltd.

Pereltsvaig, A. and Lewis, M. 2015. *The Indo-European Controversy: Facts and Fallacies in Historical Linguistics*. Cambridge: Cambridge University Press.

Peška, J. 2013. Two new burial sites of Bell Beaker Culture with exceptional finds from Eastern Moravia/Czech Republic, chapter 6 in Prieto-Martinez and Salanova (eds) 2013, 61–72.

Pezron, [P. Y.]. 1706. *The Antiquities of Nations, More particularly of the Celtae or Gauls, Taken to be Originally the same People as our Ancient Britains, Englished by Mr. Jones*. London: Janeway.

Piggott, S. 1995. Wood and the wheelwright, chapter 18 in Green (ed.) 1995, 321–27.

Piguet M. and Besse, M. 2009. Chronology and Bell Beaker common ware, *Radiocarbon*, 51 (2), 817–30.

Pliny the Elder. *Natural History*, trans. J. Bostock and H. T. Riley. 6 vols. 1855–57. London: H. G. Bohn.

Plutarch. The Life of Caesar, in *The Fall of the Roman Republic: Six Lives by Plutarch*, trans. R. Warner. 1958. Harmondsworth: Penguin.

Polyaenus. *Stratagems of War*, trans. R. Shepherd. 1793. London: George Nicol.

Polybius. *The Histories*, trans. R. Waterfield with notes by B. McGing. 2010. Oxford: Oxford University Press.

Pomponius Mela's Description of the World, ed. F. E. Romer. 1998. Ann Arbor: University of Michigan Press.

Prescott, C. 2012. Third millennium transformations in Norway: modelling an interpretive platform, chapter 10 in Prescott and Glørstad (eds) 2012, 115–27.

Prescott, C. and Glørstad, H. (eds). 2012. *Becoming European*. Oxford and Oakville: Oxbow Books.

Price, T. D., Knipper, C., Grupe, G. and Smrcka, V. 2004. Strontium isotopes and prehistoric human migration: the Bell Beaker period in Central Europe, *European Journal of Archaeology*, 7 (1), 9–40.

Prieto-Martínez, M. P. 2012. Perceiving changes in the third millennium BC in Europe through pottery, chapter 4 in Prescott and Glørstad (eds) 2012, 30–47.

Prieto-Martínez, M. P. and Salanova, L. (eds) 2013. *Current Researches on Bell Beakers: Proceedings of the 15th International Bell Beaker Conference: From Atlantic to Ural. 5th–9th May 2011. Poio (Pontevedra, Galicia, Spain)*. Santiago de Compostela.

Prósper, B. M. 2010/2011. The Hispano-Celtic divinity ILVRBEDA, gold mining in western Hispania and the syntactic context of Celtiberian arkatobezom 'silver mine', *Die Sprache*, 49 (1), 53–83.

Prósper, B. M. 2014. Sifting the evidence: new interpretations on Celtic and Nonceltic personal names of western Hispania in the light of phonetics, composition and suffixation, in *Continental Celtic Word Formation. The Onomastic Data*, J. L. G. Alonso (ed.), 181–200. Salamanca: Ediciones Universidad de Salamanca.

Ptolemy, Claudius. *The Geography*. No reliable complete English translation is in print. That used is trans. E. L. Stevenson. 1932. New York: New York Public Library.

Querré, G. and Convertini, F. 1998. Apports des études céramologiques en laboratoire à la connaissance du Campaniforme: résultats, bilan et perspectives, *Bulletin de la Société préhistorique française*, 95 (3), 333–42.

Raftery, B. 2005. Iron-Age Ireland, chapter 6 in Ó Cróinín (ed.) 2005, 134–81.

Raghavan, M. et al. 2014. Upper Palaeolithic Siberian genome reveals dual ancestry of Native Americans, *Nature*, 505, 87–91.

Rance, P. 2001. Attacotti, Déisi and Magnus Maximus: the case for Irish federates in Late Roman Britain, *Britannia*, 32, 243–70.

Rankin, D. 1987. *Celts and the Classical World*. London and New York: Routledge.

Reaney, P. H. and Wilson, R. M. 1997. *Oxford Dictionary of English Surnames* (3rd ed.). Oxford: Oxford University Press.

Redmonds, G., King T. and Hey, D. 2011. *Surnames, DNA and Family History*. Oxford and New York: Oxford University Press.

Rees, B. R. 1998. *Pelagius: Life and Letters*. Woodbridge: Boydell Press.

Renfrew, C. 1987. *Archaeology and Language: The Puzzle of Indo-European Origins*. London: Jonathan Cape.

Res Gestae Divi Augusti, in *Compendium of Roman History. Res Gestae Divi Augusti*, trans. F. W. Shipley. 1924. (Loeb Classical Library). Cambridge, MA: Harvard University Press.

Reynolds, S. 1983. Medieval origines gentium and the community of the realm, *History*, 68, 375–90.

Ringe, D., Warnow, T. and Taylor, A. 2002. Indo-European and computational cladistics, *Transactions of the Philological Society*, 100 (1), 59–129.

Ríos, P. 2013. New dating of the Bell Beaker Horizon in the region of Madrid, chapter 9 in Prieto-Martínez and Salanova (eds) 2013, 97–109.

Ritchie, J. N. G. and W. F. 1995. The army, weapons and fighting, chapter 4 in Green (ed.) 1995.

Rivet, A. L. F. and Smith, C. 1979. *The Place-Names of Roman Britain*. London: Batsford.

Robb, J. 2009. People of stone: stelae, personhood and society in prehistoric Europe, *Journal of Archaeological Method and Theory*, 16 (3), 162–83.

Roberts, B. 2008. Creating traditions and shaping technologies: understanding the earliest metal objects and metal production in Western Europe, *World Archaeology*, 40 (3), 354–72.

Roberts, B.W. 2009. Production networks and consumer choice in the earliest metal of Western Europe, *Journal of World Prehistory*, 22 (4), 461–81.

Roberts, S., Sofaer, J. and Kiss, V. 2008. Characterization and textural analysis of Middle Bronze Age Transdanubian inlaid wares of the Encrusted Pottery Culture, Hungary: a preliminary study, *Journal of Archaeological Science*, 35 (2), 322–30.

Rocca, R. et al. 2012. Discovery of Western European R1b1a2 Y chromosome variants in 1000 Genomes project data: an online community approach, *PLoS ONE* 7 (7), e41634.

Rojo-Guerra, M. Á. et al. 2006. Beer and Bell Beakers: drinking rituals in Copper Age inner Iberia, *Proceedings of the Prehistoric Society*, 72, 243–65.

Roller, D. W. 2006. *Through the Pillars of Herakles: Greco-Roman Exploration of the Atlantic*. New York and London: Routledge.

Rolley, C. (ed.) 2003. *The Tombe Princière de Vix*. Paris: Société des Amis du Musée du Châtillonais.

Ross, A. P. 1981. The Table of Nations in Genesis 10 – Its content, *Bibliotheca Sacra*, vol. 138.

Ruzickova, P. 2009. Bow-shaped pendants of the Bell Beaker Culture, *Acta Archaeologica Carpathica*, 44, 37–72.

Salanova, L. 2004. The frontiers inside the western Bell Beaker block, in Czebreszuk (ed.) 2004, 63–75.

Salanova, L. 2008. Le temps d'une diffusion: la céramique campaniforme en Europe, in *Construire le temps. Histoire et méthodes des chronologies et calendriers des derniers millénaires avant notre ère en Europe occidentale. Actes du XXXe colloque international de Halma-Ipel, UMR 8164 (CNRS, Lille 3, MCC)*, 7–9 décembre 2006, Lille, A. Lehoërff (ed.), 135–47. Glux-en-Glenne: Bibracte.

Salanova, L. et al. 2011. Archaeometric analysis and Bell Beaker pottery circulation: a synopsis of the results in Western Europe. Paper presented at the 15th Bell Beaker International Congress – From Atlantic to Ural, 5–9 May 2011.

Sarauw, T. 2007. Male symbols or warrior identities? The archery burials of the Danish Bell Beaker Culture, *Journal of Anthropological Archaeology*, 26 (1), 65–87.

Sarauw, T. 2008. Danish Bell Beaker pottery and flint daggers – the display of social identities?, *European Journal of Archaeology*, 11 (1), 23–47.

Schiffels, S. et al. 2014. Insights into British and European population history from ancient DNA sequencing of Iron Age and Anglo-Saxon samples from Hinxton, England. Paper presented at the American Society of Human Genetics Annual Meeting, October 8–22, 2014.

Schloen, D. and Fink, A. S. 2009. New excavations at Zincirli Höyük in Turkey (Ancient Sam'al) and the discovery of an inscribed mortuary stele, *Bulletin of the American Schools of Oriental Research*, no. 356, 1–13.

Schrijver, P. C. H. 2006. Review of G. Meiser, *Veni Vidi Vici: Die Vorgeschichte des lateinischen Perfektsystems*, in *Kratylos*, 51, 46–64.

Schrijver, P. 2007. What Britons spoke around 400 AD, in *Britons in Anglo-Saxon England*, N. J. Higham (ed.), 165–71. Woodbridge: Boydell Press.

Scozzari, R. et al. 2012. Molecular dissection of the basal clades in the human Y chromosome phylogenetic tree, *PLoS ONE* 7 (11): e49170.

Seguin-Orlando, A. et al. 2014, Genomic structure in Europeans dating back at least 36,200 years, *Science*, 6 November 2014.

Senna-Martinez, J. C. et al. 2011. First Bronzes of North-West Iberia: The Date from Fraga dos Corvos Habitat Site, in *Povoamento e Exploração de Recursos Mineiros na Europa Atlântica Ocidental/Settlement and Mining in the Atlantic Western Europe. Proceedings of the First International Congress, Braga*, 10 December of 2010, C. B. Martins et al. (eds), 381–94. Braga: CITEM, APEQ, FEUP.

Shepherd, I. 2012. Is there a Scottish Chalcolithic, chapter 11 in Allen, Gardiner and Sheridan 2012, 164–71.

Sheridan, A. 2008. Upper Largie and Dutch-Scottish connections during the Beaker period, in *Between Foraging and Farming: An Extended Broad Spectrum of Papers Presented to Leendert Louwe Kooijmans* (Analecta Praehistorica Leidensia, 40), H. Fokkens et al. (eds), 247–60. Leiden: University of Leiden.

Sherratt, A. 1981. Plough and pastoralism: aspects of the secondary products revolution, chapter 10 in *Pattern of the Past: Studies in Honour of David Clarke*. I. Hodder, G. Isaac and N. Hammond (eds), 261–305. Cambridge: Cambridge University Press.

Sherratt, A. 1986. Two new finds of wooden wheels from later Neolithic and Early Bronze Age Europe, *Oxford Journal of Archaeology*, 5 (2), 243–48.

Sherratt, A. 1987. Cups that cheered, in *Bell Beakers of the Western Mediterranean* (BAR International Series 287), W. H. Waldren and R. C. Kennard (eds), Oxford: British Archaeological Reports, 81–114. Revised and reprinted as: Cups that cheered: the introduction of alcohol to prehistoric Europe, in A. Sherratt, 1997. *Economy and Society in Prehistoric Europe: Changing Perspectives*, 376–402. Princeton: Princeton University Press.

Shisha-Halevy, A. 2003. Celtic syntax, Egyptian-Coptic syntax, in *Das Alte Ägypten und seine Nachbarn: Festschrift Helmut Satzinger*, M. R. M. Hasitzka, J. Diethart and G. Dembski (eds), 245–302. Krems: Österreichisches Literaturforum.

Shrimpton, G. S. 1991. *Theopompus The Historian*. McGill: Queens University Press.

Sikora, M. J., Colonna, V., Xue, Y. and Tyler-Smith, C. 2013. Modeling the contrasting Neolithic male lineage expansions in Europe and Africa, *Investigative Genetics*, 4:25.

Silva, L. 2013. *Viriathus: and the Lusitanian Resistance to Rome 155–139 BC*. Barnsley: Pen and Sword Military.

Simmons, I. and Tooley, M. (eds). 1981. *The Environment in British Prehistory*. London: Duckworth.

Sims-Williams, P. 2006. *Ancient Celtic Place-Names in Europe and Asia Minor* (Publications of the Philological Society, 39). Oxford and Boston: Blackwell Publishing.

Sims-Williams, P. 2007. Common Celtic, Gallo-Brittonic and Insular Celtic, in *Gaulois et Celtique Continental*, P.-Y. Lambert and G.-J. Pinault (eds), 309–54. Geneva: Droz.

Skene, W. F. (ed. and trans.). 1868. *The Four Ancient Books of Wales*. 2 vols. Edinburgh: Edmonston and Douglas.

Smith, W. (ed.). 1854. *Dictionary of Greek and Roman Geography*. London: Walton and Maberly/John Murray.

Smyntyna, O. V. 2007. Late Mesolithic of the Ukrainian part of the Lower Danube region: New perspectives of human adaptation and interpretation of natural environments, *Quaternary International* 167–68, 114–20.

Solinus. *Collectanea Rerum Memorabilium*, ed. T. Mommsen. 1895. Berolini [Bern]: Weidmann.

Stevens, C. J. and Fuller, D. Q. 2012. Did Neolithic farming fail? The case for a Bronze Age agricultural revolution in the British Isles, *Antiquity*, 86 (333), 707–22.

Strabo. *The Geography*, trans. H. L. Jones. 1917–32. 8 vols (Loeb Classical Library). Cambridge, MA: Harvard University Press.

Struble, E. J. and Herrmann, V. R. 2009. An eternal feast at Sam'al: the new Iron Age mortuary stele in context, *Bulletin of the American Schools of Oriental Research*, 356, 15–49.

Stupak, D. 2006. Chipped flint technologies in Swiderian complexes of the Ukrainian Polissya Region, *Archaeologia Baltica*, 7, 109–19.

Summerfield, T. 2011. Filling the Gap: Brutus in the Historia Brittonum, The Anglo-Saxon Chronicle MS F and Geoffrey of Monmouth, *The Medieval Chronicle 7*, 85–102. Amsterdam and New York: Rodopi.

Szécsényi-Nagy, A. et al. 2015. Tracing the genetic origin of Europe's first farmers reveals insights into their social organization, *Proceedings of the Royal Society B*, 282 (1805), 20150339.

Tacitus. *Agricola, Germania*, trans. H. Mattingly, rev. with intro and notes by J. B. Rives. 2009. London and New York: Penguin Books.

Tacitus. *Annals*. Available in a number of translations into English. A recent edition is trans. J. C. Yardley. 2008. Oxford and New York: Oxford University Press.

Táin Bó Cúailnge survives in three recensions, the third of which is found only in fragmentary form. The first two have been published in several translations, of which the most recent are: C. O'Rahilly (ed. and trans.), *Táin Bó Cualnge from the Book of Leinster* [Recension 2], 1970, and C. O'Rahilly, *Táin Bó Cúailnge. Recension I*, 1976. Dublin: School of Celtic Studies, Dublin Institute for Advanced Studies. Accessible translations combining elements of both recensions are *The Táin*, trans. T. Kinsella, 1969, Dublin: Dolmen Press and 1970, Oxford: Oxford University Press; and *The Táin*, trans. C. Carson, 2007, London: Penguin Classics.

Talbert, R. J. A. 2000. *Map-by-Map Directory to Accompany Barrington Atlas of the Greek and Roman World*. Princeton: Princeton University Press.

Taylor, J. 1980. *Bronze Age Goldwork of the British Isles*. Cambridge and New York: Cambridge University Press.

Taylor, J. J. 1994. The Oliver Davis Lecture: the first Golden Age of Europe was in Ireland and Britain (circa 2400–1400 BC), *Ulster Journal of Archaeology*, Third Series, 57, 37–60.

Telegin, D. Ya. and Mallory, J. P. 1994. *The Anthropomorphic Stelae of the Ukraine: The Early Iconography of the Indo-Europeans*. Journal of Indo-European Studies Monograph 11. Washington: Institute for the Study of Man.

Ternes, E. 1992. The Breton language, chapter 7 in *The Celtic Languages*, D. MacAulay (ed.), 371–452. Cambridge: Cambridge University Press.

Tertullian. *De Anima* (c. AD 203), trans. by P. Holmes as *A Treatise on the Soul*, in *Translations of the Writings of the Fathers Down to AD 325*. 1870. Edinburgh: T. & T. Clark.

Thissen, L. 1993. New insights in Balkan-Anatolian connections in the Late Chalcolithic: old evidence from the Turkish Black Sea littoral, *Anatolian Studies*, 43, 207–37.

Thomas, C. 1981. *Christianity in Roman Britain to AD 500*. Berkeley and Los Angeles: University of California Press.

Thomason, S. G. 2001. *Language Contact: An Introduction*. Edinburgh: Edinburgh University Press.

Thornton, D. E. 2003. *Kings, Chronologies, and Genealogies: Studies in the Political History of Early Medieval Ireland and Wales*. Oxford: Unit for Prosopographical Research, Linacre College.

Thorpe, L. (ed. and trans.). 1966. Geoffrey of Monmouth, *The History of the Kings of Britain*. Harmondsworth: Penguin.

Tian, C. et al. 2008. Analysis and application of European genetic substructure using 300 K SNP information, *PLoS Genetics*, 4 (1), e4.

Tian, C. et al. 2009. European population genetic substructure: further definition of ancestry informative markers for distinguishing among diverse European ethnic groups, *Molecular Medicine*, 15 (11–12), 371–83.

Tinner, W. et al. 2003. Climatic change and contemporaneous land-use phases north and south of the Alps 2300 BC to 800 AD, *Quaternary Science Reviews* 22, 1447–60.

Tinsley, H. 1981. The Bronze Age, in Simmons and Tooley (eds) 1981, 210–49.

Tomlin, R. S. O. 1992. Voices from the Sacred Spring, *Bath History*, 4, 7–24.

Toner, G. 2000. Identifying Ptolemy's Irish places and tribes, in *Ptolemy: Towards a Linguistic Atlas of the Earliest Celtic Place-Names of Europe*, D. N. Parsons and P. Sims-Williams (eds), 73–82. Aberystwyth: CMCS.

Turek, J. 2006. Beaker barrows and the houses of dead, in *Archaeology of Burial Mounds*, L. Šmejda (ed.), 170–79. Plzeň, Czech Republic: University of West Bohemia.

Turek, J. 2012. Origin of the Bell Beaker phenomenon: the Moroccan connection, chapter 8 in H. Fokkens and F. Nicolis (eds), *Background to Beakers: Inquiries into Regional Cultural Backgrounds of the Bell Beaker Complex*. Leiden: Sidestone Press.

Turner, J. 1981. The Iron Age, in Simmons and Tooley (eds) 1981, 250–81.

Uhlich, J. 2007. More on the linguistic classification of Lepontic, in *Gaulois et Celtique Continental*, P.-Y. Lambert and G.-J. Pinault (eds), 373–412. Geneva: Droz.

Valério, M. 2014. The interpretive limits of the Southwestern script, *Journal of Indo-European Studies*, 42 (3 & 4), 439–67.

Vander Linden, M. 2007. What linked the Bell Beakers in third millennium BC Europe?, *Antiquity*, 81 (312), 343–52.

Vasil'ev, S. 1999. The Siberian mosaic: Upper Paleolithic adaptations and change before the Last Glacial Maximum, chapter 14 in *Hunters of the Golden Age: The Mid Upper Palaeolithic of Eurasia 30,000-20,000 BP* (Analecta Praehistorica Leidensia, 31), W. Roebroeks, M. Mussi, J. Svoboda and K. Fennema (eds), 173–95. Leiden: University of Leiden.

Veluščsek, A. 2004. Past and present lake dwelling studies in Slovenia: Ljubljansko barje (the Ljubljana Marsh), chapter 5 in *Living on the Lake in Prehistoric Europe: 150 Years of Lake-Dwelling Research*, F. Menotti (ed.), 69–82. Abingdon and New York: Routledge.

Verger, S. 2006. La grande tombe de Hochdorf, mise en scène funéraire d'un cursus honorum tribal hors pair, *Siris*, 7, 5–44.

Vergnaud, L. 2013. The Bell Beaker funeral group from Sierentz 'Les Villas d'Aurèle' (Haut-Rhin, France), chapter 5 in Prieto-Martinez and Salanova (eds) 2013, 51–59.

Villar, F. 2000. *Indoeuropeos y no Indoeuropeos en la Hispania prerromana*. Salamanca: Ediciones Universidad de Salamanca.

Villar, F. 2004. The Celtic Language of the Iberian Peninsula, in *Studies in Baltic and Indo-European Linguistics in Honor of William R. Schmalstieg*, P. Baldi and P. U. Dini (eds), 243–74. Amsterdam: John Benjamins.

Vitali, D. 1991. The Celts in Italy, in Moscati et al. (eds) 1991, 220–35.

Vouga, P. 1923. *La Tène. Monographie de la station publiée au nom de la Commission des Fouilles de La Tène*. Leipzig: Karl W. Hiersemann.

Všianský, D., Kolář, J. and Petřika, J. 2014. Continuity and changes of manufacturing traditions of Bell Beaker and Bronze Age encrusted pottery in the Morava river catchment (Czech Republic), *Journal of Archaeological Science*, 49, 414–22.

Walsh, A. 1991. Excavation at the Black Pig's Dyke, *Clogher Record*, 14 (1), 9–26.

Warner, R. 1990. The 'Prehistoric' Irish Annals?, *Archaeology Ireland*, 4 (1), 30–33.

Warner. R., Moles, N. and Chapman, R. 2010. Evidence for early Bronze Age tin and gold extraction in the Mourne Mountains, County Down, *Journal of the Mining Heritage Trust of Ireland*, 10, 29–36.

Watkins, C. 1966. Italo-Celtic revisited, in *Ancient Indo-European Dialects* H. Birnbaum and J. Puhvel (eds), 29–50. Berkeley: University of California Press.

Watkins, C. 2001. An Indo-European linguistic area and its characteristics: Ancient Anatolia. Areal diffusion as a challenge to the comparative method?, in *Areal Diffusion and Genetic Inheritance: Problems in Comparative Linguistics*, A. Y. Aikhenvald and R. M. W. Dixon (eds), 44–63. Oxford: Oxford University Press.

Wei, W. et al. 2013. A calibrated human Y-chromosomal phylogeny based on resequencing, *Genome Research*, 23(2), 388–95.

Whitehouse, N. et al. 2014. Neolithic agriculture on the European western frontier: the boom and bust of early farming in Ireland, *Journal of Archaeological Science*, 51, 181–205.

Wilde, S. 2014. Direct evidence for positive selection of skin, hair, and eye pigmentation in Europeans during the last 5,000 y, *PNAS*, 111 (13), 4832–37.

William of Newburgh, *The History of English Affairs*, Book 1, ed. with trans. and commentary by P. G. Walsh and M. J. Kennedy. 1988. Warminster: Aris.

Winney, B. et al. 2012. People of the British Isles: preliminary analysis of genotypes and surnames in a UK-control population, *European Journal of Human Genetics*, 20, 203–10.

Włodarczak, P. 2009. Radiocarbon and dendrochronological dates of the Corded Ware culture, *Radiocarbon*, 51 (2), 737–49.

Woodward, A. and Hunter, J. 2011. *An Examination of Prehistoric Stone Bracers from Britain*. Oxford: Oxbow Books.

Woolf, A. 2007. *From Pictland to Alba 789-1070* (The New Edinburgh History of Scotland 2). Edinburgh: Edinburgh University Press.

Wright, D. M. 2009. A set of distinctive marker values defines a Y-STR signature for Gaelic Dalcassian families, *Journal of Genetic Genealogy*, 5 (1), 1–7.

Zavaroni, A. 2009. Footprints as a symbol of a divine guide of souls: focus on the Scandinavian rock art, Papers presented at the XXIII Valcamonica Symposium 2009, 420–29.

Sources of Illustrations

Images are listed by figure numbers.

Title page: Musée de l'Oise, Beauvais; **1** Drazen Tomic, after Koch 2006, p. 373; **2** British Museum, London; **3** from Francis Grose, *The Antiquities of England and Wales*, new edition, Vol. IV, c. 1784; **4** Joseph Christian-Leyendecker for *The Century Illustrated Magazine*, January 1907; **5** National Monuments Service, Ireland. Department of Arts, Heritage and the Gaeltacht; **6** National Museum of Wales, Cardiff; **7** British Library, London; **8** Drazen Tomic, adapted from Soares 2010; **9** Drazen Tomic, after Richard Rocca; **10** Private Collection; **11** Drazen Tomic, based on Koch 2007; **12** Musée Cantonal d'Archéologie, Neuchâtel; **13** from P. Vouga, *La Tène*, 1923; **14** British Library, London; **15** Musée d'Archéologie Nationale, Paris; **16** Nationalmuseet, Copenhagen; **17** Francois Guillot/AFP/Getty Images; **18** Heritage Image Partnership Ltd/Alamy; **19** Drazen Tomic; **20** José-Manuel Benito Álvarez; **21** Wessex Archaeology. Drawing by Elizabeth James; **22** National Museum of Ireland, Dublin; **23** Drazen Tomic, adapted from Myres 2011; **24** Drazen Tomic; **25** Drazen Tomic, based on Sims-Williams 2006; **26** adapted from Nahkleh, Ringe and Warnow; **27** Drazen Tomic; **28** David Bezzina; **29** Drazen Tomic, after Inizan 2012; **30** Drazen Tomic, adapted from Lazaridis 2014; **31** Drazen Tomic, adapted from David Anthony 2007; **32** Dnipropetrovsk National Historical Museum named after D. I. Yavornytsky, Ukraine; **33** Drazen Tomic, with information from Telegin and Mallory figs 2, 19, and Dimitriadis, G. 2008. Looking for metals: megalithic monuments between reality and mythology, in *Geoarchaeology and Archaeomineralogy. Proceedings of the International Conference, 29-30 October 2008 Sofia*, R. I. Kostov, B. Gaydarska, M. Gurova (eds), 205–10. St. Ivan Rilski: Sofia, fig. 3; **34** Histria Museum, Constanta; **35** Musées Cantonaux du Valais, Sion. Photo Hervé Paitier; **36** Musée Fenaille, Rodez; **37** Drazen Tomic; **38** DRCC-Museu da Guarda; **39** British Library, London; **40** David Bezzina, after Kunst 2001; **41** Muzeul Naţional de Istorie a României, Bucharest; **42** Drazen Tomic; **43** Museo de Valladolid; **44** Landesmuseum Württemberg, Stuttgart; **45**, **46** Drazen Tomic, adapted from Cunliffe 2008; **47** Erich Lessing/akg-images; **48** Landesmuseum Württemberg, Stuttgart; **49** Photo Keltenmuseum Hochdorf/Enz, Eberdingen; **50 above** Musée du Pays Châtillonnais, Châtillon-sur-Seine; **50 below** Musée du Pays Châtillonnais, Châtillon-sur-Seine/Gianni Dagli Orti/The Art Library; **51**, **52** akg-images; **53** Drazen Tomic, after Koch 2007; **56** DEA Picture Library/Getty Images; **57** Čestmír Štuka; **58**, **59** The Trustees of the British Museum, London; **60** Drazen Tomic, after Cunliffe 1997, fig. 55; **61** Staatliche Museen zu Berlin; **62** Posavski Muzej, Brežice; **63** Musei Capitolini, Rome; **64** Drazen Tomic, after Lorria and Zapatero 2005, from Albertos 1990; **65** Private Collection; **66** Drazen Tomic, after Richard Rocca; **67** ML Design; **68** Werner Forman/Corbis; **69**, **70**, **71** Drazen Tomic; **72** Musée Calvet d'Avignon; **73** Musée Crozatier, Le Puy-en-Velay; **74** Drazen Tomic; **75** Museum of London/The Art Archive; **76** Drazen Tomic; **77** Meigle Sculptured Stone Museum, Perthshire; **78** Drazen Tomic; **79** LVR - LandesMuseum, Bonn. Photo Jürgen Vogel; **80** The Trustees of the British Museum, London; **81** Miss G. D. Jones; **82** Carmarthenshire County Museum, Abergwili. Photo Dara Jasumani; **83** National Museum of Ireland, Dublin; **85** Drazen Tomic, after *Atlas of Irish History*, 2nd ed. (2000), p. 19; **86** Patrick Frilet/Marka/SuperStock; **87** ML Design, based on Campbell, John and Wormald 1982, fig. 50; **88** Royal Commission on the Ancient and Historical Monuments of Wales (RCAHMW); **89**, **90** Drazen Tomic; **91** Trinity College Library, Dublin; **92** Drazen Tomic, after Koch 2007, §24, §390; **93**, **94** Drazen Tomic; **95** National Portrait Gallery, London; **96** from Edward Lhuyd, *Archaeologia Britannica*, Vol. 1, 1702; **97** Victoria and Albert Museum, London; **98** *The Illustrated London News*, 1862; **99** Fred Tanneau/AFP/Getty Images; **100** Educational Images/UIG/Getty Images; **101** Hemis/Alamy.

Acknowledgments

Colin Ridler of Thames & Hudson had the idea for this book, Jim Mallory acted as midwife to its birth, while Miranda Aldhouse-Green and David Miles supplied expert comments, which is not to say that any of them shares all the views expressed herein. James Honeychuck was kind enough to proofread the first two chapters. Thanks are due to Alan Reilly for generously sharing his research on pressure blade-making and pointing out other useful papers. On the genetic side, I am grateful to Sir Conor O'Brien, Baron Inchiquin, for permission to include his Y-DNA haplogroup, and to Dennis Wright for consultation on it. Kenneth Nordtvedt was as helpful as always on the estimated dating of subclades of Y-DNA haplogroup I. DNA distribution maps for R1b-U152 and R1b-L21 were initially created by Richard Rocca.

Index

Numbers in *italic* refer to illustrations; numbers in **bold** refer to maps

Aedui 149–50; **71**
Aeneas 24
Afontova Gora man 69, 70, 71, 73
Agricola (governor of Britain) 156–58; **76**
agriculture, spread of 66–67
Alaric the Goth 163
Alba, kingdom of 184
Alban, St 162–63
Albanian language 104
alcohol 49–50
Aldhelm, abbot of Malmesbury 180
Alesia, siege of 151–52
Alexander the Great, and Celts 129–30
Alps 32, 33, 82–83, 86, 114, 115, 128
Altai Mountains 76
Alteuropäisch see Old European (IE)
amber 53, 104–05, 107, 110
Ambiani 68
Ambrona Valley (Spain) 50
America 70
Amesbury Archer 53, 56; *21*
Ammianus Marcellinus 123
Anatolia 75–76, 136
  Galatian Celts 131–33
  PIE homeland theory 66–67
ancestral north Eurasians (ANE) 70, 73; *30*
ancient DNA, European
  earliest dates for 44–45
  Indo-European origins 202
  Insular Celts and 202
  and spread of R1b-L21 27
  Yamnaya culture 76
Andronovo culture 78
Angles 13, 174; **78**
Anglesey (Ynys Môn) 22, 177, 178
Anglo-Saxons
  and Britons 174–77
  genetics 175
  see also Saxons
animals, draught 74
Annales Cambriae (Welsh Chronicles) 23
annals 19, 21
Annals of the Four Masters 19–20

Annals of Ulster 168
Anthony, David 68
Antoninus Pius, emperor 156
Antonine Wall 156
Aosta, necropolis 89–90, 97, 115; *53*
Aquae Sulis (Bath) 163
Aquitani 31; *71*
Aragon 135
Arbroath, Declaration of (1320) 182
archaeology 7
  and literature 18–20
archery equipment 52, 53
Argantonios 43
Ariovistus 149–50
Aristotle 31, 102
Arkaim 78
Arles, Christian Council 163
Armenian language 77; *31*
Armorica 180–81, 187; **89**
armour 102–03
  see also weapons
Arras 140
Arras culture, Yorkshire 38; **55**
arrows/arrowheads 53, 112; *21*
arsenic-rich copper 51, 74, 89
art, Celtic 118–19; *57, 58,* 83
Art Nouveau, Celtic art and 196
Artchorp, Irish genealogy 168
Arthur, British war leader 22, 23
Arverni 149, 151–52; *71*
Asia Minor, *Galatoi* (Galatians) 131–33
Assyrians 67
Asterix 151
Athenaeus of Naucratis 131
Atlantic Bronze Age 100
Atrebates 140, 154–55; **74, 76**
Attacotti 159, 161; **78**
Attalus I, of Pergamon 132; **63**
Aubrey, John 3
Augustine of Hippo, St 163
Augustorium (Limoges) 40
Aulus Plautius 154–55; **74, 76**
Austria 128
Auxilius (missionary to Ireland) 167–68
Avienus, Rufus Festus, *Ora Maritima* 46

Aylesford-Swarling culture 140
axes 52, 75, 91
Aztecs 70

Baetica 134
Baia de Cris (Romania) 82
Baikal, Lake 69, 71; *29*
Balkan languages 77; **31**
Balkans 60
  collapse of farming 75–76
  La Tène culture 128–31
  metallurgy 84
  Yamnaya culture 72
Baltic 104–05
Barrington Atlas of the Greek and Roman World (2000) 59
Basque language 31
Bathanattus 131
Bede, the Venerable
  Dál Riata 182–83
  Picts 182–83, 194
  Ecclesiastical History of the English People 28, 174, 194
beehive quern stones 137
beer, Bell Beaker and 49–50
Belgae 31, 60, 123–24, 133; *71*
  against Rome 150–51
  coins 140; 68
  in Britain 139–40; 68
  language 133
  see also Gauls
Belgium 30
Bell Beaker 48–56, 73; 20; *19*
  eastern and western 97–98
  language 57–61; **23**
  mobility 56, 115
  and stelae 89–91; *39*
Bell Beaker routes, and development of Celtic cultures 94–99, 115; **42**
Bell Beaker ware 48–51, 73, 89; 20; *19*
  All Over Corded (AOC) 73, 76, 91–92
  Epi-Bell-Beaker in Portugal 52
  geographic locations 51, 91
  Maritime 91–93, 96, 98; *40*
  origins of 91–94
  Protruding Foot Beaker (PFB) 92
  style of ornamentation 91–92
belts 82, 91; *34*
Benraw (Ireland) 98
Berber language 95, 96
Beringia land bridge 70

Bernicia, Angle kingdom 13; **87**
Bettelbühl necropolis 106–07
birch bark hat 107; *48*
birds, and Celts 122; *58*
Bithynia 131
Black Pig's Dyke (Armagh) 18; **57**
Black Sea 25, 60, 70, 75, 77, 93, 103; **31, 33, 45**
boar's tusks 97
Bohemia 117, 118, 120; **55** 144, 148; *57*
Bolgios 130
Botteghino (Italy) 83
Boudica 36, 110
bow 89, 91
Bragança district (Portugal), bronze workings 52
Brennos, attack on Delphi 130–31
Breton language 21, 31, 116, 187–88; **92**
Bretons 209–10
Brian Boru 207–09
bridles 104
Brigantes 155–56; **67, 74, 76**
Britain
  ancient genome sequences 175
  British and Anglo-Saxon kingdoms **87**
  Celtic name for 45–46
  chariot burials 36, 38, 124
  gold 53
  ogham 164, 165; 82
  Saxon provinces 175; **87**
  wine trade 125–26; 59
  Yr Hen Ogledd (The Old North) 175, 187
Britannia (Roman province) 12, 21, 59, 152–61, 170
  attacked by barbarians 158, 159–61; **78**
  Celtic place-names 59, 123, 137–38, 168; **25**
  Irish raiders 163–64
  leaves Roman empire 161
  Pritani 169–70
  Roman conquest of 153–61; **74, 76**
  Saxon provinces 175
British Celts, DNA profile 26–27
British Isles
  Christian Celts 162–85
  development of Celtic 116